BUDDHIST
BIRTH-STORIES

BUDDHIST
BIRTH-STORIES

(JĀTAKA TALES)

Translated from

Prof. V. Fausböll's edition of the Pali text by

RHYS DAVIDS

BKP

BHARATIYA KALA PRAKASHAN

DELHI (INDIA)

First Revised Edition : 2005

ISBN : 81-8090-073-8

Published by : **C.P. Gautam**
for **BHARATIYA KALA PRAKASHAN**
3421-A, IInd Floor, Narang Colony,
Tri Nagar, Delhi-110035.
Phone : 27393083, 30967505 (O)
27522129 (R)

Laser Typesetting by: Twinkle Graphics, Delhi-110088.

Printed by : BDH Printer at Salasar Imaging Systems
Delhi-35. Ph : 31045804

Editorial Note

This essay and the following translation were published in 1880 as a volume in *Trübner's Oriental Series.* That volume contained, further, the beginning of a much longer work, namely the translation of the so-called Jātaka. This is a collection of upwards of 550 folk-lore tales which forms part of the Buddhist canonical scriptures. The tales are in prose, each explaining a much more ancient poem of two or more lines. The allusions in the verses cannot be understood without the explanation given in the prose. Over and above this explanation there is added to each story an episode said to be from the life of the founder of what is now called Buddhism. Something has occurred which the founder likens to an episode in the long past, when, in a former life the actors in the present episode and he himself were engaged. In this way a moral, something like those in our fables, is drawn. At the same time the immensely long evolution in the full life or lives of all men and in particular of such a superman as the founder is brought out.

The original volume has long been out of print. The writer, passing on to other pioneer work, handed over the long task of the Jātaka translation to the late Professor E.B. Cowell. Under his editorship and up to his death the work was carried out by a group of translators and was issued during 1895-1907 by the Cambridge University Press. Naturally the remainder of the original volume herewith re-issued could not take its proper place at the head of the complete translation.

It has long been out of print. But neither the introductory essay nor the translation of the Nidāna-kathā or Jātaka introductory chronicle has been superseded. Hence it has seemed good to the house of Routledge, in taking up the mantle of the house of Trübner, to issue a fresh edition of both. Hereby a service is rendered to all inquirers into the history of Indian literature and especially into a phase of it which has held much significance in the Buddhist tradition and is of no small interest for the general mind of to-day.

Jātāka means 'birth-let', 'birth-er', or collectively 'birth-anea'. And the 'story of the lineage' is a biography of Gotama Buddha so far as it includes those earth-lives which he was said to have lived under preceding Buddhas, and also the life he lived as himself a Buddha down to the time when his new church had won a footing. It is not from a modern standpoint a logically necessary preface. We should deem ourselves better instructed had the compilers of prefaces and following stories told us something about the sources of story and verse and episode.

But for the old-world orthodox Buddhist, rapt in contemplation of his Great Man (*mahā-purisa*) the chief end of the work–discounting the endless entertainment afforded then (and even now) by the stories–was to throw light on that notable object of his worship. The stories were episodes in the founding and grounding, down an immemorial past, of that wonderful product, the character of a Tathāgata of 'him-who-had-thus-come'. The introductory narrative is chiefly concerned with the two great milestones in his career : the milestone when the conscious will to become a helper of men first awoke, and the milestone when that will had reached such perfection that he could become such a helper.

This narrative came to be called the Discourse of the Nidāna. In translating Nidāna by 'lineage',[1] a verbal difficulty has been solved more by the spirit of the contents than by the letter of the title. The word *nidāna* is usually rendered by cause, source, base, origin. None of these would convey a meaning to English readers. In Buddhist perspective the narrative reveals a long, long line of ancestors. These are not ancestors 'after the flesh'. These are not ancestors by what we reckon as heredity. We merge the individual in the family, the tribe, the race. In Buddhism the *line of the individual* stands out much more strongly, in startling incongruity with its church's rejection of 'the man'. These are ancestors of 'dead selves' through whom, again and

1. Rhys Davids left the word untranslated.

again reborn, the 'man' whose will is set on the best he knows, may rise as 'on stepping stones to higher things'. 'Dead selves' is a poor wording, but by it Tennyson meets the Buddhist point of view not inaptly. The word *nidāna* suggests something serial, or connected in line. *Dā* is 'to bind'; *ni* means 'along'. And so we get the notion of chain or series of antecedents. And that, in the matter of living ascent or descent, is lineage.

The Nidāna Kathā, as forming a running commentary on the *Buddhavaṃsa* (chronicle of the Buddhas), itself a canonical book, is a later comer into the Canon. In its treatment of the Buddha-legend–and the story of the life of the very real founder had by that time become legendary–it occupies a midway house between the biographical fragments in Vinaya and chief Nikāyas, and those later more highly embroidered 'lives' of which there are not a few. The nimbus and thc rays and the beauty of the figure have come in. But the narrative is still relatively simple. The historical question of Jātaka literature may be followed up in Rhys Davids's *Buddhist India*, 2nd ed., 1903, in Oldenberg's 'The Ākhyāna Type and the Jātakas', *Jl. Pali Text Society*, 1912, and in Dr. Winternitz's art : Jātaka, *Ency. Religion and Ethics* and his *Geschichte der Indischen Litteratur* II, pt. 1, p. 89, and 149, 1913.

The revising in this re-issue has been solely of a number of small details in transliteration, in closer accuracy of translation, and in discarding certain renderings in this, his earliest published translation, which Rhys Davids had in later works himself discarded.

C.A.F. Rhys Davids

Table of Contents

Supplementary Tables

Introduction

It is well known that amongst the Buddhist Scriptures there is one book in which a large number of old stories, fables, and fairy-tales lie enshrined in an edifying commentary; and have thus been preserved for the study and amusement of later times. How this came about is not at present quite certain. The belief of orthodox Buddhists on the subject is this : The Buddha, as occasion arose, was accustomed throughout his long career to explain and comment on the events happening around him by telling of similar events that had occurred in his own previous births. The experience, not of one lifetime only, but of many lives, was always present to his mind; and it was this experience he so often used to point a moral, or adorn a tale. The stories so told are said to have been reverently learned and repeated by his disciples; and after his death 550 of them were gathered together in one collection, called the Book of the 550 Jātakas or Birthlets. The commentary to these gives for each Jātaka, or Birth Story, an account of the event in Gotama's life which led to his first telling that particular story. Both text and commentary were then handed down, in the Pāli language in which they were composed, to the time of the Council of Patna (held in or about the year 250 B.C.); and they were carried in the following year to Ceylon by the great missionary Mahinda, the son of Asoka. There the commentary was written down in Singhalese, the Aryan dialect spoken in Ceylon; and was retranslated into its present form in the Pāli language in the fifth century of our era. But the text of the Jātaka stories themselves has been throughout preserved in its original Pāli form.

Unfortunately this orthodox Buddhist belief as to the history of the Book of Birth Stories rests on a foundation of quicksand. The Buddhist belief, that most of their sacred books were in existence immediately after the Buddha's death, is not only not supported, but is contradicted by the evidence of those books themselves. It may be necessary to state what that belief is, in order to show the importance which the Buddhists attach to the book; but in order to estimate the value we ourselves should give it, it will be necessary by critical, and more round about methods to endeavour to arrive at some more reliable conclusion. Such an investigation cannot, it is true, be completed until the whole series of the Buddhist Birth Stories shall have become accessible in the original Pāli text, and the history of those stories shall have been traced in other sources. With the present inadequate information at our command, it is only possible to arrive at probabilities. But it is therefore the more fortunate that the course of the inquiry will lead to some highly interesting and instructive results.

In the first place, the fairy tales, parables, fables, riddles, and comic and moral stories, of which the Buddhist Collection–known as the *Jātaka Book*–consists, have been found, in many instances, to bear a striking resemblance to similar ones current in the West. Now in many instances this resemblance is simply due to the fact that the *Western stories were borrowed from the Buddhist ones.*

To this resemblance much of the interest excited by the Buddhist Birth Stories is, very naturally, due. As, therefore, the stories translated in the body of this volume do not happen to contain among them any of those most generally known in England, I insert here one or two specimens which may at the same time afford some amusement, and also enable the reader to judge how far the alleged resemblances do actually exist.

It is absolutely essential for the correctness of such judgment that the stories should be presented exactly as they stand in the original. I am aware that a close and literal translation involves the disadvantage of presenting the stories in a style which will probably seem strange, and even wooden, to the modern reader. But it cannot be admitted that, even for purposes of comparison, it would be sufficient to reproduce the stories in a modern form which should aim at combining substantial accuracy with a pleasing dress.

And the *Book of Birth Stories* has a value quite independent of the fact that many of its tales have been transplanted to the West. It contains a record of the every-day life, and every-day thought, of the people among whom the tales were told : it is *the oldest, most complete, and most important collection of folk-lore extant.*

The whole value of its evidence in this respect would be lost, if a translator, by slight additions in some places, slight omissions in others, and slight modifications here and there, should run the risk of conveying erroneous impressions of early Buddhist beliefs, and habits, and modes of thought. It is important, therefore, that the reader should understand, before reading the stories I intend to give, that while translating sentence by sentence, rather than word by word, I have never lost sight of the importance of retaining in the English version, as far as possible, not only the phraseology, but the style and spirit of the Buddhist story-teller.

Rhys Davids

PART I

THE BOOK OF BIRTH STORIES, AND MIGRATION TO THE WEST

THE ASS IN THE LION'S SKIN

Sīha-Chamma Jātaka

(Fausböll, no. 189)

Once upon a time, while Brahma-datta was reigning in Benāres, the future Buddha was born one of a peasant family; and when he grew up, he gained his living by tilling the ground.

At that time a hawker used to go from place to place, trafficking in goods carried by an ass. Now at each place he came to, when to take the pack down from the ass's back he used to clothe him in a lion's skin, and turn him loose in the rice and barley-fields, and when the watchmen in the fields saw the ass, they dared not go near him, taking him for a lion.

So one day the hawker stopped in a village; and whilst he was getting his own breakfast cooked, he dressed the ass in a lion's skin, and turned him loose in a barley-field. The watchmen in the field dared not go up to him; but going home, they published the news. Then all the villagers came out with weapons in their hands; and blowing chanks, and beating drums, they went near the field and shouted. Terrified with the fear of death, the ass uttered a cry–the cry of an ass!

And when he knew him then to be ass, the future Buddha pronounced the First Stanza :

"This is not a lion's roaring,
Nor a tiger's, nor a panther's;
Dressed in a lion's skin,
'Tis a wretched ass that roars!"

But when the villagers knew the creature to be an ass, they beat him till his bones broke; and, carrying off the lion's skin, went away. Then the hawker came, and seeing the ass fallen into so bad a plight, pronounced the Second Stanza :

"Long might the ass,
Clad in a lion's skin,
Have fed on barley green.
but he brayed!
And that moment he came to ruin."

And even while he was yet speaking the ass died on the spot!

This story will doubtless sound familiar enough to English ears; for a similar tale is found in our modern collections of so-called *Aesop's Fables.*[1] Professor Benfey has further traced it in mediaeval French, German, Turkish, and Indian literature.[2] But it may have been much older than any of these books; for the fable possibly gave rise to a proverb of which we find traces among the Greeks as early as the time of Plato.[3] Lucian gives the fable in full, localizing it at Kume, in South Italy,[4] and Julien has given us a Chinese version in his *Avadānas.*[5] Erasmus, in his work on proverbs,[6] alludes to the fable; and so also does our own Shakespeare in *King John.*[7] It is worthy of mention that in one of the later story-books–in a Persian translation, that is, of the *Hitopadeśa*–there is a version of our fable in which it is the vanity of the ass in trying to sing which leads to his disguise being discovered, and thus brings him to grief.[8] But Professor Benfey has shown,[9] that this version is simply the rolling into one of the present tale and of another also widely prevalent, when an ass by trying to sing earns for himself, not thanks, but blows.[10] I shall hereafter attempt to draw some conclusions from the history of the story. But I would here point out that the fable could scarcely have originated in any country in which lions were not common; and that the Jātaka story gives a reasonable explanation of the ass being dressed in the skin, instead of saying that he dressed himself in it, as is said in our *Aesop's Fables.*

The reader will notice that the "moral" of the tale is contained in two stanzas, one of which is put into the mouth of the Bodisat or future Buddha. This will be found to be the case in all the Birth Stories, save that the number of the stanzas differs, and that they are usually all spoken by the Bodisat. It should also be noticed that the identification of the peasant's son with the Bodisat, which is of so little importance to the story, is the only part of it which is essentially Buddhistic. Both these points will be of importance further on.

The introduction of the human element takes this story, perhaps, out of the class of fables in the most exact sense of that word. I therefore add a story containing a fable proper, where animals speak and act like men.

THE TALKATIVE TORTOISE

Kacchapa Jātaka

(Fausböll, no. 215)

Once upon a time, when Brahma-datta was reigning in Benāres, the future Buddha was born in a minister's family; and when he grew up, he became the king's adviser in things temporal and spiritual.

Now this king was very talkative : while he was speaking, others had no opportunity for a word. And the future Buddha, wanting to cure this talkativeness of his, was constantly seeking for some means of doing so.

At that time there was living, in a pond in the Himālaya mountains, a tortoise. Two young hangsas (*i.e.* wild ducks[11]) who came to feed there, made friends with him. And one day, when they had become very intimate with him, they said to the tortoise :

"Friend tortoise! the place where we live, at the Golden Cave on Mount Beautiful in the Himālaya country, is a delightful spot. Will you come there with us?"

"But how can I get there?"

"We can take you, if you can only hold your tongue, and will say nothing to anybody."[12]

"O! that I can do. Take me with you."

"That's right," said they. And making the tortoise bite hold of a stick, they themselves took the two ends in their teeth, and flew up into the air.[13]

Seeing him thus carried by the hangsas, some villagers called out, "Two wild ducks are carrying a tortoise along on a stick!" Whereupon the tortoise wanted to say, "If my friends choose to carry me, what is that to you, you wretched slaves!" So just as the swift flight of the wild ducks had brought him over the king's palace in the city of Benāres, he let go of the stick he was biting, and falling in the open courtyard, split in two! And there arose a universal cry : "A tortoise has fallen in the open courtyard, and has split in two!"

The king, taking the future Buddha, went to the place, surrounded by his courtiers, and looking at the tortoise, he asked the Bodisat : "Teacher! how comes he to be fallen here?"

The future Buddha thought to himself : "Long expecting, wishing to admonish the king, have I sought for some means of doing so. This tortoise must have made friends with the wild ducks; and they must have made him bite hold of the stick, and have flown up into the air to take him to the hills. But he, being unable to hold his tongue when he hears any one else talk, must have wanted to say something, and let go the stick; and so must have fallen down from the sky, and thus lost his life." And saying "Truly, O king! those who are called chatter-boxes–people whose words have no end–come to grief like this," he uttered these verses :

"Verily the tortoise killed himself
Whilst uttering his voice;
Though he was holding tight the stick,
By a word himself he slew.

"Behold him then, O excellent by strength!
And speak wise words, not out of season.
You see how, by his talking overmuch,
The tortoise fell into this wretched plight!"

The king saw that he was himself referred to and said : "O Teacher! are you speaking of us?"

And the Bodisat spoke openly, and said : "O great king! be it thou, or be it any other, whoever talks beyond measure meets with some mishap like this."

And the king henceforth refrained himself, and became a man of few words.

This story too is found also in Greek, Latin, Arabic, Persian, and in most European languages,[14] though, strangely enough, it does not occur in our books of *Aesop's Fables.* But in the *Aesop's Fables* is usually included a story of a tortoise who asked an eagle to teach him to fly; and being dropped, split in two![15] It is worthy of notice that in the Southern recension of the *Pañca Tantra* it is eagles, and not wild ducks or swans, who carry the tortoise;[16] and there can, I think, be little doubt that the two fables are historically connected.

Another fable, very familiar to modern readers, is stated in the commentary to have been first related in ridicule of a kind of Mutual Admiration Society existing among the opponents of the Buddha. Hearing the monks talking about the foolish way in which Devadatta and Kokālika went about among the people ascribing each to the other virtues which neither possessed, he is said to have told this tale.

THE JACKAL AND THE CROW

Jambu-Khādaka Jātaka

(Fausböll, no. 294)

Long, long ago, when Brahma-datta was reigning in Benāres, the Bodisat had come to life as a treefairy, dwelling in a certain grove of jambu-trees.

Now a crow was sitting there one day on the branch of a jambu-tree, eating the jambu-fruits, when a jackal coming by, looked up, and saw him.

"Ha!" thought he. "I'll flatter that fellow, and get some of those jambus to eat." And thereupon he uttered this verse in his praise :

"Who may this be, whose rich and pleasant notes

Proclaim him best of all the singing-birds?
Warbling so sweetly on the jambu-branch,
Where like a peacock he sits firm and grand!"

Then the crow, to pay him back his compliments, replied in this second verse :

"'Tis a well-bred young gentleman, who understands
To speak of gentlemen in terms polite!
Good Sir!–whose shape and glossy coat reveal
The tiger's offspring–eat of these, I pray!"

And so saying, he shook the branch of the jambu tree till he made the fruit to fall.

But when the fairy who dwelt in that tree saw the two of them, now they had done flattering one another, eating the jambus together, he uttered a third verse :

"Too long, forsooth, I've borne the sight
Of these poor chatterers of lies–
The refuse-eater and the offal-eater
Belauding each other!"

And making himself visible in awful shape, he frightened them away from the place!

It is easy to understand that, when this story had been carried out of those countries where the crow and the jackal are the common scavengers, it would lose its point; and it may very well, therefore, have been shortened into the fable of the fox and the Crow and the piece of cheese. On the other hand, the latter is so complete and excellent a story that it would scarcely have been expanded, if it had been the original, into the tale of the Jackal and the Crow.[17]

The next tale to be quoted is one showing how a wise man solves a difficulty. I give it from a Singhalese version of the fourteenth century, which is nearer to the Pāli than any other as yet known.[18] It is an episode in the long Jātaka called.

THE BIRTH AS "GREAT PHYSICIAN"[19]

Mahosadha Jātaka

(Fausböll, no. 546)

A woman, carrying her child, went to the future Buddha's tank to wash. And having first bathed the child, she put on her upper garment and descended into the water to bathe herself.

Then a Yakshinī[20] seeing the child, had a craving to eat it. And taking the form of a woman, she drew near, and asked the mother :

"Friend, this *is* a *very* pretty child, is it one of yours?"

And when she was told it was, she asked if she might nurse it. And this being allowed, she nursed it a little, and then carried it off.

But when the mother saw this, she ran after her, and cried out : "Where are you taking my child to?" and caught hold of her.

The Yakshiṇī boldly said; "Where did you get the child from? It is mine!" And so quarrelling, they passed the door of the future Buddha's Judgment Hall.

He heard the noise, sent for them, inquired into the matter, and asked them whether they would abide by his decision. And they agreed. Then he had a line drawn on the ground; and told the Yakshiṇī to take hold of the child's arms, and the mother to take hold of its legs; and said : "The child shall be hers who drags him over the line."

But as soon as they pulled at him, the mother, seeing how he suffered, grieved as if her heart would break. And letting him go, she stood there weeping.

Then the future Buddha asked the bystanders : "Whose hearts are tender to babes? those who have borne children, or those who have not?"

And they answered : "O Sire! the hearts of mothers are tender."

Then he said : "Who, think you, is the mother? she who has the child in her arms, or she who has let go?"

And they answered : "She who has let go is the mother."

And he said : "Then do you all think that the other was the thief?"

And they answered : "Sire! we cannot tell."

And he said : "Verily this is a Yakshiṇī, who took the child to eat it."

And they asked : "O Sire! how did you know it?"

And he replied : "Because her eyes winked not, and were red, and she knew no fear, and had no pity, I knew it."

And so saying, he demanded of the thief : "Who are you?

And she said : "Lord! I am a Yakshiṇī."

And he asked : "Why did you take away this child?"

And she said : "I thought to eat him, O my Lord!"

And he rebuked her, saying : "O foolish woman! For your former sins you have been born a Yakshiṇī, and now do you still sin!" And he laid a vow upon her to keep the Five Commandments, and let her go.

But the mother of the child exalted the future Buddha, and said : "O my Lord! O Great Physician! may thy life be long!" And she went away, with her babe clasped to her bosom.

The Hebrew story, in which a similar judgment is ascribed to Solomon, occurs in the Book of Kings, which is probably older than the time of Gotama. We shall consider below what may be the connexion between the two.

The next specimen is a tale about lifeless things endowed with miraculous powers; perhaps the oldest tale in the world of that kind which has been yet published. It is an episode in.

SAKKA'S PRESENTS

Dadhi-Vāhana Jātaka

(Fausböll, no. 186)

Once upon a time, when Brahma-datta was reigning in Benāres, four brothers, Brāhmans, of that kingdom, devoted themselves to an ascetic life; and having built themselves huts at equal distances in the region of Himālaya mountains, took up their residence there.

The eldest of them died, and was reborn as the god Sakka.[21] When he became aware of this, he used to go and render help at intervals every seven of eight days to the others. And one day, having greeted the eldest hermit, and sat down beside him, he asked him : "Reverend Sir, what are you in need of?"

The hermit, who suffered from jaundice, answered : "I want fire!" So he gave him a double-edged hatchet.

But the hermit said : "Who is to take his, and bring me firewood?"

Then Sakka spoke thus to him : "Whenever, reverend Sir, you want firewood, you should let go the hatchet from your hand and say : 'Please fetch me firewood : make me fire!' And it will do so."

So he gave him the hatchet; and went to the second hermit, and asked : "Reverend Sir, what are you in need of?"

Now the elephants had made a track for themselves close to his hut. And he was annoyed by those elephants, and said : "I am much troubled by elephants, and said : "I am much troubled by elephants; drive them away."

Sakka, handing him a drum, said : "Reverend Sir, if you strike on this side of it, your enemies will take to flight; but if you strike on this side, they will become friendly, and surround you on all sides with an army in fourfold array."[22]

So he gave him the drum; and went to the third hermit, and asked : "Reverend Sir, what are you in need of?"

He was also affected with jaundice, and said, therefore : "I want sour milk."

Sakka gave him a milk-bowl, and said : "If you wish for anything, and turn this bowl over, it will become a great river, and pour out such a torrent, that it will be able to take a kingdom, and give it to you."

And Sakka went away. But thenceforward the hatchet made fire for the eldest hermit; when the second struck on side of his drum, the elephants ran away; and the third enjoyed his curds.

Now at that time a wild boar, straying in a forsaken village, saw a gem of magical power. When he seized this in his mouth, he rose by its magic into the air, and went to an island in the midst of the ocean. And thinking "Here now I ought to live", he descended, and took up his abode in a convenient spot under un Udumbara-tree. And one day, placing the gem before him, he fell asleep at the foot of the tree.

Now a certain man of the land of Kāsi had been expelled from home by his parents, who said : "This fellow is of no use to us." So he went to a seaport, and embarked in a ship as a servant to the sailors. And the ship was wrecked; but by the help of a plank he reached that very island. And while he was looking about for fruits, he saw the boar asleep; and going softly up, he took hold of the gem.

Then by its magical power he straightway rose right up into the air! So, taking a seat on the Udumbara-tree, he said to himself : "Methinks this boar must have become a sky-walker through the magic of this gem. That's how he got to be living here! It's plain enough what I ought to do; I'll first of all kill and eat him, and then I can get away!"

So he broke a twig off the tree, and dropped it on his head. The boar woke up, and not seeing the gem, ran about, trembling, this way and that way. The man seated on the tree laughed. The boar, looking up, saw him, and dashing his head against the tree, died on the spot.

But the man descended, cooked his flesh, ate it, and rose into the air. And as he was passing along the summit of the

Himālaya range, he saw a hermitage; and descending at the hut of the eldest hermit, he stayed there two or three days, and waited on the hermit; and thus became aware of the magic power of the hatchet.

"I must get that", thought he. And he showed the hermit the magic power of his gem, and said : "Sir, do you take this, and give me your hatchet." The ascetic, full of longing to be able to fly through the air,[23] did so. But the man, taking the hatchet, went a little way off, and letting it go, said : "O hatchet! cut off that hermit's head, and bring the gem to me!" And it went, and cut off the hermit's head, and brought him the gem.

Then he put the hatchet in a secret place, and went to the second hermit, and stayed there a few days. And having thus become aware of the magic power of the drum, he exchanged the gem for the drum; and cut off *his* head too in the same way as before.

Then he went to the third hermit, and saw the magic power of the milk-bowl; and exchanging the gem for it, caused *his* head to be cut off in the same manner. And taking the gem, and the hatchet, and the drum, and the milk-bowl, he flew away up into the air.

Not far from the city of Benāres he stopped, and sent by the hand of a man a letter to the king of Benāres to this effect : "Either do battle, or give me up your kingdom!"

No sooner had he heard that message than the king sallied forth, saying : "Let us catch the scoundrel!"

But the man beat one side of his drum, and a fourfold army stood around him! And directly he saw that the king's army was drawn out in battle array, he poured out his milk-bowl; and a mighty river arose, and the multitude, sinking down in it, were not able to escape! Then letting go to hatchet, he said : "Bring me the king's head!" And the hatchet went, and brought the king's head, and threw it at his feet; and no one had time even to raise a weapon!

Then he entered the city in the midst of his great army, and caused himself to be anointed king, under the name of Dadhi-vāhana (Bringer of Milk), and governed the kingdom with righteousness.[24]

The story goes on to relate how the king planted a wonderful mango, how the sweetness of its fruit turned to sourness through the too-close proximity of bitter herbs (!), and how the Bodisat, then the king's minister, pointed out that evil communications corrupt good things. But it is the portion above translated which deserves notice as the most ancient example known of those tales in which inanimate objects are endowed with magical powers; and in which the seven league boots, or the wishing cup, or the vanishing hat, or the wonderful lamp, render their fortunate possessors happy and glorious. There is a very tragical story of a wishing cup in the Buddhist Collection,[25] where the wishing cup, however, is turned into ridicule. It is not unpleasant to find that beliefs akin to, and perhaps the result of, fetish-worship, had faded away, among Buddhist story-tellers, into sources of innocent amusement.

In this curious tale the hatchet, the drum, and the milk-bowl are endowed with qualities much more fit for the use they were put to in the latter part of the story, than to satisfy the wants of the hermits. It is common ground with satirists how little, save sorrow men would gain if they could have anything they chose to ask for. But, unlike the others we have quoted, the tale in its present shape has a flavour distinctively Buddhist in the irreverent way in which it treats the great god Sakka, the Jupiter of the pre Buddhistic Hindus. It takes for granted too, that the hero ruled in righteousness; and this is as common in the Jātakas as the 'lived happily ever after' of modern love stories.

This last idea recurs more strongly in the Birth Story called.

A LESSON FOR KING

Rājovāda Jātaka

(Fausböll, no. 151)

Once upon a time, when Brahmadatta was reigning in Benāres, the future Buddha returned to life in the womb of his chief queen; and after the conception ceremony had been performed, he was safely born. And when the day came for choosing a name, they called him Prince Brahmadatta. He grew up in due course; and when he was sixteen years old, went to Takkasilā,[26] and became accomplished in all arts. And after this father died he ascended the throne, and ruled the kingdom with righteousness and equity. He gave judgments without partiality, hatred, ignorance, or fear.[27] Since he thus reigned with justice, with justice also his ministers administered the law. Lawsuits being thus decided with justice, there were none who brought false cases. And as these ceased, the noise and tumult of litigation ceased in the king's court. Though the judges sat all day in the court, they had to leave without any one coming for justice. It came to this, that the Hall of Justice would have to be closed!

Then the future Buddha thought : "From my reigning with righteousness there are none who come for judgment; the bustle has ceased, and the Hall of Justice will have to be closed. It behoves me, therefore, now to examine into my own faults; and if I find that anything is wrong in me, to put that away and practise only virtue."

Thenceforth he sought for some one to tell him his faults; but among those around him he found no one who would tell him of any fault, but heard only his own praise.

Then he thought : "It is from fear of me that these men speak only good things, and not evil things," and he sought among those people who lived outside the palace. And finding no fault-finder there, he sought among those who lived outside the city, in the suburbs, at the four gates.[28] And there too finding no one to find fault, and hearing only his own praise, he determined to search the country places.

So he made over the kingdom to his ministers, and mounted his chariot; and taking only his charioteer, left the city in disguise. And searching the country through, up to the very boundary, he found no faultfinder, and heard only of his own virtue; and so he turned back from the outermost boundary, and returned by the high road towards the city.

Now at that time the king of Kosala, Mallika by name, was also ruling his kingdom with righteousness; and when seeking for some fault in himself, he also found no fault-finder in the palace, but only heard of his own virtue! So seeking in country places, he too came to that very spot. And these two came face to face in a low cart-track with precipitous sides, where there was no space for a chariot to get out of the way!

Then the charioteer of Mallika the king said to the charioteer of the king of Benāres : "Take thy chariot out of the way!"

But he said : "Take thy chariot out of the way, O charioteer! In this chariot sitteth the lord over the kingdom of Benāres, the great king Brahmadatta."

Yet the other replied : "In this chariot, O charioteer, sitteth the lord over the kingdom of Kosala, the great king Mallika. Take thy carriage out of the way, and make room for the chariot of our king!"

Then charioteer of the king of Benāres thought : "They say then that he too is a king! What is now to be done?" After some consideration, he said to himself, "I know a way. I'll find out how old he is, and then I'll let the chariot of the younger be got out of the way, and so make room for the elder."

And when he had arrived at that conclusion, he asked that charioteer what the age of the king of Kosala was. But on inquiry he found that the ages of both were equal. Then he inquired about the extent of his kingdom, and about his army, and his wealth, and his renown, and about the country he lived in, and his caste and tribe and family. And he found that both were lords of a kingdom three hundred leagues in extent; and that in respect of army and wealth and renown, and the countries in which they lived, and their caste and their tribe and their family, they were just on a par!

Then he thought : "I will make way for the most righteous." And he asked : "What kind of righteousness has this king of yours?"

And the other saying : "Such and such is our king's righteousness", and so proclaiming his king's wickedness as goodness, uttered the First Stanza :

The strong he overthrows by strength,
The mild by mildness, Mallika;
The good by goodness he o'ercomes,
The wicked by the wicked too.
Such is the nature of this king!
Move out of the way, O charioteer!

But the charioteer of the king of Benāres asked him : "Well, have you told all the virtues of your king?"

"Yes", said the other.

"If these are his *virtues,* where are then his faults?" replied he.

The other said : "Well, for the nonce, they shall be faults, if you like! But pray, then, what is the kind of goodness your king has?"

And then the charioteer of the king of Benāres called unto him to hearken, and uttered the Second Stanza :

Anger he conquers by not-anger,
By goodness he conquers what is not good;
The stingy he conquers by giving gifts,
By truth he meets the speaker of lies.
Such is the nature of this king!
Move out of the way, O charioteer!"

And when he had thus spoken, both Mallika the king and his charioteer alighted from their chariot. And they took out the horses, and removed their chariot, and made way for the king of Benāres!

But the king of Benāres exhorted Mallika the king, saying : "Thus and thus is it right to do." And returning to Benāres, he practised charity, and did other good deeds, and so when his life was ended he passed away to heaven.

And Mallika the king took his exhortation to heart; and having in vain searched the country through for a fault-finder, he too returned to his own city, and practised charity and other good deeds; and so at the end of his life he went to heaven.

The mixture in this Jātaka of earnestness with dry humour is very instructive. The exaggeration in the earlier part of the story; the hint that law depends in reality on false cases; the suggestion that to decide cases justly would be itself put an end not only to "the block in the law courts", but even to all lawsuits; the way in which it is brought about that two mighty kings should meet, unattended, in a narrow lane; the cleverness of the first charioteer in getting out of his difficulties; the brand-new method of settling the delicate question of precedence–a method which, logically carried out, would destroy the necessity of such questions being raised at all;–all this is the amusing side of the Jātaka. It throws, and is meant to throw, an air of unreality over the story; and it is none the less humour because it is left to be inferred, because it is only an aroma which might easily escape unnoticed, only the humour or naïve absurdity and of clever repartee.

But none the less also is the story-teller thoroughly in earnest; he really means that justice is noble, that to conquer evil by good is the right thing, and that goodness is the true measure of greatness. The object is edification also, and not amusement only. The lesson itself is quite Buddhistic. The first four lines of the Second Moral are indeed included, as verse 223, in the *Dhammapada* ór "Scripture Verses", perhaps the most sacred and most widely learnt book of the Buddhist Bible; and the distinction between the two ideals of virtue is in harmony with all Buddhist ethics. It is by no means, however, exclusively Buddhistic. It gives expression to an idea that would be consistent with most of the later religions; and is found also in the great Hindu Epic, the *Mahā Bhārata,* which has been called the Bible of the Hindus.[29] It is true that further on in that poem is found the opposite sentiment, attributed in our story to the king of Mallika;[30] and that the higher teaching is in one of the latest portions of the *Mahā Bhārata,* and probably of Buddhist origin. But when we find that the Buddhist principle of overcoming evil by good was received, as well as its opposite, into the Hindu poem, it is clear that this lofty doctrine was by no means repugnant to the best among the Brahmans.[31]

It is to be regretted that some writers on Buddhism have been led away by their just admiration for the noble teaching of Gotama into an unjust depreciation of the religious system of which his own was, after all, but the highest product and result. There were doubtless among the Brāhmans uncompromising advocates of the worst privileges of caste, of the most debasing belief in the efficacy of rites and ceremonies; but this verse is only one among many others which are incontestable evidence of the wide prevalence also of a spirit of justice, and of an earnest seeking after truth. It is, in fact, inaccurate to draw any hard-and-fast line between the Indian Buddhists and their countrymen of other faiths. After the first glow of the Buddhist reformation had passed away, there was probably as little difference between Buddhist and Hindu as there was between the two kings in the story which has just been told.

THE KALILAG AND DAMNAG LITERATURE

Among the other points of similarity between Buddhists and Hindus, there is one which deserves more especial mention here–that of their liking for the kind of moral-comic tales which form the bulk of the Buddhist Birth Stories. That this partiality was by no means confined to the Buddhists is apparent from the fact that books of such tales have been amongst the most favourite literature of the Hindus. And this is the more interesting to us, as it is these Hindu collections that have most nearly preserved the form in which many of the Indian stories have been carried to the West.

The oldest of the collections now extant is the one already referred to, the *Pancha Tantra*, that is, the '*Five Books*', a kind of Hindu *Pentateuch* or *Pentamerone*. In its earliest form this work is unfortunately no longer extant; but in the sixth century of our era a book very much like it formed part of a work translated into Pahlavi, or Ancient Persian; and thence, about 750 A.D., into Syriac, under the title of *Kalilag and Damnag*, and into Arabic under the title *Kalilah and Dimnah*.[32]

These tales, though originally Buddhist, became great favourites among the Arabs; and as the Arabs were gradually brought into contact with Europeans, and penetrated into the South of Europe, they brought the stories with them; and we soon afterward find them translated into Western tongues. It would be impossible within the limits of this preface to set out in full detail the intricate literary history involved in this statement; and while I must refer the student to the Tables appended to this Introduction for fuller information, I can only give here a short summary of the principal facts.

It is curious to notice that it was the Jews to whom we owe the earliest versions. Whilst their mercantile pursuits took them much amongst the followers of the Prophet, and the comparative nearness of their religious beliefs led to a freer intercourse than was usually possible between Christians and Moslems, they were naturally attracted by a kind of literature such as this–Oriental in morality, amusing in style, and perfectly free from Christian legend and from Christian dogma. It was also the kind of literature which travellers would most easily become acquainted with, and we need not therefore be surprised to hear that a Jew, named Symeon Seth, about 1080 A.D., made the first translation into a European language, viz. into modern Greek. Another Jew, about 1250, made a translation of a slightly different recension of the *Kalilah and Dimnah* into Hebrew; and a third, John of Capua, turned this Hebrew version into Latin between 1263 and 1278. At about the same time as the Hebrew version, another was made direct from the Arabic into Spanish, and a fifth into Latin; and from these five versions translations were afterwards made into German, Italian, French, and English.

The title of the second Latin version just mentioned is very striking–it is "Aesop the Old." To the translator, Baldo, it evidently seemed quite in order to ascribe these new stories to the traditional teller of similar stories in ancient times; just as witty sayings of more modern times have been collected into books ascribed to the once venerable Joe Miller. Baldo was neither sufficiently enlightened to consider a good story the worse for being an old one, nor sufficiently scrupulous to hesitate at giving his new book the advantage it would gain from its connexion with a well-known name.

Is it true, then, that the so-called *Aesop's Fables*–so popular still, in spite of many rivals, among our Western children–are merely adaptations from tales invented long ago to please and to instruct the child like people of the East? I think I can give an answer, though not a complete answer, to the question.

Aesop himself is several times mentioned in classical literature, and always as the teller of stories or fables. Thus Plato says that Socrates in his imprisonment occupied himself by turning the stories (literally myths) of Aesop into verse :[33] Aristophanes four times refers to his tales :[34] and Aristotle quotes in one form a fable of his, which Lucian quotes in another.[35] In accordance with these references, classical historians fix the date of Aesop in the sixth century B.C.;[36] but some modern critics, relying on the vagueness and inconsistency of the traditions, have denied his existence altogether. This is, perhaps, pushing scepticism too far; but it may be admitted that he left no written works, and it is quite certain that if he did, they have been irretrievably lost.

Notwithstanding this, a learned monk of Constantinople, named Planudes, and the author also of numerous other works, did not hesitate, in the first half of the fourteenth century, to write a work which he called a collection of *Aesop's Fables*. This was first printed at Milan at the end of the fifteenth century; and two other supplementary collections have subsequently appeared.[37] From these, and especially from the work of Planudes, all our so-called *Aesop's Fables* are derived.

Whence then did Planudes and his fellow-labourers draw their tales? This cannot be completely answered till the source of each one of them shall have been clearly found, and this has not yet been completely done. But Oriental and classical scholars have already traced a goodly number of them; and the general results of their investigations may be shortly stated.

Babrius, a Greek poet, who probably lived in the first century before Christ, wrote in verse a number of fables, of which a few fragments were known in the Middle Ages.[38] The complete work was fortunately discovered by Mynas in the year 1824, at Mount Athos; and both Bentley and Tyrwhitt from the fragments, and Sir George Cornewall Lewis in his well-known edition of the whole work, have shown that several of Planudes' *Fables* are also to be found in Babrius.[39]

It is possible, also, that the Aesopian fables of the Latin poet Phaedrus, who in the title of his work calls himself a freedman of Augustus, were known to Planudes. But the work of Phaedrus, which is based on that of Babrius, existed only in very rare MSS. till the end of the sixteenth century,[40] and may therefore have easily escaped the notice of Planudes.

On the other hand, we have seen that versions of Buddhist Birth Stories, and other Indian tales, had appeared in Europe before the time of Planudes in Greek, Latin, Hebrew, and Spanish; and many of his stories have been clearly traced back to this source.[41] Further, as I shall presently show, some of the fables of Babrius and Phaedrus, found in Planudes, were possibly derived by those authors from Buddhist sources. And lastly, other versions of the Jātakas, besides those which have been mentioned as coming through the Arabs, had reached Europe long before the time of Planudes; and some more of his stories have been traced back to Buddhist sources through these channels also.

What is at present known, then, with respect to the so-called *Aesop's Fables*, amounts to this–that none of them are really Aesopean at all; that the collection was first formed in the Middle Ages; that a large number of them have been already traced back, in various ways, to our Buddhist Jātaka Book; and that almost the whole of them are probably derived in one way or another from Indian sources.

It is perhaps worthy of mention, as a fitting close to the history of the so-called *Aesop's Fables,* that those of his stories which Planudes borrowed indirectly from India have at length been restored to their original home, and bid fair to be popular even in this much-altered form. For not only has an Englishman translated a few of them into several of the many languages spoken in the great continent of India,[42] but Narāyan Balkrishṇa Godpole, B.A., one of the Masters of the Government High School at Ahmadnagar, has lately published a second edition of his translation into Sanskrit of the common English version of the successful spurious compilations of the old monk of Constantinople!

THE BARLAAM AND JOSAPHAT LITERATURE

A complete answer to the question with which the last digression started can only be given when each one of the two hundred and thirty-one fables of Planudes and his successors shall have been traced back to its original author. But–whatever that complete answer may be–the discoveries just pointed out are at least most strange and most instructive. And yet if I mistake not, the history of the Jātaka Book contains hidden amongst its details a fact more unexpected and more striking still.

In the eighth century the Khalif of Bagdad was that Almansur at whose court was written the Arabic book *Kalilah and Dimnah,* afterwards translated by the learned Jews I have mentioned into Hebrew, Latin, and Greek. A Christian, high in office at his court, afterwards became a monk, and is well known, under the name of St. John of Damascus, as the author in Greek of many theological words in defence of the orthodox faith. Among these is a religious romance called *Barlaam and Jōasaph,* giving the history of an Indian prince who was converted by Barlaam and became a hermit. This history, the reader will be surprised to learn, is taken from the life of the Buddha; and Joasaph is merely the Buddha under another name, the word Joasaph, or Josaphat, being simply a corruption of the word Bodisat, that title of the future Buddha so constantly repeated in the Buddhist Birth Stories.[43] Now a life of the Buddha forms the introduction to our Jātaka Book, and St. John's romance also contains a number of fables and stories, most of which have been traced back to the same source.[44]

This book, the first religious romance published in a Western language, became very popular indeed, and, like the Arabic *Kalilah and Dimnah,* was translated into many other European languages. It exists in Latin, French, Italian, Spanish, German, English, Swedish, and Dutch. This will show how widely it was read, and how much its moral tone pleased the taste of the Middle Ages. It was also translated as early as 1204 into Icelandic, and has even been published in the Spanish dialect used in the Philippine Islands!

Now it was a very ancient custom among Christians to recite at the most sacred part of their most sacred service (in the so-called Canon of the Mass, immediately before the consecration of the Host) the names of deceased saints and martyrs. Religious men of local celebrity were inserted for this purpose in local lists, called Diptychs, and names universally honoured throughout Christendom appeared in all such catalogues. The confessors and martyrs so honoured are now said to be *canonized,* that is, they have become enrolled among the number of Christian saints mentioned in the 'Canon', whom it is the duty of every Catholic to revere, whose intercession may be invoked, who may be chosen as patron saints, and in whose honour images and altars and chapels may be set up.[45]

For a long time it was permitted to the local ecclesiastics to continue the custom of inserting such names in their 'Diptychs', but about 1170 a decretal of Pope Alexander III confined the power of canonization, as far as the Roman Catholics were concerned,[46] to the Pope himself. From the different Diptychs various martyrologies, or lists of persons so to be commemorated in the 'Canon', were composed to supply the place of the merely local lists or Diptychs. For, as time went on, it began to be considered more and more improper to insert new names in so sacred a part of the Church prayers; and the old names being well known, the Diptychs fell into disuse. The names in the Martyrologies were at last no longer inserted in the Canon, but are repeated in the service called the 'Prime', though the term 'canonized' was still used of the holy men mentioned in them. And when the increasing number of such Martyrologies threatened to lead to confusion, and to throw doubt on the exclusive power of the Popes to canonize, Pope Sixtus the Fifth (1585-90) authorized a particular *Martyrologium,* drawn up by Cardinal Baronius, to be used throughout the Western Church. In that work are included not only the saints first canonized at Rome, but all those who, having been already canonized elsewhere, were then acknowledged by the Pope and the College of Rites to be saints of the Catholic Church of Christ. Among such, under the date of the 27th November, are included 'The holy Saints Barlaam and Josaphat, of India, on the borders of Persia, whose wonderful acts Saint John of Damascus has described.'[47]

Where and when they were first canonized, I have been unable, in spite of much investigation, to ascertain. Petrus de Natalibus, who was Bishop of Equilium, the modern Jesolo, near Venice, from 1370 to 1400, wrote a Martyrology called *Catalogus Sanctorum;* and in it, among the 'saints', he inserts both Barlaam and Josaphat, giving also a short account of them derived from the old Latin translation of St. John of Damascus.[48] It is from this work that Baronius the compiler of the authorized Martyrology now in use, took over the names of these two saints, Barlaam and Josaphat. But, so far as I have been able to ascertain, they do not occur in any martyrologies or lists of saints of the Western Church older than that of Petrus de Natalibus.[49]

In the corresponding manual of worship still used in the Greek Church, however, we find, under 26th August, the name 'of the holy Iosaph, so of Abenēr, king of India.'[50] Barlaam is not mentioned, and is not therefore recognized as a saint in the Greek Church. No history is added to the simple statement I have quoted; and I do not know on what authority it rests. But there is no doubt that it is in the East, and probably among the records of the ancient church of Syria, that a final solution of this question should be sought.[51]

Some of the more learned of the numerous writers who translated or composed new works on the basis of the story of Josaphat, have pointed out in their notes that he had been canonized;[52] and the hero of the romance is usually called St. Josaphat in the titles of these works, as will be seen from the Table of the Josaphat literature below. But Professor Liebrecht, when identifying Josaphat with the Buddha, took no notice of this; and it was Professor Max Müller, who has done so much to infuse the glow of life into the dry bones of Oriental scholarship, who first pointed out the strange fact–almost incredible, were it not for the completeness of the proof–that Gotama the Buddha, under the name of St. Josaphat, is now officially recognized and honoured and worshipped throughout the whole of Catholic Christendom as a Christian saint!

I have now followed the Western history of the Buddhist Book of Birth Stories along two channels only. Space would fail me, and the reader's patience perhaps too, if I attempted to do more. But I may mention that the inquiry is not by any means exhausted. A learned Italian has proved that a good many of the stories of the hero known throughout Europe as *Sinbad the Sialor* are derived from the same inexhaustible treasury of stories, witty and wise;[53] and a similar remark applies also to other well known Tales included in the *Arabian Nights.*[54] La Fontaine, whose charming versions of the Fables are so deservedly admired, openly acknowledge his indebtedness to the French versions of *Kalilah and Dimnah*; and Professor Benfey and others have traced the same stories, or ideas drawn from them, to Poggio, Baccaccio, Gower, Chaucer, Spenser, and many other later writers. Thus, for instance, the three caskets and the pound of flesh in *The Merchant of Venice,* and the precious jewel which in *As you Like It* the venomous toad wears in his head,[55] are derived from the Buddhist tales. In a similar way it has been shown that tales current among the Hungarians and the numerous peoples of Slavonic race have been derived from Buddhist sources, through translations made by or for the Huns, who penetrated in the time of Genghis Khān into the East of Europe.[56] And finally yet other Indian tales, not included in the *Kalilag and Damnag* literature, have been brought into the opposite corner of Europe, by the Arabs of Spain.[57]

There is only one other point on which a few words should be said. I have purposely chosen as specimens one Buddhist Birth Story similar to the Judgment of Solomon; two which are found also in Babrius; and one which is found also in Phaedrus. How are these similarities, on which the later history of Indian Fables throws no light, to be explained?

As regards the cases of Babrius and Phaedrus, it can only be said that the Greeks who travelled with Alexander to India may have taken the tales there, but they may equally well have brought them back. We only know that at the end of the fourth, and still more in the third century before Christ, there was constant travelling to and fro between the Greek dominions in the East and the adjoining parts of India, which were then Buddhist, and that the Birth Stories were already popular among the Buddhists in Afghanistan, where the Greeks remained for a long time. Indeed, the very region which became the seat of the Graeco-Bactrian kings takes, in all the Northern versions of the Birth Stories, the place occupied by the country of Kāsi in the Pāli text–so that the scene of the tales is laid in that district. And among the innumerable Buddhist remains still existing there, a large number are connected with the Birth Stories.[58] It is also in this very district, and under the immediate successor of Alexander, that the original of the *Kalilah and Dimnah* was said by its Arabian translators to have been written by Bidpai. It is possible that a smaller number of similar stories were also current among the Greeks; and that they not only heard the Buddhist ones, but told their own. But so far as the Greek and the Buddhist stories can at present be compared, it seems to me that the internal evidence is in favour of the Buddhist versions being the originals from which the Greek versions were adapted. Whether more than this can be at present said is very doubtful : when the Jātakas are all published, and the similarities between them and classical stories shall have been fully investigated, the contents of the stories may enable criticism to reach a more definite conclusion.

The case of Solomon's judgment is somewhat different. If there were only one fable in Babrius on Phaedrus identical with a Buddhist Birth Story, we should suppose merely that the same idea had occurred to two different minds : and there would thus be no necessity to postulate any historical connexion. Now the similarity of the two judgments stands, as far as I know, in complete isolation; and the story is not so curious but that two writers may have hit upon the same idea. At the same time it is just possible that when the Jews were in Babylon they may have told, or heard, the story.

Had we met with this story in a book unquestionably later than the Exile, we might suppose that they heard the story there; that some one repeating it has ascribed the judgment to King

Solomon, whose great wisdom was a common tradition among them; and that it had thus been included in their history of that king. But we find it in the *Book of Kings,* which is usually assigned to the time of Jeremiah, who died during the Exile; and it should be remembered that the chronicle in question was based for the most part on traditions current much earlier among the Jewish people, and probably on earlier documents.

If, on the other hand, they told it there, we may expect to find some evidence of the fact in the details of the story as preserved in the Buddhist story-books current in the North of India, and more especially in the Buddhist countries bordering on Persia. Now Dr. Dennys, in his *Folk-lore of China,* has given us a Chinese Buddhist version of a similar judgment, which is most probably derived from a Northern Buddhist Sanskrit original; and though this version is very late, and differs so much in its details from those of both the Pāli and Hebrew tales that it affords no basis itself for argument, it yet holds out the hope that we may discover further evidence of a decisive character. This hope is confirmed by the occurrence of a similar tale in the *Gesta Romanorum* a medieval work which quotes *Barlaam and Josaphat,* and is otherwise largely indebted in an indirect way to Buddhist sources.[59] It is true that the basis of the judgment in that story is not the love of a mother to her son, but the love of a son to his father. But that very difference is encouraging. The orthodox compilers of the 'Gests of the Romans'[60] dared not have so twisted the sacred record. They could not therefore have taken it from our Bible. Like all their other tales, however, this one was borrowed from somewhere; and its history, when discovered, may be expected to throw some light on this inquiry.

I should perhaps point out another way in which this tale may possibly be supposed to have wandered from the Jews to the Buddhists, or from India to the Jews. The land of Ophir was probably in India. The Hebrew names of the apes and peacocks said to have been brought thence by Solomon's coasting-vessels are merely corruptions of Indian names; and Ophir must therefore have been either an Indian port (and if so, almost certainly at the mouth of the Indus, afterwards a Buddhist country) or an entrepôt, further west, for Indian trade. But the very gist of the account of Solomon's expedition by sea is its unprecedented and hazardous character; it would have been impossible even for him without the aid of Phoenician sailors; and it was not renewed by the Hebrews till after the time when the account of the judgment was recorded in the *Book of Kings.* Any intercourse between his servants and the people of Ophir must, from the difference of language, have been of the most meagre extent; and we may safely conclude that it was not the means of the migration of our tale. It is much more likely, if the Jews heard or told the Indian story at all, and before the time of the captivity, that the way of communication was overland. There is every reason to believe that there was a great and continual commercial intercourse between East and West from very early times by way of Palmyra and Mesopotamia. Though the intercourse by sea was not continued after Solomon's time, gold of Ophir,[61] ivory, jade, and Eastern gems still found their way to the West; and it would be an interesting task for an Assyrian or Hebrew scholar to trace the evidence of this ancient overland route in other ways.

SUMMARY

To sum up what can at present be said on the connexion between the Indian tales, preserved to us in the Book of Buddhist Birth Stories, and their counterparts in the West :

1. In a few isolated passages of Greek and other writers, earlier than the invasion of India by Alexander the Great, there are references to a legendary Aesop, and perhaps also allusions to stories like some of the Buddhist ones.
2. After Alexander's time a number of tales also found in the Buddhist collection became current in Greece, and are preserved in the poetical versions of Babrius and Phaedrus. They are probably of Buddhist origin.
3. From the time of Babrius to the time of the first Crusade no migration of Indian tales to Europe can be proved to have taken place. About the latter time a translation into

Arabic of a Persian work containing tales found in the Buddhist book was translated by Jews into Greek, Hebrew, and Latin. Translations of these versions afterwards appeared in all the principal languages of Europe.

4. In the eleventh or twelfth century a translation was made into Latin of the legend of *Barlaam and Josaphat,* a Greek romance written in the eighth century by St. John of Damascus on the basis of the Buddhist Jātaka book. Translations, poems, and plays founded on this work were rapidly produced throughout Western Europe.

5. Other Buddhist stories not included in either of the works mentioned in the two last paragraphs were introduced into Europe both during the Crusades and also during the dominion of the Arabs in Spain.

6. Versions of other Buddhist stories were introduced into Eastern Europe by the Huns under Genghis Khān.

7. The fables and stories introduced through these various channels became very popular during the Middle Ages, and were used as the subjects of numerous sermons, story-books, romances, poems, and edifying dramas. Thus extensively adopted and circulated, they had a considerable influence on the revival of literature, which, hand in hand with the revival of learning, did so much to render possible and to bring about the Great Reformation. The character of the hero of them–the Buddha, in his last or in one or other of his supposed previous births–appealed so strongly to the sympathies, and was so attractive to the minds of medieval Christians, that he became, and has ever since remained, an object of Christian worship. And a collection of these and similar stories–wrongly, but very naturally, ascribed to a famous story-teller of the ancient Greeks–has become the common property, the household literature, of all the nations of Europe; and, under the name of *Aesop's Fables,* has handed down, as a first moral lesson-book and as a continual feast for our children in the West, tales first invented to please and to instruct our far-off cousins in the distant East.

REFERENCES

1. James's *Aesop's Fables* (London, Murray, 1852), p. 111; La Fontaine, Book v, no. 21; Aesop (Greek text, ed. Furia, 141, 262; ed. Coriae, 113); Babrius (Lewis, vol. ii, p. 43).
2. Benfey's *Pancha Tantra,* Book iv, no. 7 in the note on which, at vol. i, p. 462, he refers to Halm, p. 333; Robert, in the *Fables inédites du Moyen Age,* vol. i, p. 360; and the Turkish *Tūtīnāmah* (Rosen, vol. ii, p. 149). In India it is found also in the Northern Buddhist Collection called *Kathā Sarit Sāgara,* by Somadeva; and in *Hitopadeśa* (iii, 2, Max Müller, p. 110).
3. *Kratylos,* 411 (ed. Tauchnitz, ii, 275).
4. Lucian, *Piscator,* 32
5. Vol. ii, no. 91.
6. *Adagia,* under *Asinus apud Cumanos.*
7. Act ii, scene 1; and again, Act iii, scene 1.
8. De Sacy, *Notes et Extraits,* x, 1, 247.
9. loc. cit., p. 463.
10. *Pancha Tantra,* v, 7. Professor Weber (*Indische Studien,* iii, 352) compares Phaedrus (Dressler, App. vi.2) and Erasmus's *Adagia* under *Asinus ad Lyrum.* See also *Tūtī-nāmah* (Rosen ii, 218); and I would add Varro, in Aulus Gellius, iii, 16; and Jerome, Ep. 27 : *Ad Marcellam.*
11. Often rendered swan, a favourite bird in Indian tales, and constantly represented in Buddhist carvings. It is the original golden Goose. See Jātaka, no. 136.
12. There is an old story of a Fellow of Magdalen College, Oxford, who inherited a family living. He went in great trouble to Dr. Routh, the Head of his College, saying that he doubted whether he could hold, at the same time, the Living and the Fellowship. "You can hold anything," was the reply, "if you can only hold your tongue." And he held *all three.*
13. In the *Vinīla Jātaka* (no. 160) they similarly carry a crow to the Himālaya mountains.
14. *Pañca Tantra,* vol. 1, p. 13, where Professor Benfey (i, 239-41) traces also the later versions in different languages. He mentions Wolff's German translation of the *Kalilah and Dimnah,* vol. i, p. 91; Knatehbull's English version, p. 146; Simeon Seth's Greek version, p. 28; John of Capua's *Directorium Humanoe Vitoe* D, 5b; the German translation of this last (Ulm, 1483), F. viii, 6; the

Spanish translation, xix a; *Firenzuola,* 65; *Doni,* 93; *Anvār i Suhaili,* p. 159; *Le Livre des Lumiéres* (1664, 8vol), 124; *Le Cabinet des Fées,* xvii, 309. See also *contes et Fables Indiennes de Bidpai et de Lokman,* ii, 112; La Fontaine, x, 3 (where the ducks fly to America!); and Bickell's *Kalilag and Dimnag,* p. 24. In India it is found in *Somadeva,* and in the *Hitopadesa,* iv, 2 (Max Müller, p. 125). See also *Julien,* i, 71.

15. This version is found in *Babrius* (Lewis, i. 122); *Phoedrus,* ii, 7, and vii, 14 (Orelli, 55, 128); and in the Aesopaean collections (fur. 193; Coriae, 61) and in *Abstemius,* 108.
16. Dubois, p. 109.
17. See La Fontaine, Bk. i, no. 2, and the current collections of *Aesop's Fables* (e.g. James's ed., p. 136). It should be added that the *Jambukhādaka-sangyutta* in the *Sangyutta Nikāya* has nothing to do with our fable. The 'jambu-eater' or that story is an ascetic, who lives on jambus, and is converted by a discussion on Nirvāna.
18. The Singhalese text will be found in the *Sidat Sangarāwa,* p. clxxvi.
19. Literally "the great medicine". The Bodisat of that time received this name because he was born with a powerful drug in his hand–an omen of the cleverness in device by which, when he grew up, he delivered people from their misfortunes. Compare my *Buddhism,* p. 187.
20. The Yakshas, products of witchcraft and cannibalism, are beings of magical power, who feed on human flesh. The male Yaksha occupies in Buddhist stories a position similar to that of the wicked geni in the *Arabian Nights;* the female Yakshiṇī, who occurs more frequently, usually plays the part of siren.
21. Not quite the same as Jupiter. Sakka is a very harmless and gentle kind of god, not a jealous god, nor given to lasciviousness or spite. Neither is he immortal : he dies from time to time; and, if he has behaved well, is reborn under happy conditions. Meanwhile somebody else, usually one of the sons of men who has deserved it, succeeds, for a hundred thousand years or so, to his name and place and glory. Sakka can call to mind his experiences in his former birth, a gift in which he surpasses most other beings. He was also given to a kind of practical joking, by which he tempted people, and has become a mere beneficent fairy.
22. That is, infantry, cavalry, chariots of war, and elephants of war. Truly a useful kind of present to give to a pious hermit!

23. The power of going through the air is usually considered in Indian legends to be the result, and a proof, of great holiness, and long-continued penance. So the hermit thought he would get a fine reputation cheaply.
24. Compare *Mahā-bhārata,* xii, 1796.
25. Fausböll, no. 291.
26. This is the well-known town in the Panjāb, called by the Greeks Taxila, and famed in Buddhist legend as the great university of ancient India, as Nālanda was in later times.
27. Literally "without partiality and the rest", that is, the rest of the *agatis,* the actions forbidden to judges (and to kings as judges).
28. The gates opening towards the four "directions", that is, the four cardinal points of the compass.
29. *Mahā-Bhārata,* v, 1518. Another passage at iii, 13253, is very similar.
30. *Mahā-Bhārata,* xii, 4052. See Dr. Muir's *Metrical Translations from Sanskrit Writers* (1879), pp. xxxi, 88, 275, 356.
31. Similar passages will also be found in Lao Tse, Douglas's *Confucianism,* etc., p. 197; *Pancha Tantra,* i, 247 (277) = iv, 72; in Stobaeus, quoted by Muir, p. 356; and in St. Matthew, v, 44-6; while the Mallika doctrine is inculcated by Confucius (Legge, *Chinese Classics.* i, 152).
32. The names are corruptions of the Indian names of the two jackals, Karaṭak and Damanak, who take a principal part in the first of the fables.
33. *Phoedo,* p. 61. Comp. Bentley, *Dissertation on the Fables of Aesop,* p. 136.
34. *Vespoe,* 566, 1259, 1401 sqq.; and *Aves,* 651 sqq.
35. Arist., *de part, anim.,* iii, 2; Lucian, *Nigr.,* 32.
36. Herodotus (ii, 134) makes him contemporary with King Amasis of Egypt, the beginning of whose reign is placed in 569 B.C.; Plutarch (*Sept. Sap. Conv.,* 152) makes him contemporary with Solon, who is reputed to have been born in 638 B.C.; and Dioenes Laertius (i, 72) says that he flourished about the fifty-second Olympaid, *i.e.,* 572-69 B.C. Compare Clinton, *Fast. Hell.,* i, 237 under the year B.C. 572), and i, 239 (under B.C. 534).
37. One at Heidelberg in 1610, and the other at Paris in 1810. There is a complete edition of all these fables, 231 in number, by T.Gl. Schneider, Breslau, 1812.

38. See the editions by De Furia, Florence, 1809; Schneder, in an appendix to his edition of *Aesop's Fables,* Breslau, 1812; Berger, München, 1816; Knoch, Halle, 1835; and Lewis, *Philolog. Museum,* 1832, i, 280-304.
39. Bentley, loc. cit.; Tyrwhitt, *De Babrio,* etc., Lond., 1776. The edition of the newly-found MS. are by Lachmann, 1845; Orelli and Baiter, 1845; G.C. Lewis, 1846; and Schneidewin, 1853.
40. It was first edited by Pithou, in 1596; also by Orelli, Zürieh, 1831. Comp. Oesterley, *Phoedrus and die Aesop. Fabel im Mittelalter.*
41. By Silvestre de Sacy, in his edition of *Kalilah and Dimnah,* Paris, 1816; Loiseleur Deslongchamps, in his *Essai sur les Fables Indiennes, et sur leur Introd. en Europe,* Paris, 1838; Prof. Benfey, in his edition of the *Pañca Tantra,* Leipzig, 1859; Prof. Max Müller, *On the Migration of Fables, Contemporary Review,* July, 1870; Prof. Weber, *Ueber den Zusammenhang indischer Fabeln mit Griechischen, Indische Studien,* iii, 337 sqq.; Adolf Wagener, *Essai sur les rapport entre les apologues del' Inde et de la Gréce,* 1853; Otto Keller, Ueber *die Geschichte der Griechischen Fabeln,* 1862.
42. J. Gilchrist, *The Oriental Fabulist, or Polyglot Translations of Aesop's and other Ancient Fables from the English Language into Hindustani, Persian, Arabic, Bhakka, Bongla, Sanscrit, etc., in the Roman Character,* Calcutta, 1803.
43. Joasaph is in Arabic written also Yūdasatf; and this, through a confusion between the Arabic letter *Y* and *B,* is for Bodisat. See, for the history of these changes, Reinaud, *Memoire sur l' Inde,* 1849, p. 91; quoted with approbation by Weber, *Indische Streifen,* iii, 57.
44. The Buddhist origin was first pointed out by Laboulaye in the *Débats,* July 1859; and more fully by Liebrecht, in the *Jahrbuch für romanische and englische Literatur,* 1860. See also Littré, *Journal des Savans,* 1865, who fully discusses, and decides in favour of the romance being really the work or St. John of Damascus. I hope, in a future volume, to publish a complete analysis of St. John's work; pointing out the resemblances between it and the Buddhist lives of Gotama, and giving parallel passages wherever the Greek adopts not only the Buddhist ideas, but also Buddhist expressions.

45. Pope Benedict XIV, in *De servorum Dei beatificatione et beatorum canonisatione,* lib. i, cap. 45; regnier, *De ecclesid Christi,* in Migne's *Theol. Curs. Compl.,* iv, 710.
46. *Decrėt. Greg.* lib. iii, tit. xlvi, confirmed and explained by decrees of Urban VIII (13th March, 1625, and 5th July, 1634) and of Alexander VII (1659).
47. p. 177 of the edition of 1873, bearing the official approval of Pope Pius IX, or p. 803 of the Cologne edition of 1610.
48. *Cat. Sanct.,* Leyden ed. 1542, p. cliii.
49. The author added the following in his copy. They occur in the works of Usnard, a Benedictine, who wrote about 875 (published by Greven in 1515, and by Molanus in 1568). In the *Month* for 1881, p. 141, Father Coleridge. S.J., wrote that they occur in a Slavonic calendar of the 15th century, preserved in the Ecclesiastical Academy at Petrograd, and in several later Slavonic martyrologies, but not in the Menologium drawn up by Cardinal Girlet, from which the compilers of the Roman martyrology drew their notices of the saints of the Greek church. This work was published shortly before theirs. Coleridge says, that there may have been such saints, and that the Buddhist story may have been added to theirs, or derived from it.–Editor.
50. p. 160 of the part for the month of August of the authorized *Μηvaῖov* of the Greek Church, published at Constantinople, 1843. "*Τον όσίον' Ιωάσαφ, víov' Αβενηρ τον βασλεως της' Ινδίας.*"
51. For the information in the last three pages I am chiefly indebted to my father, the Rev. T.W. Davids, without whose generous aid I should not have attempted to touch this obscure and difficult question.
52. See, for instance, Billius, and the italian Editor, of 1734.
53. Comparetti, *Ricerche intorne al Libro di Sindibad,* Milano, 1869. Compare Landsberger, *Die Fabeln des Sophos,* Posen, 1859.
54. See Benfey, *Pantscha Tantra,* vol. i, Introduction, *passim.*
55. Act ii, sc. 1. Prof. Benfey, in his *Pantscha Tantra,* i, 213-20, has traced this idea far and wide. Dr. Dennys, in his *Folklore of China,* gives the Chinese Buddhist version of it.
56. See Benfey's *Introduction to Pañca Tantra,* §§ 36, 397, 1, 92, 166, 186. Ralston's translation of Tibetan stories throws further light on this, at present, rather obscure subject.
57. See for example Jāt. i, No. 30 : Muṇika-Jātaka. Benfey (*Pañca Tantra,* p. 228 f.) has traced stories somewhat analogous

throughout European literature, but the Jātaka itself is, he says, found almost word for word in an unpublished Hebrew book by Berachia ben Natronai, only that two donkeys take the place of the two oxen. Berachia lived in the 12th-13th century, in Provence.

The story of the monkey and his heart, in Jātaka ii, No. 208, occurs in a Japanese version given in Andrew Lang's *Violet Fairy Book,* p. 275, 'The Monkey and the Jellyfish,' sea and liver replacing Ganges and heart.–Editor.

58. The legend of Sumedha's self-abnegation (see below, p. 93) is laid near Jelālabad; and Mr. William Simpson has discovered on the spot two bas-reliefs representing the principal incident in the legend.
59. No. xlv. p. 80, of Swan and Hooper's popular edition; no. xlii, p. 167, of the critical edition published for the Early English Text Society in 1879 by S.J.H. Herrtage, who has added a valuable historical note at p. 477.
60. This adaptation of the Latin title is worthy of notice. If of course means "Deeds"; but, as most of the stories are more or less humorous, the word *Gest,* now spelt *Jest,* acquired its present meaning.
61. *Psalm* xiv, 9; *Isaiah* xiii, 12; *Job* xxii, 24, xxviii, 16.

PART II

ON THE HISTORY OF THE BIRTH STORIES IN INDIA

In the previous part of this Introduction I have attempted to point out the resemblances between certain Western tales and the Buddhist Birth Stories, to explain the reason of those resemblances, and to trace the history of the Birth Story literature in Europe. Much remains yet to be done to complete this interesting and instructive history; but the general results can already be stated with a considerable degree of certainty, and the literature in which further research will have to be made is accessible in print in the public libraries of Europe.

For the history in India of the *Jātaka Book* itself, and of the stories it contains, so little has been done that one may say it has still to be written; and the authorities for further research are only to be found in manuscripts very rare in Europe, and written in languages for the most part but little known. Much of what follows is necessarily therefore very incomplete and provisional.

In some portions of the Brāhmanical literature, later than the *Vedas*, and probably older than Buddhism, there are found myths and legends of a character somewhat similar to a few of the Buddhist ones. But, so far as I know, no one of these has been traced either in Europe or in the Buddhist Collection.

One the other hand, there is every reason to hope that in the older portions of the Buddhist Scriptures a considerable number of the tales also included in the *Jātaka Book* will be found in identical or similar forms; for even in the few fragment of the Piṭakas as yet studied, several Birth Stories have already been discovered.[1] These occur in isolated passages and, except the story of King Mahā Sudassana and that in Anguttara, i, p. 111, have not as yet become Jātakas–that is, no character in the story is identified with the Buddha in one or other of his supposed previous births. But one book included in the Pāli Piṭakas consists entirely of real Jātaka stories, all of which are found in our Collection.

The tile of this work is *Cariyā-piṭaka;* and it is constructed to show when, and in what births. Gotama had acquired the Ten Great Perfections (Generosity, Goodness, Renunciation, Wisdom, Firmness, Patience, Truth, Resolution, Kindness, and Equanimity), without which he could not have become a Buddha. In striking analogy with the modern view, that true growth in moral and intellectual power is the result of the labours, not of one only, but of many successive generations, so the qualifications necessary for the making of a Buddha, like the characters of all the lesser mortals, cannot be acquired during, and do not depend upon the actions of, one life only, but are the last result of many deeds performed through a long series of consecutive lives.[2]

To each of the first two of these Ten Perfections a whole chapter of this work is devoted, giving, in verse, ten examples of the previous births in which the Bodisat or future Buddha had plactised Generosity and Goodness respectively. The third chapter gives only fifteen examples of the lives in which he acquired the other eight of the Perfections. It looks very much as if the original plan of the unknown author had been to given ten Birth Stories for each of the Ten Perfections. And, curiously enough, the Northern Buddhists have a tradition that the celebrated teacher Aṣvagosha began to write a work giving ten Births for each of the Ten Perfections, but died when he had versified only thirty-four.[3] Now there is a Sanskrit work called *Jātaka Mālā,* as yet unpublished,[4] but of which there are several MSS. in Paris and in London, consisting of thirty-five Birth Stories in mixed prose and verse, in illustration of the Ten Perfections.[5] It would be premature to attempt to draw any conclusions from coincidences, but the curious reader will find in a Table below a comparative view of the titles of the Jātakas comprised in the Chariyā Piṭaka and in the Jātaka Mālā.[6]

There is yet another work in the Pāli Piṭakas which constantly refers to the Jātaka theory. The Buddhavaṃsa,[7] which is a history of all the Buddhas, gives an account also of the life of the Bodisat in the character he filled during the lifetime of each of twenty-four of the previous Buddhas. It is on that work that a great part of the Pāli Introduction to our *Jātaka Book* is based, and most of the verses in the first fifty pages of the present translation are quotations from, the Buddhavaṃsa. From this source we thus have authority for twenty-four Birth Stories, corresponding to the last twenty-four of the twenty-seven previous Buddhas,[8] besides the thirty-four in illustration of the Perfections, and the other isolated ones I have mentioned.

Beyond this it is impossible yet to state what proportion of the stories in the *Jātaka Book* can thus be traced back to the earlier Pāli Buddhist literature; and it would be out of place to enter here upon any lengthy discussion of the difficult question as to the date of those earlier records. The provisional conclusion was to the age of the Sutta and Vinaya reached by Dr. Oldenberg in the very able introduction prefixed to his edition of the text of the *Mahā Vagga,* and summarized at p. xxxviii of that work, will be sufficient for our present purposes. It may be taken as so highly probable as to be almost certain, that all those Birth Stories which are not only found in the so-called *Jātaka Book* itself, but are also referred to in these other parts of the Pāli Piṭ akas, are at least older than the council of Vesāli.[9]

The Council of Vesāli was held about a hundred years after Gotama's death, to settle certain disputes as to points of discipline and practice which had arisen among the members of the Older. The exact date of Gotama's death is uncertain;[10] and in the tradition regarding the length of the interval between that event and the Council, the "hundred years" is of course a round number. But we can allow for all possibilities, and still keep within the bounds of certainty, if we fix the date of the Council of Vesāli at within thirty years of 350 B.C.

The members of the Buddhist Order of Mendicant Monks were divided at that Council–as important for the history of Buddhism as the Council of Nice is for the history of Christianity–into two parties. One side advocated the relaxation of the rules of the Order in ten particular matters, the others adopted the stricter view. In the accounts of the matter, which we at present only possess from the successors of the stricter party (or, as they call themselves, the orthodox party), it is acknowledged that the other, the later side, were in the majority; and that when that older and more influential members of the Order decided in favour of the orthodox view, the others held a council of their own, called, from the numbers of those who attended it, the Great Council.

Now the oldest Ceylon Chronicle, the *Dīpavaṃsa,* which contains the only account as yet published of what occurred at the Great Council, says as follows :[11] "The monks of the Great Council turned the religion upside down;

They broke up the original Scriptures, and made a new recension :

A discourse put in one place they put in another;

They distorted the sense and the teaching of the Five Nikāyas.

Those monks–knowing not what had been spoken at length, and what concisely,

What was the obvious, and what was the higher meaning–

Attached new meaning to new words, as if spoken by the Buddha,

And destroyed much of the spirit by holding to the shadow of the letter.

In part they cast aside the Sutta and the Vinaya so deep,

And made an imitation Sutta and Vinaya, changing this to that.

The Pariwāra abstract, and the Six Books of abhidhamma;

The Paṭisambhidā, the Niddesa, *and a portion of the Jātaka*–

So much they put aside, and made others in their place!"

The animus of this description is sufficiently evident; and the *Dīpavaṃsa,* which cannot have been written earlier than the fourth century after the commencement of our era, is but poor evidence of the events of seven centuries before. But it is the best we have; it is acknowledged to have been based on earlier sources, and it is at least reliable that, according to Ceylon tradition, a book called the Jātaka existed at the time of the Councils of Vesāli.

As the Northern Buddhists are the successors of those who held the Great Council, we may hope before long to have the account of it from the other side, either from the Sanskrit or from the Chinese.[12] Meanwhile it is important to notice that the fact of a *Book of Birth Stories* having existed at a very early date is confirmed, not only by such stories being found in other parts of the Pāli Piṭakas, but also by ancient monuments.

Among the most interesting and important discoveries which we owe to recent archaeological researches in India must undoubtedly be reckoned those of the Buddhist carvings on the railings round the dome-shaped relic shrines of Sānchi, Amaravatī, and Bharhut. There have been there found, very boldly and clearly sculptured in deep bas-relief figures which were at first thought to represent merely scenes in Indian life. Even so their value as records of ancient civilization would have been of incalculable value; but they have acquired further importance since it has been proved that most of them are illustrations of the sacred Birth Stories in the Buddhist Jātaka book–are scenes, that is, from the life of Gotama in his last or previous births. This would be incontestable in many cases from the carvings themselves, but it is rendered doublysure by the titles of Jātakas having been found inscribed over a number of those of the bas-reliefs which have been last discovered–the carvings, namely, on the railing at Bharhut.

It is not necessary to turn aside here to examine into the details of these discoveries. It is sufficient for our present inquiry into the age of the Jātaka stories that these ancient bas-reliefs afford indisputable evidence that the Birth Stories were already at the end of the third century B.C., considered so sacred that they were chosen as the subjects to be represented round the most sacred Buddhist buildings, and that they were already popularly known under the technical name of "Jātakas". A detailed statement of all the Jātakas hitherto discovered on these Buddhist railings, and other places, will be found in one of the Tables appended to this Introduction; and it will be noticed that several of those tales translated below in this volume had thus been chosen, more than two thousand years ago, to fill places of honour round the relic shrines of the Great Teacher.

One remarkable fact apparent from that Table will be that the Birth Stories are sometimes called in the inscriptions over the bas-reliefs by names different from those given to them in the *Jātaka Book* in the Pāli Piṭakas. This would seem, at first sight, to show that, although the very stories as we have them must have been known at the time when the bas beliefs were carved, yet the present collection, in which different names are clearly given at the end of each story, did not then exist. But, on the other hand, we not only find in the Jātaka Book itself very great uncertainty as to the names–the same stories being called in different parts of the Book by different titles[13]–but one of these very bas-reliefs has actually inscribed over it two distinct names in full![14]

The reason for this is very plain. When a fable about a lion and a jackal was told (as in no. 157) to show the advantage of a good character, and it was necessary to choose a short title for it, it was called "The Lion Jātaka", or "The Jackal Jātaka", or even "The Good Character Jātaka"; and when a fable was told about a tortoise, to show the evil results which follow on talkativeness (as in no. 215), the fable might as well be called "The Chatterbox Jātaka" as "The Tortoise Jātaka", and the fable is referred to accordingly under both those names. It must always have been difficult, if not impossible, to fix upon a short title which should at once characterize the lesson to be taught, and the personages through whose acts it was taught; and different names would thus arise, and become interachangeable. It would be wrong therefore to attach too much importance to the difference of the names on the bas-reliefs and in the *Jātaka Book.* And in translating the titles we need not be afraid to allow ourselves a latitude similar to that which was indulged in by the early Buddhists themselves.

There is yet further evidence confirmatory of the *Dīpavaṃsa* tradition. The Buddhist Scriptures are sometimes spoken of as consisting of nine different divisions, or sorts of texts (*Angānī*), of which the seventh is *Jātakas,* or *The Jātaka Collection* (*Jātakaṃ*). This division of the Sacred Books is mentioned, not only in the *Dīpavaṃsa* itself, and in the *Sumangala Vilāsinī,* but also in the *Anguttara Nikāya* (one of the later works included in the Pāli Piṭakas, and in the *Saddharma Puṇḍarīka* (a late, but standard Sanskrit work of the Northern Buddhists).[15] It is common, therefore, to both of the two sections of the Buddhist Church; and it follows that it was probably in use before the great schism took place between them, possibly before the Council of Vesāli itself. In any case it is conclusive as to the existence of a collection of Jātakas at a very early date.

The text of the *Jātaka Book,* as now received among the Southern Buddhists, consists, as will be seen from the translation, not only of the stories, but of an elaborate commentary, containing a detailed Explanation of the verse or verses which occur in each of the stories; an Introduction to each of them, giving the occasion on which it is said to have been told; a conclusion, explaining the connexion between the personages in the Introductory Story and the characters in the Birth Story; and finally, a long general Introduction to the whole work. It is, in fact, an edition by a later hand of the earlier stories; and though I have called it concisely the *Jātaka Book* its full title is *The Commentary on the Jātakas.*

We do not know either the name of the author of this work, or the date when it was composed. The meagre account given at the commencement of the work itself (below, p. 81) contains all our present information on these points. Childers, who is the translator of this passage (below, p. lxxix), has elsewhere ascribed the work to Buddhaghosa[16]; but I venture to think that this is, to say the least, very uncertain.

We have, in the thirty-seventh chapter of the *Mahāvaṃsa,*[17] a perhaps almost contemporaneous account of Buddhaghosa's literary work; and it is there distinctly stated, that after writing in India the *Atthasālinī* (a commentary on the *Dhammasanganī,* the first of the *Six Books of the Abhidhamma Piṭataka*), he went to Ceylon (about 430 A.D.) with the express intention of translating the Singhalese commentaries into Pāli. There he studied under the Thera Sanghapāli, and having proved his efficiency by his great work *The Path of Purity* (*Visuddhi-Magga,* a compendium of doctrine), he was allowed by the monks in Ceylon to carry out his wish, and translate the commentaries. The Chronicle then goes on to say that he did render "the whole Singhalese Commentary" into Pāli. But it by no means follows, as has been too generally supposed, that he was the author of all the Pāli Commentaries we now possess. He translated, it may be granted, the *Commentaries on the Vinaya Piṭaka* and on the four great divisions (Nikāyas) of the *Sutta Pitaka;* but these works together with those mentioned above, would amply justify the very general expression of the chronicler. The *Singhalese Commentary* being now lost, it is impossible to say what books were and what were not included under that expression as used in the *Mahāvaṃsa*; and to assign any Pāli commentary, other than those just mentioned, to Buddhaghosa, some further evidence more clear than the ambiguous words of the Ceylon Chronicle should be required.

What little evidence we have as regards the particular work now in question seems to me to tend very strongly in the other direction. Buddhaghosa could scarcely have commenced his labours on the Jātaka Commentary, leaving the works I have mentioned–so much more important from his point of view–undone. Now I would ask the reader to imagine himself in Buddhaghosa's position, and then to read carefully the opening words of our *Jātaka Commentary* as translated below, and to judge of himself whether they could possibly be such words as Buddhaghosa would probably, under the circumstances, have written. It is a matter of feeling; but I confess I cannot think it possible that he was the author of them. Three Elders of the Buddhist Order are the mentioned with respect, but neither the name of Revata, Buddhaghosa's teacher in India, nor the name of Sanghapāli, his teacher in Ceylon, is even referred to; and there is not the slightest allusion either to Buddhaghosa's conversion, his journey from India, the high hopes he had entertained, or the work he had already accomplished! This silence seems to me almost as convincing as such negative evidence can possibly be.

If not, however, by Buddhaghosa, the work must have been composed after his time; but probably not long after. It is quite clear from the account in the *Mahāvaṃsa* that before he came to Ceylon, the Singhalese commentaries had not been turned into Pāli; and on the other hand, the example he had set so well will almost certainly have been quickly followed. We know one instance at least, that of the *Mahāvaṃsa* itself, which would confirm this supposition; and had the present work been much later than his time, it would not have been ascribed to Buddhaghosa at all.

It is worthy of notice, perhaps, in this connexion, that the Pāli work is not a translation of the Singhalese Commentary. The author three times refers to a previous *Jātaka Commentary.* Which possibly formed part of the Singhalese work, as a separate book;[18] and in one case mentions what it says only to overrule it.[19] Our Pāli work may have been based upon it, but cannot be said to be a mere version of it. And the present Commentary agrees almost word for word, from p. 58 to p. 124 of my translation, with the *Madhura-attha-vilāsinī*, the Commentary on the *Buddhavaṃsa* mentioned above, which is not usually ascribed to Buddhaghosa.[20]

The *Jātaka Book* is not the only Pāli Commentary which has made use of the ancient Birth Stories. They occur in numerous passages of the different exegetical works composed in Ceylon, and the only commentary of which anything is known in print, that on the *Dhammapada* or *Collection of Scripture Verses,* contains a considerable number of them. Mr. Fausböll has published copious extracts from this Commentary, which may be by Buddhaghosa, as an appendix to his edition of the text; and the work by Captain Rogers, entitled *Buddhaghosa's Parables*–a translation from a Burmese book called *Dhammapada-vatthu* (that is "Stories connected with the Dhammapada")–consists almost entirely of Jātaka tales.

In Siam there is even a rival collection of Birth Stories which is called *Paṇṇāsa-Jātakan* (*The Fifty Jātakas*), and of which an account has been given us by Léon Feer;[21] and the same scholar has pointed out that isolated stories, not contained in our collection, are also to be found in the Pāli literature of that country.[22] The first hundred and fifty tales in our collection are divided into three *Paṇṇāsas,* or fifties;[23] but the Siamese collection cannot be either of these, as M. Feer has ascertained that it contains no tales beginning in the same way as any of those in either of these "Fifties".

In India itself the Birth Stories survived the fall, as some of them had probably preceded the rise, of Buddhism. Not a few of them were preserved by being included in the *Mahā Bhārata,* the great Hindu epic which became the storehouse of Indian mythology, philosophy, and folk-life. Unfortunately the date of the final arrangement of the *Mahā Bhārata* is extremely uncertain, and there is no further evidence of the continued existence of the Jātaka tales till we come to the time of the work already frequently referred to–the *Pancha Tantra.*

It is to the history of this book that Benfey has devoted that elaborate and learned Introduction which is the most important contribution to the study of this class of literature as yet published; and I cannot do better than give in his own words his final conclusions as to the origin of this popular story-book[24] :

"Although we are unable at present to give any certain information either as to the author or as to the date of the work, we receive, as it seems to me, no unimportant compensation in the fact, that it turned out,[25] with a certainty beyond doubt, to have been originally a Buddhist book. This followed especially from the chapter discussed in § 225. But it was already indicated by the considerable number of the fables and tales contained in the work, which could also be traced in Buddhist writings. Their number, and also the relation between the form in which they are told in our work, and that in which they appear in the Buddhist writings, incline us–nay, drive us–to the conclusion that the latter were the source form which our work, within the circle of Buddhist literature, proceeded.

"The proof that our work is of Buddhist origin is of importance in two ways : firstly–on which we will not here further insist–for the history of the work itself; and secondly, for the history of the work itself; and secondly, for the determination of what Buddhism is. We can find in it one more proof of that literary activity of Buddhism, to which, in my articles on 'India', which appeared in 1840,[26] I had already felt myself compelled to assign the most important place in the enlightenment and general intellectual development of India. This view has since received, from year to year, fresh confirmations, which I hope to ring together in another place; and whereby I hope to prove that the very bloom of the intellectual life of India (whether it found expression in Brahmanical or Buddhist works) proceeded substantially from Buddhism, and is contemporaneous with the epoch in which Buddhism flourished;–that is to say, from the third century before Christ to the sixth or seventh century after Christ. With that principle, said to have been proclaimed by Buddhism in its earliest years, 'that only *that* teaching of the Buddha's is true which contraveneth not sound reason,'[27] the autonomy of man's Intellect was, we may fairly say, effectively acknowledged; the whole relation between the realms of the knowable and of the unknowable was subjected to its control; and notwithstanding that the actual reasoning powers, to which the ultimate appeal was thus given, were in fact then not altogether sound, yet the way was pointed out by which Reason could, under more favourable circumstances, begin to liberate itself from its failings. We are already learning to value in the philosophical endeavours of Buddhism, the labours, sometimes indeed quaint, but aiming at thoroughness and worthy of the highest respect, of its severe earnestness in inquiry. And that, side by side with this, the merry jests of light, and even frivolous poetry and conversation, preserved the cheerfulness of life, is clear from the prevailing tone of our work, and still more so from the probable Buddhist origin of those other Indian story-books which have hitherto become known to us."

Benfey then proceeds to show that the *Pancha Tantra* consisted originally, not of five, but of certainly eleven, perhaps of twelve, and just possibly of thirteen books; and that its original design was to teach princes right government and conduct.[28] The whole collection had then a different title descriptive of this design; and it was only after a part became detached from the rest that part was called, for distinction's sake, the *Pancha Tantra* (*The Five Books*). When this occurred it is impossible to say. But it was certainly the older and larger collection, not the present Pancha Tantra, which travelled into Persia, and became the source of the whole of the extensive *Kalilag and Damnag* literature.[29]

The Arabian authors of the work translated (through the ancient Persian) from this older collection assign it to a certain Bidpai; who is said to have composed it in order to instruct Dabschelim, the successor of Alexander in his Indian possessions, in worldly wisdom.[30] There may well be some truth in this tradition. And when we consider that the *Barlaam and Josaphat* literature took its origin at the same time, and into the same place, as the *Kalilag and Damnag* literature; that both of them are based upon Buddhist originals taken to Bagdad in the sixth century of our era; and that it is precisely such a book as the *Book of Birth Stories* from which they could have derived all that they borrowed; it is difficult to avoid connecting these facts together by the supposition that the work ascribed to Bidpai may, in fact, have been a selection of those Jātaka stories bearing more especially on the conduct of life, and preceded, like our own collection, by a sketch of the life of the Buddha in his last birth. Such a supposition would afford a reasonable explanation of some curious facts which have been quite inexplicable on the existing theory. If the Arabic *Kalilah and Dimnah* was an exact translation, in our modern sense of the word translation, of an exact translation of a Buddhist work, how comes it that the various copies of the *Kalilah and Dimnah* differ so greatly, not only among themselves, but from the lately discovered Syriac *Kalilag and Damnag,* which was also, according to the current hypothesis, a translation of the same original?–how comes it that in these translations from a Buddhist book there are no references to the Buddha, and no expressions on the face of them Buddhistic? If, on the other hand, the later writers had merely derived their subject-matter from a Buddhist work or works, and had composed what were in effect fresh works on the basis of such an original as has been suggested, we can understand how the different writers might have used different portions of the material before them, and might have described any expressions too directly in contradiction with their own religious beliefs.

The first three of those five chapters of the work ascribed to Bidpai which make up the *Pancha Tantra,* are also found in a form slightly different, but, on the whole, essentially the same, in two other Indian Story books–the *Kathā-Sarit-Sāgara* (*Ocean of the Rivers of Stories*), composed in Sanskrit by a Northern Buddhist named Somadeva in the twelfth century, and in the well-known *Hitopadeśa*, which is a much later work. If Somadeva had had the *Pancha Tantra* in its present form before him, he would probably have included the whole five books in his encyclopaedic collection; and the absence from the *Kathā-Sarit-Sāgara* of the last two books would tend to whom that when he wrote his great work the *Pancha Tantra* had not been composed, or at least had not reached the North of India.

Somadeva derived his knowledge of the three books he does not give from the *Vṛihat-Kathā,* a work ascribed to Guṇādhya, written in the Paiṣāchī dialect, and probably at least as early as the sixth century.[31] This work, on which Somadeva's whole poem is based, is lost. But Dr. Bühler has lately discovered another Sanskrit poem, based on that earlier work, written in Kashmïr by Kshemendra at the end of the eleventh century, and called, like its original, *Vṛihat-Kathā;* and as Somadeva wrote quite independently of this earlier poem, we may hope that a comparison of the two Sanskrit works will afford reliable evidence of the contents of the old *Vṛihat-Kathā.*[32]

I should also mention here that another well-known work, the *Vetāla-Pañca-Viṃsatī* (*The Twenty-five Tales of a Demon*), is contained in both the Sanskrit poems, and was therefore probably also in Guṇādhya's collection; but as no Jātaka stories have been as yet traced in it, I have simply included it for purposes of reference in Appendix, Table I, together with the most important of those of the later Indian storybooks of which anything is at present known.

There remains only to add a few words on the mode in which the stories, whose history in Europe and in India I have above attempted to trace, are presented to us in the *Jātaka Book.*

Each story is introduced by another explaining where and why it was told by Buddha; the Birth Story itself being called the *Atīta-vatthu* (*Story of the Past*) and the Introductory Story the *Paccuppannavatthu* (*Story of the Present*). There is another book in the Pāli *Piṭakas* called *Apadāna*, which consists of tales about the lives of certain early Buddhists; and many of the Introductory Stories in the *Jātaka Book* (such, for instance, as the tale about Little Roadling, no. 4, or the tale about Kumāra Kassapa, no. 12) differ very little from these *Apadānas.* Other of the Introductory Stories (such, for instance, as no. 17) seem to be mere repetitions of the principal idea of the story they introduce, and are probably derived from it. That the Introductory Stories are entirely devoid of credit is clear from the fact that different Birth Stories are introduced as having been told at the same time and place, and in answer to the same question. Thus no less than ten stories are each said to have been told to a certain love-sick monk as a warning to him against his folly;[33] the closely allied story given below as the Introduction to Birth Story no. 30 appears also as the Introduction to at least four others :[34] and there are many other instances of a similar kind.[35]

After the two stories have been told, there comes a Conclusion, in which the Buddha identifies the personages in the Birth Story with those in the Introductory Story; but it should be noticed that in one or two cases characters mentioned in the *Atītavatthu* are supposed not to have been reborn on earth at the time of the *Paccuppanna-vatthu.*[36] And the reader must of course avoid the mistake of importing Christian idea into this Conclusion by supposing that the identity of the persons in the two stories is owing to the passage of a "soul" from the one to the other. Buddhism does not teach the transmigration of souls. Its doctrine (which is somewhat intricate, and for a fuller statement of which I must refer to my *Manual of Buddhism*[37]) would be better summarized as the transmigration of character; for it is entirely independent of the early and widely prevalent notion of the existence within each human body of a distinct soul, or ghost, or spirit. The Bodisat, for instance, is not supposed to have a soul, which, on the death of one body, is transferred to another; but to be the inheritor of the character acquired by the previous

Bodisats. The insight and goodness, the moral and intellectual perfection which constitute Buddhahood, could not, according to the Buddhist theory, be acquired in one lifetime; they were the accumulated result of the continual effort of many generations of successive Bodisats. The only thing which continues to exist when man dies is his *Karma,* the result of his words and thoughts and deeds (literally his "doing"); and the curious theory that this result is concentrated in some new individual is due to the older theory of soul.

In the case of one Jātaka (Fausböll, no. 276), the Conclusion is wholly in verse; and in several cases the Conclusion contains a verse or verses added by way of moral. Such verses, when they occur, are called *Abhisambuddha-gāthā.* or *Verses spoken by the Buddha,* not when he was still only a Bodisat, but when he had become a Buddha. They are so called to distinguish them from the similar verses inserted in the Birth Story, and spoken there by the Bodisat. Each story has its verse or verses, either in the *Atīta-vatthu* or in the Conclusion, and sometimes in both. The number of cases in which all the verses are *Abhisambuddhagāthā* is relatively small (being only one in ten of the Jātakas published[38]); and the number of cases in which they occur together with verses in the *Atītavatthu* is very small indeed (being only five out of the three hundred Jātakas published[39]); in the remaining two hundred and sixty-five the verse or verses occur in the course of the Birth Story and are most generally spoken by the Bodisat himself.

There are several reasons for supposing that these verses are older than the prose which now forms their setting. The Ceylon tradition goes so far as to say that the original *Jālaka Book* consisted of the verses alone; that the Birth Stories are Commentary upon them; and the Introductory Stories, the Conclusions and the *Pada-gata-sannaya,* or word-for-word explanation of the verses, are Commentary on this commentary.[40] And archaic forms and forced constructions in the verses (in striking contrast with the regulatory and simplicity of the prose parts of the book), and the corrupt state in which some of the verses are found, seem to point to the conclusion that the verses are older.

But I venture to think that, though the present form of the verses may be older than the present form of the Birth Stories, the latter, or most of the latter, were in existence first; that the verses, at least in many cases, were added to the stories after they had become current; and that the Birth Stories without verses in them at all–those enumerated in the list in note 1 on the previous page, where the verses are found only in the Conclusion–are, in fact, among the oldest, if not the oldest, in the whole collection. For anyone who takes the trouble to go through that list seriatim will find that it contains a considerable number of those stories which, from their being found also in the Pāli *Piṭtakas* or in the oldest European collections, can already be proved to belong to a very early date. The only hypothesis which will reconcile these facts seems to me to be that the Birth Stories, though probably originally older than the verses they contain, were handed down in Ceylon till the time of the compilation of our present *Jātaká Book* in the Singhalese language; whilst the verses on the other hand were not translated, but were preserved as they were received, in Pāli.

There is another group of stories which seems to be older than most of the others; those, namely, in which the Bodisat appears as a sort of chorus, a moralizer only, and not an actor in the play, whose part may have been an addition made when the story in which it occurs was adopted by the Buddhists. Such is the fable above translated of "The Ass in the Lion's Skin", and most of the stories where the Bodisat is a *rukkha-devatā*–the fairy or genius of a tree.[41] But the materials are insufficient at present to put this forward as otherwise than a mere conjecture.

The arrangement of the stories in our present collection is a most unpractical one. They are classified, not according to their contents, but according to the number of verses they contain. Thus, the First division (Nipāta) includes those one hundred and fifty of the stories which have only one verse; the Second, one hundred stories, each having two verses; the Third and Fourth, each of them fifty stories containing respectively three and four verses each; and so on, the number of stories in each division decreasing rapidly after the number of verses exceeds four; and the whole of the five hundred and fifty Jātakas being contained in the twenty-two Nipātas. Even this division, depending on so unimportant a factor as the number of the verses, is not logically carried out; and the round numbers of the stories in the first four divisions are made up by including in them stories which, according to the principle adopted, should not properly be placed within them. Thus several Jātakas are only mentioned in the first two Nipātas to say that they will be found in the later ones;[42] and several Jātakas given with one verse only in the First Nipāta are given again with more verses in those that follow;[43] and occasionally a story is even repeated, with but little variation, in the same Nipāta.[44]

On the other hand, several Jātakas, which count only as one story in the present enumeration, really contain several different tales or fables. Thus, for instance, the *Kulāvaka Jātaka* (*On Mercy to Animals*) consists of several stories woven, not very closely, into one. The most striking instance of this is the *Ummagga Jātaka,* of which the Singhalese translation by the learned Baṭuwan Tudāwa occupies two hundred and fifty pages octavo, and consists of a very large number (I have not counted them, and there is no index, but I should think they amount to more than one hundred and fifty) of most entertaining anecdotes. Although therefore the Birth Stories are spoken of as "The five hundred and fifty Jātakas", this is merely a round number reached by an entirely artificial arrangement, and gives no clue to the actual number of stories. It is probable that our present collection contains altogether (including the Introductory Stories where they are not mere repetitions) between two and three thousand independent tales, fables, anecdotes, and riddles.

Nor is the number 550 any more exact (though the discrepancy in this case in not so great) if it be supposed to record, not the number of stories, but the number of distinct births of the Bodisat. In the *Kulāvaka Jātaka,* just referred to (the tale *On Mercy to Animals*), there are two consecutive births of the future Buddha; and on the other hand, none of the six Jātakas mentioned in note 1, p. lxxiii, represents a distinct birth at all–the Bodisat is in them the same person as he is in the later Jātakas in which those six are contained.

From the facts as they stand it seems at present to be the most probable explanation of the rise of our *Jātaka Book* to suppose that it was due to the religious faith of the Indian Buddhists of the third or fourth century B.C., who not only repeated a number of fables, parables, and stories ascribed to the Buddha, but gave them a peculiar sacredness and a special religious significance by indentifying the best character in each with the Buddha himself in some previous birth. From the time when this step was taken, what had been merely parables or fables became "Jātakas", a word invented to distinguish, and used only of, those stories which have been thus sanctified. The earliest use of that word at present known is in the inscriptions on the Buddhist Tope at Bhārhut; and from the way in which it is there used it is clear that the word must have then been already in use for some considerable time. But when stories thus made sacred were popularly accepted among people so accustomed to literary activity as the early Buddhists, the natural consequence would be that the Jātakas should have been brought together into a collection of some kind; and the probability of this having been done at a very early date is confirmed, firstly, by the tradition of the difference of opinion concerning a *Jātaka Book* at the Councils of Vesāli; and secondly by the mention of a *Jātaka Book* in the ninefold division of the Scriptures found in the *Anguttara Nikāya* and in the *Saddharma Puṇḍarīka.* To the compiler of this, or of some early collection, are probably to be ascribed the Verses, which in some cases at least are later than the Stories.

With regard to some of the Jātakas, among which may certainly be included those found in the Pāli *Piṭakas,* there may well have been a tradition, more or less reliable, as to the time and the occasion at which they ere supposed to have been uttered by the Buddha. These traditions will have given rise to the earliest Introductory Stories, in imitation of which the rest were afterwards invented; and these will then have been handed down as commentary on the Birth Stories, till they were finally made part of our present collection by its compiler in Ceylon. That (either through their later origin, or their having been much more modified in transmission) they represent a more modern point of view than the Birth Stories themselves, will be patent to every reader. There is a freshness and simplicity about the *Stories of the Past* that is sadly wanting in the *Stories of the Present;* so much so, that the latter (and this is also true of the whole long Introduction containing the life of the Buddha) may be compared more accurately with mediaeval Legends of the Saints that with such simple stories as *Aesop's Fables,* which still bear a likeness to their forefathers, the *Stories of the Past.*

The Jātakas so constituted were carried to Ceylon in the Pāli language, when Buddhism was first introduced into that island (a data that is not quite certain, but may be taken provisionally as about 250 B.C.); and the whole was there translated into a preserved in the Singhalese language (except the verses, which were left untranslated) until the compilation in the fifth century A.D., and by an unknown author, of the Pāli *Jātaka Book,* the translation of which into English is commenced in this volume.

When we consider the number of elaborate similes by which the arguments in the Pāli Suttas are enforced, there can be no reasonable doubt that the Buddha was really accustomed to teach much by the aid of parables, and it is not improbable that the compiler was quite correct in attributing to him that subtle sense of good-natured humour which led to his inventing, as occasion aroses, some fable or some tale of a previous birth, to explain away existing failures in conduct among the monks, or to draw a moral from contemporaneous events. It is even already possible to point to some of the Jātakas as being probably the oldest in the collection; but it must be left to future research to carry out in ampler detail the investigation into the comparative date of each of the stories, both those which are called *Stories of the Past* and those which are called *Stories of the Present.*

Besides the points which the teaching of the Jātakas has in common with that of European moralists and satirists, it inculcates two lessons peculiar to itself–firtly, the powerful influence of inherited character; and secondly, the essential likeness between man and other animals. The former of these two ideas underlies both the central Buddhist doctrine of Karma and the theory of the Buddhas, views certainly common among all the early Buddhists and therefore probably held by Gotama himself. And the latter of the two underlies and explains the sympathy with animals so conscious in these tales, and the frequency with which they lay stress upon the duty of kindness, and even of courtesy, to the brute creation. It is curious to find in these records of a strange and ancient faith such kind feeling after, such vague foreshadowing of beliefs only now beginning to be put forward here in the West; but it is scarcely necessary to point out that the paramount value to us now of the Jātaka stories is historical.

In this respect their value does not consist only in the evidence they afford of the intercommunion between East and West, but also, and perhaps chiefly, in the assistance which they will render to the study of folk-lore–that is, of the beliefs and habits of men in the earlier stages of their development. The researches of Tylor and Waitz and Pischel and Lubbock and Spencer have shown us that this is the means by which it is most easily possible rightly to understand and estimate many of the habits and beliefs still current among ourselves. But the chief obstacle to a consensus of opinion in such studies is the insufficiency and inaccuracy of the authorities on which the facts depend. While the ancient literature of peoples more advanced usually ignores or passes lightly over the very details most important from this point of view, the account of modern travellers among the so-called savage tribes are often at best very secondary evidence. It constantly happens that such a traveller can only tell us the impression conveyed to his mind of that which his informant holds to be the belief or custom of the tribe. Such native information may be inaccurate, incomplete, or misleading; and it reaches us only after filtration though a European mind more or less able to comprehend it rightly.

But in the Jātakas we have a nearly complete picture, and quite uncorrupted and unadulterated by European intercourse, of the social life and customs and popular beliefs of the common people of Aryan tribes closely related to ourselves, just as they were passing through the first stages of civilization.

The popularity of the Jātakas as amusing stories may pass away. How can it stand against the rival claims of the fairy tales of science, and the entrancing, many-sided story of man's gradual rise and progress? But though these less fabulous and more attractive stories will increasingly engage the attention of ourselves and of our children, we may still turn with appreciation to the ancient *Book of the Buddhist Jātaka Tales* as a priceless record of the childhood of our race.

I avail myself of this opportunity of acknowledging my indebtedness to several friends whose assistance has been too continuous to be specified on any particular page. Robert Childers, whose premature death was so great a blow to Pāli studies, and whose name I never think of without a feeling of reverent and grateful regret, had undertaken the translation of the Jātakas, and the first thirty-three pages are from his pen. They are the last memento of his earnest work : they stand exactly as he left them. The Rev. J. Estlin Carpenter, who takes a deep interest in this and cognate subjects, has been kind enough to read through all the proofs, and I owe to his varied scholarship many useful hints. And my especial thanks, and the thanks of any readers this work may meet with, are above all due to Victor Fausböll, without whose *editio princeps* of the Pāli text, the result of self-denying labours spread over many years, this translation would not have been undertaken.

REFERENCES

1. Thus, for instance, the *Maṇu Kaṇṭha Jātaka* (Fausböll, no. 253) is taken from a story which is in both the Pāli and the Chinese versions of the *Vinaya Pitaka* (Oldenberg, p. xlvi); the *Tittira Jātaka* (Fausböll, no. 37, translated below) occurs almost word for word in the *Culla Vagga* (vi, 6, 3-5); the *Khandhavatta Jātaka* (Fausböll, no. 203) is a slightly enlarged version of *Culla Vagga,* v. 6; the *Sukhavihāri Jātaka* (Fausböll, no. 10, translated below) is founded on a story in the *Culla Vagga* (vii, 1, 4-6); the *Mahā-sudassana Jātaka* (Fausböll, no. 95) is derived from the Sutta of the same name in the *Dīgha Nikāya* (translated by me in 'Sacred Books of the East', vol. xi); the *Makhā Deva Jātaka* (Fausböll, no. 9, translated below) from the Sutta of the same name in the *Majjhima Nikāya* (no. 83); and the *Sakunagghi Jātaka* (Fausböll, no. 168) from a parable in the *Saiipaṭṭhāna Vagga* of the Sanyutta Nikaya.

Compare the writer's *Buddhist India,* ch. xi, Lond 1903, for an enlarged restatement of the views here briefly put forward.

2. See on this belief below, pp. 141-4, where the verses 259-69 are quotations from the *Chariyā-Piṭaka.*
3. Tāranātha's *Geschichte des Buddhismus* (a Tibetan work of the eighteenth century, translated into German by Schiefner), p. 92.
4. Since edited by E. Kern, Harvard Or. Series, i, 1891. Translation by J.S. Speyer, *S. Bks. of the Buddhists,* i. 1895.–Ed.
5. Fausböll's *Five Jātakas,* pp. 58–68, where the full text of one Jātka is given and Léon Feer, *Etude sur les Jātaka,* p. 57.
6. See p. 53.
7. The Pali Text Society published an edition by Rd. Morris, 1882.–Ed.
8. See the list of the Buddhas below, p. 138, where it will be seen that for the first three Buddhas we have no Birth Story.
9. This will hold good though the *Buddhavaṃsa* and the *Chariyā Piṭaka* should turn out to be later than most of the other books contained in the *Three Pāli Piṭakas.* That the stories they contain have already become Jātakas, whereas in most of the other cases above quoted the stories are still only parables, would seem to lead to this conclusion; and the fact that they have preserved some very ancient forms (such as locatives in *i*) may merely be due to the fat that they are older, not in matter and ideas, but only in form. Compare what is said below as to the verses in the Birth Stories.
10. The question is discussed at length in my *Ancient Coins and Measures of Ceylon* in *Numismata orientalia,* vol. i.
11. *Dīpavaṃsa,* v, 32 sqq.
12. There are several works enumerated by Beal in his *Catalogue of Chinese Buddhistic Works in the India Office Library* (see especially pp. 93-7, and pp. 107-9), from which we might expect to derive this information.
13. Thus no. 41 is called both *Losaka Jātaka* and *Mitta-vindaka Jātaka* (Feer, *Etude sur les Jātakas,* p. 121); no. 439 is called *Catudvāra Jataka* and also *Mitta-vindaka Jātaka* (ibid. p. 120); no. 57 is called *Vānarinda Jātaka* and also *Kumbhīla Jālaka* (Fausböll, vol. i., p. 278, and vol. ii, p. 206); no. 96 is called *Telapatta Jātaka* and also *Takkasilā Jātaka* (ibid. vol. i, p. 393, and vol. i, pp. 468, 470); no. 102, there called *Paṇṇika Jātaka,* is the same story as no. 217, there called *Seggu Jātaka;* no. 30, there called *Muṇika*

Jātaka, is the same story as no. 286, there called *Sālūka Jātaka;* no. 215, the *Kacchapa Jātaka,* is called *Bahu-Bhāṇi Jātaka* in the *Dhammapada* (p. 419); and no. 157 is called *Buṇa Jātaka, Sīha Jātaka,* and *Sigāla Jātaka.*

14. Cunningham, *The Stupa of Bharhut,* pl. xlvii. The carving illustrates a fable of a cat and a cock, and is labelled both Biḍala Jātaka and Kukkuṭa Jātaka (Cat and Cock Jātaka, no. 383).
15. See the authorities quoted in my manual, *Buddhism,* pp. 214, 215; and Dr. Morris, in *The Academy* for May, 1880.
16. In his *Pali Dictionary,* Preface, p. ix, note.
17. Turnour, pp. 250-3.
18. Fausböll, vol. i, p. 62 and p. 488; vol. ii, p. 224.
19. See the translation below.
20. I judge from Turnour's analysis of that work in the *Journal of the Bengal Asiatic Society,* 1839, where some long extracts have been translated and the contents of other passages given in abstract.
21. *Etude sur les Jātakas,* pp. 62-5.
22. *Ibid.*, pp. 66-71.
23. This is clear from vol. i, p. 410 of Fausböll's text, where, at the end of the 100th tale, we find to words *Majjhima-paṇṇāsa-konitthito,* that is "End of the Middle Fifty." At the end of the 50th tale (p. 261) there is a corresponding entry, *Paṭhamo paṇṇāso.* "First Fifty"; and though there is no such entry at the end of the 150th tale, the expression "Middle Fifty" shows that there must have been, at one time, such a division as is above stated.
24. *Pantscha Tantra,* Theodor Benfey, Leipzing, 1859, p. xi.
25. That is, in the course of Benfey's researches.
26. In *Ersch and Grüber's Encyklopoedie, especially* at pp. 255 and 277.
27. Wassiliew, *Der Buddhismus,* p. 68.
28. Compare the title of the Birth Story above, p. xxii : "A Lesson for Kings."
29. See above.
30. Knatchbull, p. 29.
31. Dr. Fitz-Edward Hall's *Vāsavadatta,* pp. 22-4.
32. Dr. Eühler in *The Indian Antiquary,* i, 302; v, 29; vi, 269.
33. Nos. 61-3, 147, 159, 193, 196, 198-9, 263.

34. Nos. 106, 145, 191, 286.
35. Nos. 58, 73, 142, 194, 220, and 277, have the same Introductory Story.

    And so nos. 60, 104, 116, 161.

    And nos. 127-8, 138, 173, 175.
36. See the "Pāli note" at the end of Jātaka no. 91.
37. pp. 99-106.
38. Nos. 1-5, 28-9, 37, 55-6, 68, 85, 87-8, 97, 100, 114, 136, (total, eighteen in the *Eka-Nipāta*); 156 (= 55-6), 196, 202, 237 (= 68), 241 (total, five in the *Duka-Nipāta*); 255-6, 258, 264, 284, 291, 300 (total, seven in the *Tika-Nipāta,* and thirty altogether).
39. Nos. 152, 168, 179, 233, 286.
40. This belief underlines the curious note forming the last words of the *Mahāsupina Jātaka,* i, 345 : "Those who held the Council after the death of the Blessed One placed the lines beginning *usabhā rukkhā* in the commentary, and then, making the other lines beginning *lābūni* into one verse, they put (the Jātaka) into the *Eka-Nipāta* (the chapter including all those Jātakas which have only one verse)."
41. See, for instance, below, pp. 212, 228, 230, 317; above, p. xii; and Jātaka, no. 113.
42. Nos. 110-12, 170, 192 in the *Ummagga Jātaka,* and no. 264 in the *Suruci Jātaka.*
43. No. 30 = No. 286. No. 68 = No. 237.

    No. 34 = No. 216. No. 86 = No. 290.

    No. 46 = No. 268. No. 102 = No. 217.

    No. 57 = No. 224. No. 145 = No. 198.
44. So No. 82 = No. 104.

    So No. 99 = No. 101.

    So No. 134 = No. 135.

    So No. 195 = No. 225.

    So No. 294 = No. 295.

    Compare the two stories nos. 23 and 24 translated below.

THE STORY OF THE LINEAGE

The Nidānakathā

[vv. 1-11] The Apaṇṇaka and other births, which in times gone by were recounted on various occasions by the great illustrious Sage, and in which during a long period our Teacher and Leader, desirous of the salvation of manking, fulfilled the vast conditions of Buddhahood,[1] were all collected together and added to the canon of Scripture by those who made the recension of the Scriptures and rehearsed by them under the name of The Jātaka. Having bowed at the feet of the Great Sage, the lord of the world, by whom in innumerable existences[2] boundless benefits were conferred upon mankind, and having paid reverence to the Doctrine, and ascribed honour to the Order, the receptacle of all honour; and having removed all dangers by the efficacy of that meritorious act of veneration and honour referring to the Three Gems, I proceed to recite a Commentary upon this Jātaka, illustrating as it does the infinite efficacy of the actions of great men–a commentary based upon the method of exposition current among the inmates of the Great Monastery. And I do so at the personal request of the elder Atthadassin, who lives apart from the world and ever dwells with his fraternity, and who desires the perpetuation of this chronicle of Buddha; and likewise of Buddhamitta the tranquil and wise, sprung from the race of Mahiṃsāsaka, skilled in the canons of interpretation; and moreover of the monk Buddhadeva of clear intellect May all good men lend me their favourable attention while I speak![3]

Inasmuch as this comment on the Jātaka, if it be expounded after setting forth the three Epochs, the distant, the intermediate, and proximate, will be clearly understood by those who hear it because they will have understood it from the beginning, the therefore I will expound it after setting forth the three Epochs. Accordingly from the very outset it will be well to determine the limits of these Epochs. Now the narrative of the bodhisatta's existence, from the time that at the feet of Dīpankara he formed a resolution to become a Buddha to his rebirth in the Tusita heaven after leaving his life as Vessantara, is called the Distant Epoch. From his leaving the Tusita heaven to his attainment of omniscience on the Bo-tree seat, the narrative is called the Intermediate Epoch. And the Proximate Epoch is to be found in the various places in which he sojourned (during his ministry on earth). The following is :

I : THE DISTANT EPOCH

Dūrenidāna

Tradition tells us that four asankheyyas[4] and a hundred thousand cycles ago there was a city called Amaravatī. In this city there dwelt a Brahmin named Sumedha, of good family in both sides, on the father's and the mother's side, of pure conception for seven generations back, by birth unreproached and respected, a man comely, well-favoured and amiable, and endowed with remarkeable beauty. He followed his brahminical studies without engaging in any other pursuit. His parents died while he was still young. A minister of state, who acted as steward of his property, bringing forth the roll-book of his estate, threw open the stores filled with gold and silver, gems and pearls, and other valuables, and said : "So much, young man, belonged to your mother, so much to your father, so much to your grandparents and great grandparents," and pointing out to him the property inherited through seven generations, he bade him guard it carefully. The wise Sumedha thought to himself : "After amassing all this wealth my parents and ancestors when they went to another world took not a farthing with them. Can it be right that I should make it an object to take my wealth with me when I go?" And informing the king of his intention, he caused proclamation to be made[5] in the city, gave largess to the people, and embraced the ascetic life of a hermit.

To make this matter clear the *Story of Sumedha* must here be related. This story, though given in full in the Buddhavaṃsa,[6] from its being in a metrical form, is not very easy to understand.

I will therefore relate it with sentences at intervals explaining the metrical construction.

Four asankheyyas and a hundred thousand cycles ago there was a city called Amaravatī or Amara, resounding with the ten city cries, concerning which it is said in *Buddhavaṃsa* :

12. Four asankheyyas and a hundred thousand cycles ago. A city there was called Amara, beautiful and pleasant, Resounding with the ten cries, abounding in food and drink.[7]

Then follows a stanza of *Buddhavaṃsa* enumerating some of these cries,

13. The trumpeting of elephants, the neighing of horses, (the sound of) drums, trumpets, and chariots, And viands and drinks were cried, with the invitation, "Eat and drink."

It goes on to say :

14. A city supplied with every requisite, engaged in every sort of industry, Possessing the seven precious things, thronged with dwellers of many races; The abode of devout men, like the prosperous city of the angles.

15. In the city of Amaravatī dwelt a Brahmin named Sumedha. Whose hoard was many tens of millions, blest with much wealth and store;

16. Studious, knowing the Mantras, versed in the three Vedas, Master of the science of divination and of the traditions and observances of his caste.

Now one day the wise Sumedha, having retired to the splendid upper apartment of his house, seated himself cross-legged, and fell a-thinking. "Oh! wise man,[8] grievous is rebirth in a new existence, and the dissolution of the body in each successive place where we are reborn. I am subject to birth, to decay, to disease, to death–it is right, being such, that I should strive to attain the cool great deathless Nirvāna, the tranquil, the free from birth and decay, and sickness, and grief and joy; surely there must be a road that leads to Nirvāna and releases man from becoming." Accordingly it is said :

17. Seated in seclusion, I then thought as follows :

    Grievous is rebirth and the breaking up of the body.

18. I am subject to birth, to decay, to disease, Therefore will I seek Nirvāna, undecaying, undying haven.

19. Let me leave this perishable body, this pestilent congregation of vapours, And depart without desires and without wants.

20. There is, there must be a road, it cannot but be : I will seek this road, that I may obtain release from becoming.[9]

Further he reasoned thus : "For as in this world there is pleasure as the correlative of pain, so where there is becoming there must be its opposite, the cessation of becoming; and as where there is heat there is also cold which neutralizes it, so there must be a Nirvāna[10] that extinguishes (the fires of) lust and the other passions; and as in opposition to a bad and evil condition there is a good and blameless one, so where there is evil birth there must also be a Nirvāna, called the birthless, because it puts an end to all that is called rebirth." Therefore it is said:

21. As where there is suffering there is also bliss, So where there is becoming we must look for non-becoming.

22. And as where there is heat there is also cold, So where there is the threefold fire of passion extinguishing must be sought.

23. And as coexistent with evil there is also good, Even so where there is birth[11] the cessation of birth should be sought.

Again he reasoned thus : "Just as a man who has fallen into a heap of filth, if he beholds afar off a great pond covered with lotuses of five colours; ought to seek that pond, saying : 'By what way shall I arrive there?'; but if he does not seek it the fault is not that of the pond; even so where there is the lake of the great deathless Nirvāna for the washing of the defilement of sin, if it is not sought it is not the fault of the lake. And just as a man who is surrounded by robbers, if when there is a way of escape he does not fly it is not the fault of the way but of the man; even so when there is a blessed road leading to Nirvāna for the man who is encompassed and held fast by sin, its not being sought is not the fault of the road but of the person. And as a man who is oppressed with sickness, there being a physician who can heal his disease, if he does not get cured by going to the physician that is no fault of the physician; even so if a man who is oppressed by the disease of sin seeks not a spiritual guide who is at hand and knows the road which puts and end to sin, the faults lies with him and not with the sin-destroying teacher." Therefore it is said :

24. As a man fallen among filth, beholding a brimming lake,
If he seek not that lake the faults is not in the lake;

25. So when there exists a lake of Nirvāna that washes the stains of sin,
If a man seek not that lake, the fault is not in the lake of Nirvāna.

26. As a man beset with foes, there being a way of escape,
If he flee not away, the fault is not with the road;

27. So when there is a way of bliss, if a man beset with sin
Seek not that road, the fault is not in the way of bliss.

28. And as one who is diseased, there being a physician at hand,
If he bid him not heal the disease, the fault is not in the healer :

29. So if a man who is sick and oppressed with the disease of sin,
Seek not the spiritual teacher, the fault is not in the teacher.

And again he argued : As a man fond of gay clothing, throwing off a corpse bound to his shoulders, goes away rejoicing, so must I, throwing off this perishable body, and freed from all care, enter the city of Nirvāna. And as men and women depositing filth on a dungheap do not gather it in the fold or skirt of their garments, but loathing it, throw it away, feeling no desire for it; so shall I also cast off this perishable body without regret and enter the deathless city of Nirvāna. And as seamen abandon without regret an unseaworthy ship and escape, so will I also, leaving this body, which distils corruption from its nine festering apertures, enter without regret the city of Nirvāna. And as a man carrying various sorts of jewels and going on the same road with a band of robbers, out of fear of losing his jewels withdraws from them and gains a safe road; even so this impure body is like a jewel-plundering robber, if I set my affections thereon the jewel of the good doctrine of the sublime path of holiness will be lost to me, therefore ought I to enter the city of Nirvāna, forsaking this robber-like body." Therefore it is said :

30. As a man might with loathing shake off a corpse bound upon his shoulders,
And depart, secure, independent, master of himself;

31. Even so let me depart, regretting nothing, wanting nothing,
Leaving this perishable body, this collection of many foul vapours.

32. And as men and women deposit filth upon a dungheap,
And depart regretting nothing, wanting nothing,

33. So will I depart, leaving this body filled with foul vapours,
As one leaves a cesspool after depositing ordure there.

34. And as the owners forsake the rotten bark that is shattered and leaking,
And depart without regret or longing,

35. So shall I go, leaving this body with its nine apertures ever running,
As its owners desert the broken ship.

36. And as a man carrying wares, walking with robbers,
Seeing danger of losing his wares, parts company with the robbers and gets him gone,

37. Even so is this body like a mighty robber,–
Leaving it I will depart through fear of losing good.

Having thus in nine similes pondered upon the advantages connected with retirement from the world, the wise Sumedha gave away at his own house, as aforesaid, an immense hoard of treasure to the indigent and wayfarers and sufferers, and kept open house. And renouncing all pleasures, both material and sensual, departing from the city of Amara, away from the world in Himavanta he made himself a hermitage near the mountain called Dhammaka, and built a hut and a cloister free from the five defects which are hindrances (to meditation). And with a view to obtain the power reckoned as supernormal knowledge, which is characterized by the eight casual qualities described in the words beginning "With a mind thus tranquillized,"[12] he embraced in that hermitage the ascetic life of a Rishi, casting off the cloak with its nine disadvantages, and wearing the garment of bark with its twelve advantages. And when he had thus given up the world, forsaking this hut, crowded with eight drawbacks, he repaired to the foot of a tree with its ten advantages, and rejecting all sorts of grain lived constantly upon wild fruits. And strenuously exerting himself both in sitting and in standing and in walking, within a week he became the possessor of the eight attainments, and of the five supernormal knowledges; and so, in accordance with his prayer, he attained the might of supernormal knowledge. Therefore it is said :

38. Having pondered thus I gave many thousand millions of wealth,
To rich and poor, and made my way to Himavanta.

39. Not far from Himavanta is the mountain called Dhammaka,
Here I made an excellent hermitage, and built with care a leafy hut.

40. There I built me a cloister, free from five defects,
Possessed of the eight good qualities, and attained the strength of the supernormal knowledges.

41. Then I threw off the cloak possessed of the nine faults,
And put on the raiment of bark possessed of the twelve advantages.

42. I left the hut, crowded with the eight drawbacks,
And went to the tree-foot possessed of ten advantages.[13]

43. Wholly did I reject the grain that is sown and planted,
And partook of the constant fruits of the earth, possessed of many advantages.

44. Then I strenuously strove, in sitting, in standing, and in walking,
And within seven days attained the might of the knowledges.[14]

Now while the hermit Sumedha, having thus attained the strength of supernormal knowledge, was living in the bliss of the (eight) attainments, the Teacher Dīpankara appeared in the world. At the moment of his conception, of his birth, of his attainment of Buddhahood, of his preaching his first discourse, the whole universe of ten thousand worlds trembled, shook and quaked, and gave forth a mighty sound, and the thirty-two marks showed themselves. But the hermit Sumedha, living in the bliss of the attainments, neither heard that sound not beheld those signs. Therefore it is said :

45. Thus when I had attained the consummation, while I was subjected to the teaching,
The Conqueror named Dīpankara, chief of the universe, appeared.

46. At his conception, at his birth, at his Buddhahood, at his preaching,
I saw not the four signs, plunged in the blissful trance of meditation.

At that time Dīpankara Buddha, accompanied by a hundred thousand saints, wandering his way from place to place, reached the city of Ramma, and took up his residence in the great monastery of Sudassana. And the dwellers of the city of Ramma heard it said : "Dīpankara, lord of ascetics, having attained supreme Buddhaship, and set rolling the wheel of the excellent Norm, wandering his way from place to place, has come to the town of Ramma, and dwells at the great monastery of Sudassana." And taking with them ghee and butter and other medicinal requisites and clothes and raiment, and bearing perfumes and garlands and other offerings in their hands, their minds bent towards the Buddha, the Doctrine, and the Order, inclining towards them, hanging upon them, they approached the Teacher, and worshipped him, and presenting the perfumes and other offerings, sat down on one side. And having heard his preaching of the doctrine, and invited him for the next day, they rose from their seats and departed. And on the next day, having prepared alms-giving for the poor, and having decked out the town, they repaired the road by which the Buddha was to come, throwing earth in the places that were worn away by water, and thereby levelling the surface, and scattering sand that looked like strips of silver. And they sprinkled fried paddy and flowers, and raised aloft flags and banners, of many-coloured cloths, and set up banana arches and rows of brimming jars. Then the hermit Sumedha, ascending from his hermitage, and proceeding through the air till he was above those men, and beholding the joyous multitude, exclaimed : "What can be the reason?" and alighting stood on one side and questioned the people : "Tell me, why are you adorning this road?" Therefore it is said :

47. In the region of the border districts, having invited the Buddha,
With joyful hearts they are clearing the road by which he should come.

48. And I at that time leaving my hermitage,
Rustling my barken tunic, departed through the air,

49. And seeing an excited multitude joyous and delighted,
Descending from the air I straightway asked the men,

50. The people is excited, joyous, and happy,
For whom is the road being cleared, the path, the way of his coming?

And the men replied : "Venerable Sumedha, dost thou not know? Dīpankara Buddha, having attained supreme knowledge, and set rolling the wheel of the glorious Doctrine, travelling from place to place, has reached our town, and dwells at the great monastery Sudassana; we have invited the Blessed One, and are making ready for the blessed Buddha the road by which he is to come." And the hermit Sumedha thought : "The very sound of the word Buddha is rarely met with in the world, much more the actual appearance of a Buddha; it behoves me to join these men in clearing the road." He said therefore to the men : "If you are clearing this road for the Buddha, assign to me a piece of ground, I will clear the ground in company with you."

They consented, saying : "It is well"; and perceiving the hermit Sumedha to be possessed of supernatural power, they fixed upon a swampy piece of ground, and assigned it to him, saying : "Do thou prepare this spot." Sumedha, his heart filled with joy of which the Buddha was the cause, thought within himself : "I am able to prepare this piece of ground by supernatural power, but if so prepared it will give me no satisfaction; this day it behoves me to perform menial duties"; and fetching earth he threw it upon the spot.

But ere the ground could be cleared by him–with a train of a hundred thousand miracle-working saints endowed with the six supernormal knowledges, while devas offered celestial wreaths and perfumes, while celestial hymns rang forth, and men paid their homage with earthly perfumes and with flowers and other offerings, Dīpankara endowed with the ten Forces, with all a Buddha's transcendant majesty, like a lion rousing himself to seek his prey on the Vermilion plain, came down into the road all decked and made ready for him. Then the hermit Sumedha–as the Buddha with unblenching eyes approached along the road prepared for him, beholding that form endowed with the perfection of beauty, adorned with the thirtytwo marks of a super-man, and marked with the eighty minor beauties, attended by a halo of a fathom's depth and sending forth in streams the six-hued Buddharays, linked in pairs of different colours, and wreathed like the varied lightnings that flash in the gem-studded value of heaven–exclaimed : "This day it behoves me to make sacrifice of my life for the Buddha : let not the Blessed one walk in the mire–nay, let him advance with his four hundred thousand saints trampling on my body as if walking upon a bridge of jewelled planks, this deed will long be for my good and my happiness." So saying, he loosed his hair, and spreading in the sooty mire his hermit's skin mantle, roll of matted hair and garment of bark, he lay down in the mire like a bridge of jewelled planks. Therefore it is said :

51. Questioned by me they replied, An incomparable Buddha is born into the world,
The conqueror named Dīpankara, lord of the universe,

For him the road is cleared, the way, the path of his coming.

52. When I heard the name of Buddha joy sprang up forthwith within me,
Repeating, a Buddha, a Buddha! I gave utterance to my joy.

53. Standing there I pondered, joyful and excited.
Here I will sow the seed, may the happy moment not pass away!

54. If you clear a path for the Buddha, assign to me a place,
I also will clear the road, the way, the path of his coming.

55. Then they gave me a piece of ground to clear the pathway.
Then repeating within me, a Buddha, a Buddha! I cleared the road.

56. But ere my portion was cleared, Dīpankara the great sage.
The Conqueror, entered the road with four hundred thousand saints like himself. Possessed of the six super-knowledges, pure from all taint of sin.

57. On every side men rise to receive him, many drums sound.
Men and spirits overjoyed send forth their applause.

58. Devas look upon men, men upon devas.
And both with clasped hands unpraised approach "him who had thus come."

59. Devas with deva-music, men with earthy music.
Both sending forth their strains approach "him who had thus come."

60. Devas floating in the air sprinkle down in all directions.
Erythrina flowers of deva-world, lotuses and coral flowers.

61. Men standing on the ground throw upwards in all directions
Champac and Salala flowers, Cadamba and fragrant Mesua, Punnaga, and Ketaka.

62. Then I loosed my hair, and spreading in the mire.
Bark robe and mantle of skin, lay prone upon my face.

63. Let the Buddha advance with his disciples, treading upon me.
Let him not tread in the mire, it will be for my blessing.

And as he lay in the mire, again beholding the Buddha-majesty of Dīpankara Buddha with his unblenching gaze, he thought as follows : "Were I willing, I could enter the city of Ramma as a novice in the priesthood, after having destroyed all human passions; but why should I disguise myself[15] to attain Nirvāna after the destruction of human passion? Let me rather, like Dīpankara, having risen to the supreme knowledge of the Doctrine, enable mankind to enter the Ship of the Doctrine, and so carry them across the Ocean of Going-on, and when this is done afterwards attain Nirvāna; this indeed it is right that I should do." Then having enumerated the eight conditions (necessary to the attainment of Buddhahood), and having made the resolution to become Buddha, he laid himself down. Therefore it is said

64. As I lay upon the ground this was the thought of my heart.
If I wished it I might this day destroy within me all human passions.

65. But why should I in disguise arrive at the knowledge of the Truth?
I will attain omniscience and become a Buddha, and (save) men and devas.

66. Why should I cross the ocean resolute but alone?
I will attain omniscience, and enable men and devas to cross.

67. By this resolution of mine, I a man of resolution
Will attain omniscience, and save many folk.

68. Cutting off the stream of transmigration, annihilating the three forms of rebirth.
Embarking in the ship of the Norm, I will carry across with me men and devas.[16]

And the blessed Dīpankara having reached the spot stood close by the hermit Sumedha's head. And opening his eyes possessed of the five kinds of grace as one opens a jewelled window, and beholding the hermit Sumedha lying in the mire, thought to himself : "This hermit who lies here has formed the resolution to be a Buddha; will his wish be fulfilled or not?" And casting forward his prescient gaze into the future, and considering, he perceived that four asankheyyas and a hundred thousand cycles from that time he would become a Buddha named Gotama. And standing there in the midst of the assembly he delivered this prophecy, "See ye this very austere ascetic lying in the mire?" "Yes, lord," they answered. "This man lies here having made the resolution to become a Buddha, his wish will be answered; at the end of four asankheyyas and a hundred thousand cycles hence he will become a Buddha named Gotama, and in that birth the city Kapilavatthu will be his residence, queen Māyā will be his mother, king Suddhodana his father, his chief disciple will be the there Upatissa, his second disciple the tera Kolita, the Buddha's servitor will be Ānanda, his chief female disciple the num Khemā, the second the num Uppalavaṇṇā. When he attains to years of ripe knowledge, having retired from the world and made the great exertion, having received at the foot of a banyan-tree a meal of rice milk, and partaken of it by the banks of the Neranjarā, having ascended the bo-tree seat, he will, at the foot of a fig-tree, attain Supreme Buddhahood. Therefore it is said :

70. Dīpankara, knower of all worlds, receiver of offerings.
Standing by that which pillowed my head, spoke these words :

71. See ye this very austere hermit with his matted hair.
Countless ages hence he will be a Buddha in this world.

72. Lo, "he who has thus come" departing from pleasant Kapila, having made the great effort, performed all manner of austerities.

73. Having sat at the foot of the Ajapāla tree, and there received rice pottage.
Shall approach the Neranjarā river.

74. Having received the rice pottage on the banks of the Neranjarā, the Conqueror.

Shall come by a fair road prepared for him to the foot of the Bodhi-tree.

75. Then, unrivalled and glorious, reverentially saluting the Bodhi-seat.
At the foot of a fig-tree he shall be awakened.[17]

76. The mother that bears him shall be called Māyā.
His father will be Suddhodana, he himself will be Gotama.

77. His chief disciples will be Upatissa and Kolita.
Men sane and immune, void of passion, calm-minded and intent.

78. The servitor Ānanda will attend upon the Conqueror.
Khemā and Uppalavaṇṇā will be his chief women disciples,

79. Women sane and immune, void of passion, calm-minded and intent.
The Bodhi-tree of this Buddha is known as the Assattha.

The hermit Sumedha, exclaiming : "My wish, it seems, will be accomplished", was filled with happiness. The multitudes, hearing the words of Dīpankara Buddha, were joyous and delighted, exclaiming : "The hermit Sumedha, it seems, is a Buddha-seed, a Buddha-shoot!" For thus they thought : was a man fording a river, if he is unable to cross to the ford opposite him, crosses to a ford lower down the stream, even so we, if under the dispensation of Dīpankara Buddha we fail to attain the Paths and their fruition, yet when thou shalt become Buddha we shall be enabled in thy presence to make the paths and their fruition our own"–and so they recorded their wish (for future sanctification). And Dīpankara Buddha also having praised the Bodhisatta, and made an offering to him of eight handfuls of flowers, reverentially saluted him and departed. And the Arahants also, four hundred thousand in numbers having made offerings to the Bodhisatta of perfume, and garlands, reverentially saluted him and departed. And the devas and men having made the same offerings, and bowed down to him, went their way.

And the Bodhisatta, when all had retired, rising from his seat and exclaiming : "I will study the Perfections", sat himself down cross-legged on a heap of flowers. And as the Bodhisatta sat thus, the devas in all the ten thousand worlds assembling shouted applause. "Venerable hermit Sumedha", they said, "all the ones which have manifested themselves when former Bodhisattas seated themselves cross legged, saying; 'We will study the Perfections'–all these this day have appeared : assuredly thou shalt become Buddha. This we know : to whom these omens appear, he surely will become Buddha; do thou make a strenuous effort and exert thyself" With these words they lauded the Bodhisatta with varied praises. Therefore it is said :

80. Hearing these words of the incomparable Sage. Devas and men delighted, exclaimed,
This is a Buddhaseed-seedling!

81. A great clamour arises, men and devas in ten thousand worlds.
Clap their hands, and laugh, and make obeisance with clasped hands.

82. "Should we fail," they say, "in this Buddha's dispensation,
Yet in time to come we shall stand before him.

83. As men crossing a river, if they fail to reach the opposite ford.
Gaining the lower ford cross the great river,

84. Even so we all, if we lose this Buddha, in time to come shall stand before him."

85. The world-knowing Dīpankara, the receiver of offerings,
Having celebrated my action, went his way.[18]

86. All his disciples of the Buddha that were present saluted me with reverence, Men, Nāgas, and Gandhabbas bowed down to me and departed.

87. When the Lord of the world with his following had passed beyond my sight. Then glad, with gladsome heart, I rose up from my seat.

88. Happy I am by happiness, glad with a great gladness.
Flooded with raptures then I seated myself cross-legged.

89. And even as thus I sat I thought within myself. I am trained in Jhāna, I have mastered the supernormal knowledges.

90. In a thousand worlds there are no sages that rival me. Unrivalled in miraculous powers I have reached this bliss.

91. When thus they beheld me sitting,[19] the dwellers of ten thousand worlds. Raised a mighty shout : Surely thou shalt be a Buddha!

92. The omens[20] beheld in former ages when Bodhisatta sat cross-legged. The same are beheld this day.

93. Cold is dispelled and heat ceases.
This day these things are seen,–verily thou shalt be Buddha.

94. A thousand worlds are stilled and silent.
So are they seen to-day,–verily thou shalt be Buddha.

95. The mighty winds blow not, the rivers cease to flow. These things are seen to-day,–verily thou shalt be Buddha.

96. All flowers blossom on land and sea. This day they all have bloomed,–verily thou shalt be Buddha. This day they all have bloomed,–verily thou shalt be Buddha.

97. All creepers and trees are laden with fruit. This day they all bear fruit,–verily thou shalt be Buddha.

98. Gems sparkle in earth and sky.
This day all gems do glitter,–verily thou shalt be Buddha.

99. Music earthly and deva-music.
Both these to-day send forth their strains–verily thou shalt be Buddha.

100. Flowers of every hue rain down from the sky.
This day they are seen–verily thou shalt be Buddha.

101. The mighty ocean bends itself, ten thousand worlds are shaken.
This day they both send up their roar–verily thou shalt be Buddha.

102. In hell the fires of ten thousand worlds die out.
This day these fires are quenched–verily thou shalt be Buddha.

103. Unclouded is the sun and all the stars are seen.
These things are seen to-day–verily thou shalt be Buddha.

104. Though no rain fell in water that burst forth from the earth.
This day that bursts forth from the earth–verily thou shalt be Buddha.

105. The constellations are all aglow, and the lunar mansions in the vault of heaven. Visākhā is in conjunction with the moon–verily thou shalt be Buddha.

106. Those creatures that dwell in holes and caves depart each from his lair.
This day these lairs are forsaken–verily thou shalt be Buddha.

107. There is no discontent among mortals, but they are filled with contentment.
This day all are content–verily thou shalt be Buddha.

108. Then diseases are dispelled and hunger ceases.
This day these things are seen–verily thou shalt be Buddha

109. Then Lust wastes away, Hate and Dullness perish.
This day all these are dispelled–verily thou shalt be Buddha.

110. No danger then comes near; this day this thing is seen,
By this sign we know it–verily thou shalt become Buddha.

111. No dust flies up; this day this thing is seen.
By this sign we know it, verily thou shalt be Buddha.

112. All noisome odoiurs flee away, divine fragrance brethes around. Such fragrance breathes this day–verily thou shalt be Buddha.

113. All the devas are manifested, the Formless only excepted.
This day they all are seen–verily thou shalt be Buddha.

114. All the hells become visible.
These all are seen this day–verily thou shalt be Buddha.

115. Then walls, and doors, and rocks are no impediment.
This day they have melted into space–verily thou shalt be Buddha.

116. At that moment death and birth do not take place.
This day these things are seen–verily thou shalt be Buddha.

117. Do thou make a strenuous effort, hold not back, go forward, This thing we know–verily thou shalt be Buddha.

And the Bodhisatta, having heard the words of Dīpankara Buddha and of the devas in ten thousand worlds filled with abounding vigour, thought thus within himself : "The Buddhas are beings whose word cannot fail; there is no deviation from truth in their speech. For as the fall of a clod thrown into the air, as the death of a mortal, as the sunrise at down, as a lion's roaring when he leaves his lair, as the delivery of a woman with child, as all these things are sure and certain–even so the word of the Buddhas is sure and cannot fail, verily I shall become a Buddha." Therefore it is said :

118. Having heard the words of Buddha and of the devas of ten thousand worlds.
Glad, joyous, delighted, I then thought thus within myself;

119. The Buddhas speak not doubtful words, the Conquerors speak not vain words.
There is no falsehood in the Buddhas–verily I shall become a Buddha.

120. As a clod cast into the air doth surely fall to the ground.
So the word of the glorious Buddhas is sure and everlasting.

121. As the death of all mortals is sure and constant.
So the word of the glorious Buddhas is sure and everlasting.

122. As the rising of the sun is certain when night has faded.
So the word of the glorious Buddhas is sure and everlasting.

123. As the roaring of a lion who has left his den is certain.
So the word of the glorious Buddhas is sure and everlasting.

124. As the delivery of women with child is certain.
So the word of the glorious Buddhas is sure and everlasting.

And having thus made the resolution : "I shall surely become Buddha", with a view to considering the conditions that constitute a Buddha, exclaiming : "Where are the conditions that make the Buddha, are they found above or below, in the principle or the minor directions?" studying successively the principles of all things, and beholding the first Perfection of Giving, Practised and followed by former Bodhisattas, he thus admonished himself : "Wise Sumedha, from this time forth thou must fulfil the perfection of Giving; for as a water-jar overturned discharged the water so that none remains, and cannot recover it, even so if thou, indifferent to wealth and fame, and wife and child, and goods great and small, give away to all who come and ask everything that they require till nought remains, thou shalt seat thyself at the foot of the tree of Bodhi and become a Buddha." With these words he strenuously resolved to attain the first perfection of Giving. Therefore it is said :

125. Come, I will search the Buddha-making conditions, this way and that, above and below, in all the ten directions, as far as the principles of things extend.

126. Then, as I made my search, I beheld the first the Giving perfection. The high road followed by former sages,

127. Do thou strenuously taking it upon thyself advance to this first perfection : Giving, if thou wilt attain Buddhaship.

128. As a brimming water-jar, overturned by any one. Discharges entirely all the water, and retains none within.

129. Even so, when thou seest any that ask, great, small, and middling, do thou give away all in alms, as the water-jar overthrown.

But considering further : "There must be beside this, other conditions that make a Buddha", and beholding the second perfection : Moral Practice, he thought thus : "O wise Sumedha, from this day forth mayest thou fulfil the perfection of Morality; for as the yak ox, regardless of his life, guards his bushy tail, even so thou shalt become Buddha, if from this day forward regardless of thy life thou keepest the moral precepts." And he strenuously resolved to attain the second perfection, Moral Practice. Therefore it is said :

130. The conditions of a Buddha cannot in sooth be so few. I will study the other conditions that bring Buddhaship to maturity.

131. Then studying I beheld the second Perfection of Morality Practised and followed by former sages.

132. This second one do thou strenuously undertake, and reach the perfection Moral Practice if thou wilt attain Buddhahood.

133. And as the yak cow, when her tail has got in aught entangled. Then and there awaits death, and will not injure her tail,[21]

134. So also do thou, having fulfilled the moral precepts in the four stages, Ever guard the Sīla as the yak guards her tail.

But considering further : "These cannot be the only Buddha-making condition", and beholding the third Perfection of Self-abnegation, he thought thus : "O wise Sumedha, mayest thou henceforth fulfil the perfection of Abnegation; for as man long the denizen of a prison feels no love for it, but is discontented, and wishes to live there no more, even so do thou, likening all births to a prison-house, discontented with all births, and anxious to get rid of them, set thy face toward abnegation, thus shalt thou become Buddha." And he strenuously made the resolution to attain the third Perfection of Self abnegation. Therefore it is said :

135. For the conditions that make a Buddha cannot be so few. I will study others, the conditions that bring Buddhaship to maturity.

136. Studying then I beheld the third Perfection, Abnegation practised and followed by former sages.

137. This third one do thou strenuously undertake, And reach the perfection of abnegation, if thou wilt attain Buddhahood.

138. As a man long denizen of the house of bonds, oppressed with suffering. Feels no pleasure therein, but rather longs for release,

139. Even so do thou look upon all births as prison-houses. Set thy face towards self-abnegation, to obtain release from becoming.

But considering further : "These cannot be the only Buddha-making conditions", and beholding the fourth Perfection of Wisdom, he thought thus : "O wise Sumedha, do thou from this day forth fulfil the Perfection of wisdom, avoiding no subject of knowledge, great, small, or middling,[22] do thcu approach all wise men and ask them questions; for as the medicant friar on his begging rounds, avoiding none of the families, great and small, that he frequents,[23] and wandering for alms from place to place, speedily gets food to support him, even so shalt thou, approaching all wise men, and asking them questions, become a Buddha." And he strenuously resolved to attain the fourth Perfection, Wisdom. Therefore it is said :

140. For the conditions that make a Buddha cannot be so few, I will study the other conditions that bring Buddhaship to maturity.

141. Studying then I beheld the fourth Perfection : Wisdom Practised and followed by former sages.

142. This fourth do thou strenuously undertake, and reach the Perfection of Wisdom, if thou wilt attain Buddhahood.

143. And as a monk on his begging rounds avoids no families, either small, or great, or middling, and so obtains subsistence,

144. Even so thou, constantly questioning wise men, and reaching the Wisdom Perfection, shall attain supreme Buddhaship.

But considering further : "These cannot be the only Buddha-making conditions", and seeing the fifth Perfection of Exertion, he thought thus : "O wise Sumedha, do thou from this day forth fulfil the Perfection of Exertion. As the lion, the king of beasts, in every action[24] strenuously exerts himself, so if thou in all rebirths and in all thy acts art strenuous in exertion, and not a laggard, thou shalt become a Buddha". And he made a firm resolve to attain the fifth Perfection, Exertion. Therefore it is said :

145. For the conditions of a Buddha cannot be so few, I will study the other condition which bring Buddhaship to maturity.

146. Studying then I beheld the fifth Perfection : Exertion Practised and followed by former sages.

147. This fifth do thou strenuously undertake, And reach the perfection L Exertion, if thou wilt attain Buddhahood.

148. As the lion, king of beasts, in lying, standing, and walking Is no laggard, but ever of resolute heart,

149. Even so do thou also in every existence strenuously exert thyself, And reaching the perfection, Exertion, thou shalt attain the supreme Buddhaship.

But considering further : "These cannot be the only Buddha-making conditions", and beholding the sixth Perfection of Patience, he thought to himself : "O wise Sumedha, do thou from this time forth fulfil the Perfection Patience; be thou patient in praise and in reproach. And as when men throw things pure or foul upon the earth, the earth does not feel either desire or repulsion towards them, but suffers them, endures them and consents to them, even so thou also, if thou art patient in praise and reproach shalt become a Buddha." And he strenuously resolved to attain the sixth perfection, Patience. Therefore it is said :

150. For the conditions of a Buddha cannot be so few, I will study other conditions also which bring about Buddhaship.

151. Studying then I beheld the sixth Perfection of Patience Practised and followed by former Buddhas.

152. Having strenuously taken upon thee this sixth perfection, Then with unwavering mind thou shalt attain supreme Buddhaship.

153. And as the earth endures all that is thrown upon it, Whether things pure or impure, and feels neither anger nor pity,

154. Even so enduring the prises and reproaches of all men, Going on to perfect Patience, thou shalt attain supreme buddhaship.

But further considering : "These cannot be the only conditions that make Buddha", and beholding the seventh Perfection of Truth, he although thus within himself : "O wise Sumedha, from this time forth do thou fulfil the perfection of Truth; though the thunderbolt descend upon hay head, do thou never under the influence of desire or otherwise, utter a conscious lie, for the sake of wealth or anything else. And as the planet Benus at all seasons pursues her own, even so, if thou forsake not truth and utter no lie, thou shalt become Buddha." And he strenuouly turned his mind to the seventh Perfection, Truth. Therefore it is said :

155. For these are not all the conditions of a Buddha, I will study other conditions which bring about Buddhaship.

156. Studying then I beheld the seventh Perfection of Truth Practised and followed by former Buddhas.

157. Having strenuously taken upon thyself this seventh perfection. Then free from duplicity of speech thou shalt attain supreme Buddhaship.

158. And as the Planet Venus, balanced in all her times and seasons. In the would of men and devas, departs not from her path,

159. Even so do thou no it depart from the course of truth,[25] Advancing to the perfection of Truth, thou shalt attain supreme Buddhaship.

But further considering : "These cannot be the only conditions that make a Buddha", and beholding the eighth Perfection of Resolution, he thought thus within himself : "O wise Sumedha, do thou from this time forth fulfil the perfection of Resolution; whatsoever thou resolvest be thou unshaken in that resolution. For as a mountain, the wind beating upon it in all directions, trembles not, moves not, but stands in its place, even so thou, if unswerving in thy resolution, shalt become Buddha." And he strenuously resolved to attain the eighth Perfection, Resolution. Therefore it is said :

160. For these are not all the conditions of a Buddha, I will study other conditions that bring about Buddhaship.

161. Studying then I beheld the eighth Perfection Resolution Practised and followed by former Buddhas.

162. Do thou resolutely take upon thyself this eighth perfection. Then thou being immovable shalt attain supreme Buddhaship.

163. And as the rocky mountain, immovable, firmly based, is unshaken by many winds, and stands in its own place,

164. Even so do thou also remain ever immovable in resolution, Advancing to the perfection of Resolution, thou shalt attain supreme Buddhaship.

But further considering : "These cannot be the only conditions that make a Buddha", and beholding the ninth Perfection of Good-will, he thought thus within himself : "O wise Sumedha, do thou from this time forth fulfil the perfection of Good-will, mayest thou be of one mind towards friends and foes. And as water fills with its refreshing coolness good men and had alike,[26] even so, if thou art of one mind in friendly feeling towards all mortals thou shalt become Buddha." And he strenuously resolved to attain the ninth perfection of Good-will. Therefore it is said:

165. For these are not all the conditions of a Buddha, I will study other conditions that bring about Buddhaship.

166. Studying I beheld the ninth Perfection of Good-will, Practised and followed by former Buddhas.

167. Do thou, taking resolutely upon thyself this ninth perfection, Become unrivalled in kindness, if thou wilt become Buddha.

168. And as water fills with its coolness. Good men and bad alike, and carries off all impurity.

169. Even so do thou look with friendship alike on the evil and the good. Advancing to the perfection Good-will, thou shalt attain supreme Buddhaship.

But further considering : "These cannot be the only conditions that make a Buddha", and beholding the tenth Perfection : Euqanimity, he thought thus within himself : "O wise Sumedha, from this time do thou fulfil the perfection of Equanimity, be thou of equal mind in prosperity and adversity. And as the earth is indifferent when things pure or impure are cast upon it, even so, if thou art indifferent in prosperity and adversity, thou shalt become Buddha." And he strenuously resolved to attain the tenth Perfection, Equanimity. Therefore it is said :

170. For these cannot be all the conditions of a Buddha, I will study other conditions that bring about Buddhaship.

171. Studying then I beheld the tenth Perfection; Equanimity. Practised and followed by former Buddhas.

172. If thou take resolutely upon thyself this tenth perfection, Becoming well-balanced and firm, thou shalt attain supreme Buddhaship.

173. And as the earth is indifferent to pure and impure things cast upon her. To both alike, and is free from anger and favour.

174. Even so do thou ever be evenly-balanced in joy and grief, Advancing to the perfection, Equanimity, thou shalt attain supreme Buddhaship.

Then the thought : "These are the only conditions in this world that, bringing Buddhaship to perfection and constituting a Buddha, have to be fulfilled by Boddhisattas; beside the ten Perfection there are no others. And these ten Perfections are neither in the heaven above nor in the earth below, nor are they to be found in the east, or the other quarters, but reside in my heart of flesh." Having thus realized that the Perfections were established in his heart, having strenuously resolved to keep them all, grasping them again and again, he mastered them forwards and backwards;[27] taking them at the end he went backward to the beginning, taking them at the beginning he placed them at the end,[28] taking them at the middle he carried them to the two ends, taking them at both ends he carried them to the middle. Repeating : "The Perfections are the sacrifice of limbs, the Lesser Perfections are the sacrifice of property, the Unlimited Perfections are the sacrifice of life", he mastered them as the Perfections, the Lesser Perfections and the Unlimited Perfections–like one who converts two kindred oil into one,[29] or like one who, using Mount Meru for his churning-rod, churns the great Chakkavāla ocean. And as he grasped again and again the ten Perfections, by the glow of his piety,[30] this earth, four nahutas and eight hundred thousand leagues in breadth, like a bundle of red trodden by an elephant, or a sugar-mill in motion, uttering a mighty roar, trembled, shook and quaked, and spun round like a potter's wheel or the wheel of an oil-mill. Therefore it is said :

175. These are all the conditions in the world that bring Buddhaship to perfection. Beyond these are no others, therein do thou stand fast.

176. While he grasped these conditions natural and intrinsic,[31] By the power of his piety the earth of ten thousand worlds quaked.

177. The earth sways and thunders like a suger-mill at work, Like the wheel of an oil-mill so shakes the earth.

And while the earth was trembling the people of Ramma, unable to endure it, like great Sāl-trees, overthrown by the wind that blows at the end of a cycle, fell swooning here and there, while waterpots and other vessels, revolving like a jar on a potter's wheel struck against each other and were dashed and ground to pieces. The multitudes in fear and trembling approaching the Teacher (Dīpankara) said : "Tell us, Blessed one, is this turmoil caused by Nāgas, or is it caused by either demons, or ogres, or by devas?–for this we know not, but truly this whole multitude is grievously afflicted. Pray does this portend evil to the world or good? Tell us the cause of it." The teacher hearing their words said : "Fear not nor be troubled, there is no danger to you from this. The wise Sumedha, concerning whom

I predicted this day : 'Hereafter he will be a Buddha named Gotama,' is now mastering the Perfections, and while he masters them and turns them about, by the power of his piety the whole ten thousand worlds with one accord quake and thunder." Therefore it is said :

178. All the multitude that was there in attendance on the Buddha, Trembling, fell swooning there upon the ground.

179. Many thousands of waterpots and many hundred jars. Were crushed and pounded there and dashed against each other.

180. Excited, trembling, terrified, confused, their sense disordered. The multitudes assembling, approached the Buddha.

181. Say, will it be good or evil to the world? The whole world is afflicted, ward off this (danger), thou Seer!

182. Then the great Sage Dīpankara enjoined upon them, Be confident, be not afraid at this earthquaking :

183. He of whom I foretold this day, he will be a Buddha in this world. The same is the law of the past followed by the Conquerors.

184. Therefore whole he is pondering fully then norm, the groundwork of a Buddha. This ten thousand-fold earth of men and of devas is shaken.

And the people hearing the Buddha's words, joyful and delighted, taking with them garlands, perfumes and unguents, left the city of Ramma, and went to the Bodhisatta. And having offered their flowers and other presents, and bowed to him and respectfully saluted him, they returned to the city of Ramma. And the Bodhisatta, having made a strenuous exertion of resolve, rose from the seat on which he sat. Therefore it is said :

185. Having heard the Buddha's word, their minds were straightway calmed,
All of them approaching me again paid me their homage.

186. Having taken upon me the Perfections of a Buddha, having made firm my resolve,

Having bowed to Dīpankara, I rose from my seat.

And as the Bodhisatta rose from his seat, the deva in all the ten thousand worlds having assembled and offered him garlands and perfumes, uttered these and other words of praise and blessing : "Venerable hermit Sumedha, this day thou hast made a mighty resolve at the feet of Dīpankara Buddha, mayest thou fulfil it without let or hindrance : fear not nor be dismayed, may not the slightest sickness visit thy frame, quickly exercise the Perfections and attain supreme Buddhaship. As the flowering and fruitbearing trees bring forth flowers and fruit in their season, so do thou also, not letting the right season pass by, quickly reach the supreme enlightenment," and thus having spoken, they returned each one to his deva-home. Then the Bodhisatta, having received the homage of the devas, made a strenuous exertion of resolve, saying ; "Having fulfilled then ten Perfections, at the end of four asankheyyas and a hundred thousand cycles I shall become a Buddha." And rising into the air he returned to Himavanta. Therefore it is said :

187. As he rose from his seat both devas and men. Sprinkle him with divine and earthly flowers.

188. Both devas and men pronounce their blessing : A great thing hast thou willed, mayest thou obtain it according to thy wish.

189. May all dangers be averted, may every sickness vanish, Mayest thou have no hindrance–quickly reach the supreme enlightenment.

190. As when the season is come the flowering trees blossom. Even so do thou, O mighty one, blossom with the knowledge of a Buddha.

191. As all the Buddhas have fulfilled the ten Perfections, Even so do thou, O mighty one, fulfil the ten Perfections.

192. As all the Buddhas are awakened on the seat of enlightenment, Even so be thou, O mighty one, awakened in conqueror's wisdom.

193. As all the Buddhas have set rolling the wheel of the Norm, Even so do thou, O mighty one, set it rolling.

194. As the moon on the mid-day of the month shines in her purity, Even so do thou, with thy mind at the full, shine in ten thousand worlds.

195. As the sun released by Rāhu glows fervently in his heat, Even so, having released mankind, do thou shine in all thy majesty,

196. As all the rivers find their way to the great ocean, Even so may the worlds of men and devas take refuge in thee!

197. The Bodhisatta extolled with these praises, taking on himself the ten conditions, Commencing to fulfil these conditions, entered the forest then.

End of the Story of Sumedha.

And the people of the city of Ramma, having returned to the city, kept open house to the Order with the Buddha at their head. The Teacher having preached the Doctrine to them and established them in the three Refuges and the other branches (of the faith), departing from the city of Ramma, living thereafter his allotted span of life, having fulfilled all the duties of a Buddha, in due course attained that Nirvāna in which no condition of rebirth remains. On this subject all that need be said can be learnt from the narrative in the Buddhavaṃsa, for it is said in that work :

198. Then they having entertained the Chief of the world with his Order, Took refuge in the Teacher Dīpankara.

199. Some the Buddha established in the Refuges, Some in the five Precepts, others in the ten.

200. To some he bestows the peerless doctrines of Analysis,

201. To some the Lord of men grants the eight sublime Acquisitions. On some he bestows the three Wisdoms and the six Super-knowledges.

202. In this order[32] the Great Sage exhorts the multitude. Therewith the teaching of the world's Protector was spread wise abroad.

203. He of the mighty jaw, of the broad shoulder, Dīpankara by name. Procured the salvation of many men, set them free from evil destiny.

204. Beholding persons ripe for salvation, reaching them in an instant. Even at a distance of a hundred thousand leagues, the Great Sage awakened them.

205. At the first conversion the Buddha awakened at thousand millions. At the second the Protector awakened a hundred thousand.

206. When the Buddha preached the truth in the deva-world, There took place a third conversion of nine hundred millions.

207. The Teacher Dīpankara had three assemblies, The first was a meeting of a million millions.

208. Again when the conqueror went into seclusion at Nārada Kūṭa, A thousand million spotless Arahants met together.

209. When the Mighty One dwelt on the lofty rock Sudassana, Then the Sage surrounded himself with nine hundred thousand millions.

210. At that time I was an ascetic wearing matted hair, a man of austere penances. Moving through the air, accomplished in the five superknowledges.

211. The conversion of tens of thousands, of twenties of thousands, took place, Of ones and twos the conversion were beyond computation.[33]

212. Then did the pure religion of Dīpankara Buddha become widely spread, Known to many men prosperous and flourishing.

213. Four hundred thousand, possessed the six superknowledges, endowed with miraculous powers. Ever attend upon Dīpankara, knower of the worlds.

214. Blameworthy are all they who at that time leave the human existence, Not having obtained final sanctity, still imperfect in knowledge.

215. The Word shines in the world of men and deva, made to blossom by saints such as these, Free from human passion, spotless.

216. The city of Dīpankara Buddha was called Rammavatī, The khattiya Sumedha was his father, Sumedhā his mother.

217. Sumangala and Tissa were his chief disciples, And Sāgata was the servitor of Dīpankara Buddha.

218. Nandā and Sunandā were his chief woman-disciples. The Bodhi-tree of this Buddha is called the Pipphali.[34]

219. Eighty cubits in height the Great Sage Dīpankara Shone conspicuous as a Deodar pine, or as a noble Sāl-tree in full bloom.

220. A hundred thousand years was the age of this Great Sage, And so long as he was living on earth he brought many men to salvation.

221. Having made the Truth to shine, having saved great multitudes of men, Having flamed like a mass of fire, he passed away with his disciples.

222. And all this power, this glory, these jewel-wheels on his feet, All is wholly gone–are not all existing things vanity!

223. After Dīpankara was the Leader named Koṇḍanya, Of infinite power, of boundless renown, immeasurable, unrivalled.

Next to the Dīpankara Buddha, after the lapse of one asankheyya, the Teacher Koṇḍanya appeared. He also had three assemblies of saints, in the first assembly there were a million millions, in the second ten thousand millions, in the third nine hundred millions. At that time the Bodhisatta, having been born as a universal monarch named Vijitāvin, kept open house to the priesthood with the Buddha at their head, in number a million of million. The Teacher having predicted of the Bodhisatta : "He will become of Buddha", preached the Law. He having heard the Reacher's preaching gave up his kingdom and left the world. Having mastered the three Piṭakas, having obtained the six superknowedges, and having practised Jhāna without failure, he was reborn in the Brahma world. The city of Koṇḍanya Buddha was Rammavatī, the khattiya Sunanda was his father, his mother was queen Sujātā, Bhadda and Subhadda were his two chief disciples, Anuruddha was his servitor, Tissā and Upatissā his chief woman disciples, his Bodhi-tree was the Sālakalyāṇi, his body was eighty-eight cubits high, and the duration of his life was a hundred thousand years.

After him, at the end of one asankheyya, in one and the same cycle four Buddhas were born, Mangala, Sumana, Revata and Sobhita. Mangala Buddha had three assemblies of disciples. Of these in the first there were a million million brethren, in the second ten thousand millions, in the third nine hundred millions. It is related that a step-brother of his, prince Ānanda, accompanied by an assembly of nine hundred millions, went to the Teacher to hear him preach the Law. The Teacher gave a discourse dealing successively with his various doctrines, and Ānanda and his whole retinue attained Arahantship together with the analytical knowledges. The Teacher looking back upon the meritorious works done by these men of family in former lives, and perceiving that they had merit to acquire the robe and bowl by miraculous means, stretching forth his right hand exclaimed, "Come brethren."[35] Then straightway all of them having become equipped with miraculously obtained robes and bowls, and perfect in decorum, as if they were elders of sixty years' standing, paid homage to the Teacher and attended upon him. This was his third assembly of disciples.

And whereas with other Buddhas a light shone from their bodies to the distance of eighty cubits on every side it was not so with this Buddha, but the light from his body permanently filled ten thousand worlds; trees, earth, mountains, seas, and all other things, not excepting even pots and pans and such-like articles, became as it were overspread with a film of gold. The duration of his life was ninety thousand years, and during the whole of this period the sun, moon, and other heavenly bodies could not shine by their own light, and there was no distinction between night and day. By day all living beings went about in the light of the Buddha as if in the light of the sun, and men ascertained the limits of night and day only by the flowers that blossomed in the evening and by the birds and other animals that uttered their cries in the morning. If I am asked : "What do not other Buddhas also possess this power?" I reply : "Certainly they do, for they might at will fill with their lustre ten thousand worlds or more. But in accordance with a vow made by him in a former existence, the lustre of Mangala Buddha permanently filled ten thousand worlds, just as the lustre of the others permanently extended to the distance of a fathom."

The story is that when he was performing the duties of a Bodhisatta,[36] being in an existence corresponding to the Vessantara existence,[37] he dwelt with his wife and children on a mountain like the Vanka mountain.[38] One day a demon named Kharadāṭhika,[39] hearing of the Bodhisatta's inclination to giving, approached him in the guise of a Brahmin, and asked the Bodhisatta for his two children. The bodhisatta, exclaiming : "I give my children to the Brahmin", cheerfully and joyfully gave up both children, thereby causing the ocean-girt earth to quake.[40] The demon standing by the bench at the end of the cloistered walk, while the Bodhisatta looked on, devoured the children like a bunch of roots. Not a particle of sorrow[41] arose in the Bodhisatta as he looked on the demon, and saw his mouth as soon as he opened it disgorging streams of blood like flames of fire, nay, a great joy and satisfaction welled with him as he thought : "My gift was well given." And he put up the vow : "By the merit of this deed may rays of light one day issue from me in this very way." In consequence of this prayer of his it was that the rays emitted from his body when he became Buddha filled so vast a space.

There was also another deed done by him in a former existence. It is related that, when a Boddhisatta, having visited the relic shrine of a Buddha, he exclaimed : "I ought to sacrifice my life for this Buddha", and having wrapped round the whole of his body in the same way that torches are wrapped, and having filled with clarified butter a golden vessel with jewelled wick-holders, worth a hundred thousand pieces, he lit therein a thousand wicks, and having set fire to the whole of his body beginning with his head, he spent the whole night in circumambulating the shrine. And as he thus strove till dawn not the root of a hair of his head was even heated. It was as one enters the calyx of a lotus, for religion[42] guards him who guards himself. Therefore has the Blessed One said :

224. Well doth religion protect him in sooth who follows it, Happiness bringeth along in its train religion well practised This shall be his reward by whom religion is well practised: Never goeth to misery he who doth practise religion.[43]

And through the merit of this work also the bodily lustre of this Buddha constantly extended through ten thousand worlds. At this time our Boddhisatta,[44] having been born as the Brahmin Suruci, approached the Teacher with the view of inviting him to his house, and having heard his sweet discourse, said : "Lord, take your meal with me to-morrow." "Brahmin, how many monks do you wish for?" "Nay, but how many monks have you in your escort?" At that time was the Teacher's first assembly, and accordingly he replied : "A million millions." "Lord, bring them all with you and come and take your meal at my house," The Teacher consented. The Brahmin having invited them for the next day, on his way home thought to himself : "I am perfectly well able to supply all these monks with broth and rice and clothes and such like necessaries, but how can there be room for them to sit down?"

This thought of his caused the marble throne of the deva-king, three hundred and thirty-six thousand leagues away, to become warm.[45] Sakka exclaiming : "Who wishes to bring me down from my abode?" and looking down with the deva-sight beheld the Bodhisatta, and said : "The Brahmin Suruci having invited the Order with the Buddha at their head is perplexed for room to seat them, it behoves me also to go thither and obtain a share of his merit." And having miraculouly assumed the form of a carpenter, axe in hand he appeared before the Bodhisatta, and said : "Has any one got a job to be done for hire?"

The Bodhisaṭta seeing him said : "What sort of work can you do?" "There's no art that I do not know: any house or hall that anybody orders me to build, I'll build it for him." "Very well, I've got a job to be done." "What is it, sir?" "I've invited a million million bhikkhus for tomorrow, will you build a hall to. seat them all?" "I'll build one with pleasure if you've the means of paying me." "I have, my good man." "Very well, I'll build it." And he went and began looking out for a site. There was a spot some fifty leagues in extent[46] as level as a kasiṇa circle.[47] Sakka fixed his eyes upon it, while he thought to himself : "Let a hall made of the seven precious stones rise up over such and such an extent of ground." Immediately the edifice bursting through the ground rose up. The golden pillars of this hall had silver capitals,[48] the silver pillars had golden capitals, then gem pillars had coral capitals, the coral pillars had gem capitals, while those pillars which were made of all the seven precious stones had capitals of the same. Next he said : "Let the hall have hanging wreaths of little bells at intervals", and looked again. The instant he looked a fringe of bells hung down; their musical tinkling, as they were stirred by a gentle breeze, was like a symphony of the five sort of instruments, or as when the heavenly choirs are going on. He thought : "Let there be hanging garlands of perfumes and flowers", and there the garlands hung. He thought : "Let seats and benches for a million million monks rise up through the earth", and straightway they appeared. He thought : "Let water vessels rise up a teach corner of the building", and the water vessels arose. Having by his miraculous power effected all this, he went to the Brahmin and said : "Come, sir, look at your hall, and pay me may wages."

The Boddhisatta went and looked at the hall, and as he looked his whole frame was thrilled in every part with fivefold joy. And as he gazed on the hall he thought thus within himself : "This hall was not wrought by mortal hands, but surely through my good intention, my good action, the palace of Sakka became hot, and hence this hall will have been built by the Sakka the deva-king; it is not right that in such a hall as this I should give alms for a single day, I will give alms for a whole week."

For the gift of external goods, however great, cannot give satisfaction to the Bodhisattas, but the Bodhisattas feel joy at their self-renunciation when they sever the crowned head, put out the henna-anointed eyes, cut out the heart and give it away. For when our Bodhisatta in the Sivijātaka[49] gave alms in the middle of his capital, at the four gates of the city, at a daily expenditure of five bushels of gold coins, this literality failed to arouse within him a feeling of satisfaction at his renunciation. But on the other hand, when Sakka the deva-king came to him in the disguise of a Brahmin, and asked for his eyes, then indeed, as he took them out and gave them away, laughter rose within him, nor did his heart swerve a hair's breadth from its purpose. And hence we see that as regards alms giving the Bodhisattas can have no satiety. Therefore this Bodhisatta also thinking : "I ought to give alms for seven days to a million million monks", seated them in that hall, and for a week gave them the alms called gavapâna.[50] Men alone were not able to wait upon them, but devas themselves, taking turns with men, waited upon them. A space of fifty leagues or more sufficed not to contain the monks, yet they seated themselves each by his own supernatural power. On the last day, having caused the bowls of all the monks to be washed, and filled them with butter clarified and unclarified, honey and molasses, for medicinal use, he gave them back to them, together with the three robes. The robes and cloaks received by novices and ordained priests were worth a hundred thousand.

The Teacher, when he returned thanks, considering : "This man has given such great alms, who can he be?" and perceiving that at the end of two asankheyyas and four thousand cycles he would become a Buddha named Gotama, addressing the Bodhisatta, made this prediction : "After the lapse of such and such a period thou shalt become a Buddha named Gotama." The Bodhisatta, hearing the prediction, thought : "It seems that I am to become a Buddha, what good can a householder's life do me? I will give up the world", and, treating all this prosperity like so much drivel, he received ordination at the hands of the Teacher. And having embraced the ascetic life and learnt the word of Buddha, and having attained the superknowledges and the Attainments, at the end of his life he was reborn in the Brahma world.

The city of Mangala Buddha was called Uttara; his father was the khattiya Uttara : his mother was Uttarā, Sudeva and Dhammasena were his two chief disciples; Pālita was his servitor, Sīvalī and Asokā his two chief woman disciples. The Nāga was his Bodhi-tree. His body was eighty-eight cubits high. When his death took place, after he had lived ninety thousand years, at the same instant ten thousand worlds were involved in darkness, and in all worlds there was a great cry and lamentation of men.

225. After Koṇḍanya the Leader named Mangala, Dispelling darkness in the world, held aloft the torch of religion.

And after the Buddha had died, surrounding in darkness ten thousand worlds, the Teacher named Sumana appeared. He also had three great assemblies of disciples, in the first assembly the brethren were a million millions, in the second, on the Golden Mountain, ninety million of millions, in the third eighty million of millions.

At this time the bodhisatta was the Nāga king Atula, mighty and powerful. And he, hearing that a Buddha had appeared, left the Nāga world, accompanied by his assembled kinsmen, and, making offerings with divine music to the Buddha, whose retinue was a million million brethren, and having given great gifts, bestowing upon each two garments of fine cloth, he was established in the Three Refuges. And this Teacher also foretold of him : "One day he will be a Buddha."

The city of this Buddha was named Khema : Sudatta was his father, Sirimā his mother, Saraṇa and Bhāvitatta his chief disciples, Udena his servitor, Soṇa and Upasoṇā his chief woman-disciples. The Nāga was his Bodhi-tree, his body was ninety cubits high, and his age ninety thousand years.

226. After Mangala came the Leader named Sumana. In all things unequalled, the best of all beings.

After him the Teacher Revata appeared. He also had three assemblies of disciples. In the first assembly the numbers were innumerable, in the second there were a million millions, so also in the third.

After that time the Bodhisatta having been born as the Brahmin Atideva, having heard the Teacher's preaching, was established in the Three Refuges. And raising his clasped hands to his head, having praised the Teacher's abandonment of human passion, he presented him with a monk's upper robe.

That Teacher also made the prediction : "Thou wilt become a Buddha." Now the city of this Buddha was called Sudhanyabtī, his father was the nobleman Vipula, his mother Vipulā, Varuṇa and Brahmadeva his chief disciples, Sambhava his servitor, Bhaddā and Subhaddā his chief woman-disciples, and the Nāga-tree his Bo-tree. His body was eighty cubits high, and his age sixty thousand years.

227. After Sumana came the Leader named Revata, The Conqueror unequalled, incomparable, unmatched, supreme.

After him appeared the Teacher Sobhita. He also had three assemblies of disciples; in the first assembly were a thousand million monks, in the second nine hundred millions, in the third eight hundred millions.

At that time the Bodisat, having been born as the Brahmin Ajita, and having heard the Teacher's preaching, was established in the Three Refuges, and gave a great donation to the Order of monks, with the Buddha at their head. This Teacher also prophesied to him, saying : "Thou wilt become a Buddha." Sudhamma was the name of the city of this Blessed One, Sudhamma the king was his father, Sudhammā his mother, Asama and Sunetta his chief disciples, Anoma his servitor, Nakulā and Sujātā his chief woman-disciples, and the Nāga-tree his Bo-tree; his body was fifty-eight cubits high, and his age ninety thousand years.

228. Aftet Revata came the Leader named Sobhita, Subdued and mild, unequalled and unrivalled.

After him, when an asankheyya had elapsed, three Buddhas were born in one kalpa–Anomadassin, Paduma, and Nārada. Anomadassin had three assemblies of saints; in the first were eight hundred thousand monks, in the second seven in the third six.

At that time the Bodisat was a Yakkha chief, mighty and powerful, the lord of many millions of millions of yakkhas. He, hearing that a Buddha had appeared, came and gave a great donation to the Order of monks, with the Buddha at their head.

And this Teacher also prophesied to him, saying : "Hereafter thou wilt be a Buddha." The city of Anomadassin the Blessed One was called Chandavatī, Yasava the king was his fater, Yasodharā his mother, Nisabha and Norna his chief disciples, Varuṇa his servitor, Sundarī and Sumanā his chief woman disciples, the Arjuna-tree his Bo-tree; his body was fifty-eight cubits high, his age a hundred thousand years.

229. After Sobhita came the perfect Buddha–the best of men–Anomadassin of infinite fame, glorious, difficult to surpass.

After him appeared the Teacher named Paduma. He too had three assemblies of disciples; in the first assembly were a million million monks, in the second three hundred thousand, in the third two hundred thousand of the monks dwelt at a great grove in the uninhabited forest.

At that time, whilst the Tathāgata was living in that grove, the Bodisat having been born as a lion, saw the Teacher plunged in ecstatic trance, and with trustful heart made obeisance to him, and walking round him with reverence, experienced great joy, and thrice ' ttered a mighty roar. For seven days he laid not aside the bliss arising from the tought of the Buddha, but through joy and gladness, seeking not after prey, he kept in attendance there, offering up his life. When the Teacher, after seven days, aroused himself from his trace, he looked upon the lion and thought : "he will put trust in the Order of monks and make obeisance to them; let them draw near." At that very moment the monks drew near, and the lion put faith in the Order.

The Teacher, knowing his thoughts, prophesied, saying : "Hereafter he will be a Buddha." Now the city of Paduma the Blessed One was called Champaka, his father was Paduma the king, his mother Asamā, Sāla and Upasāla were his chief disciples, Veruṇa his servitor, Rāmā and Uparāmā his chief woman disciples, the Crimson-tree his bo-tree; his body was fifty-eight cubits high, and his age was a hundred thousand years.

230. After Anomadassin came the perfect Buddha, the best of men, Paduma by name, unequalled, and without a rival.

After him appeared the Teacher named Nārada. He also had three assemblies of saints; in the first assembly were a million million monks, in the second ninety million million, in the third eighty million million.

At that time the Bodisat, having taken the vows as a sage, acquired the five Super-knowledges, and the eight sublime Acquisitions, and gave a great donation to the Order, with the Buddha at their head, making an offering of red sandal wood.

That Teacher also prophesied to him : "Hereafter thou wilt be a Buddha." The city of this Blessed One was called Dhanyavatī, his father was Sumedha the warrior, his mother Anomā, Bhaddasāla and Jetamitta his chief disciples, Bāseṭṭha his servitor, Uttarā and Paggunī his chief woman-disciples, the reat Crimson-tree was his bo-tree; his body was eightyeight cubits high, and his age was ninety thousand years.

231. After Paduma came the perfect Buddha, the best of men,
Nārada by name, unequalled and without a rival.

After Nārada the Buddha a hundred thousand world-cycles ago there appeared in one kalpa only one Buddha called Padumuttara. He also had three assemblies of disciples; in the first were a million million monks, in the second, on the Vebhāra Mountain, nine hundred thousand million, in the third eight hundred thousand million.

At that time the Bodisat, born as a Mahratta of the name of Jaṭila, gave an offering of robes to the Order with the Buddha at their head.

That Teacher also prophesied to him : "Hereafter thou wilt be a Buddha." And at the time of Padumuttara the Blessed One there were no infidels, but all, men and devas, took refuge in the Buddha. His city was called Haṁsavatī, his father was Ānanda the warrior, his mother Sujātā, Devala and Sujāta his chief disciples, Sumana his servivor, Amitā and Asamā his chief woman-disciples, the Sāl-tree his Bo-tree : his body was eighty-eight cubits high, the light from his body extended twelve leagues, and his age was a hundred thousand years.

232. After Nārada came the perfect Buddha, the best of men, padumuttara by name, the Conqueror unshaken, like the sea.

After him, when thirty thousand world-cycles had elapsed, two Buddhas, Sumedha and Sujāta, were born in one kalpa. Sumedha also had three assemblies of his saints; in the first assembly, in the city Sudassana, were a thousand million sinless ones, in the second nine hundred, the third eight hundred. At that time the Bodisat, both as the Brahmin youth named Utara, lavished eight hundred million of money he had saved in giving a great donation to the Order, with the Buddha at their head. And he then listened to the Doctrine, and accepted the Refuges, and abandoned his home, and took the vows.

That Teacher also prophesied to him, saying : "Hereafter thou wilt be a Buddha." The city of Sumedha the Blessed One was called Sudassana, Sudatta the king was his father, Sudattā his mother, Saraṇa and Sabbakāma his two chief disciples, Sāgara his servivor, Rāmā and Surāmā his two chief woman-disciples, the great Champaka-tree his Bo-tree; his body was eighty-eight cubits high, and his age was ninety thousand years.

233. After Padumuttara came the Leader named Sumedha, The Sage hard to equal, brilliant in glory, supreme in all the world.

After him appeared the Teacher Sujāta. He also had three assemblies of disciples;.in the first assembly were sixty thousand monks, in the second fifty, in the third forty.

At that time the Bodisat was a universal monarch, and hearing that a Buddha was born he went to him and heard the Doctrine, and gave to the Order, with the Buddha at their head, his kingdom of the four continents with its seven treasures and took the vows under the Teacher. All the dwellers in the land, taking advantage of the birth of a Buddha in their midst, did duty as servants in the monasteries, and continually gave great donation to the Order, with the Buddha at their head. And to him also the Teacher prophesied. The city of this Blessed One was called Sumangala, Uggata the king was his father, Pabhāvatī his mother, Sudassana and Deva his chief disciples, Nārada his servivor, Nāgā and Nāgasamālā his chief woman-disciples, and the great Bambu-tree his Bo-tree; this tree, they say, had smaller hollows and thicker wood than ordinary bambus have,[51] and in its mighty upper branches it was as brilliant as a bunch of peacocks' tails. The body of this Blessed One was fifty cubits high, and his age was ninety thousand years.

234. In that age, the Maṇḍakalpa, appeared the Leader Sujāta,
Mighty jawed and grandly framed, whose measure none
can take, and heard to equal.

After him when eighteen hundred world-cycles had elapsed, three Buddhas, Piyadassin, Atthadassin, and Dhammadassin, were born in one kalpa. Piyadassin also had three assemblies of disciples; in the first were a million million monks, in the second nine hundred million, in the third eight hundred million.

At that time the Bodisat, as a young Brahmin called Kassapa, who had thoroughly learnt the three Vedas, listened to the Teacher's preaching of the Doctrine, and built a monastery at a cost of a million million, and stood firm in the Refuges and the Precepts.

Now to him the Teacher prophesied, saying : "After the lapse of eighteen hundred kalpas thou wilt become a Buddha." The city of this Blessed One was called Anoma, his father was Sudinna the king, his mother Candā, Pālita and Sabbadassin his chief disciples, Sobhita his servivor, Sujātā and Dhammadinnā his chief woman-disciples, and the Piyangutree his Bo-tree. His body was eighty cubits high, and his age ninety thousand years.

235. After Sujātā came Piyadassin, Leader of the world, Self-
taught, hard to match, unequalled, of great glory.

After him appeared the teacher called Atthadassin. He too had three assemblies of disciples; in the first were nine million eight hundred thousand monks, in the second eight million eight hundred thousand, and the same number in the third.

At that time the Bodisat, as the mighty ascetic Susima, brought from heaven the sunshade of Mandārava flowers, and offered it to the Teacher, who prophesied also to him. The city of this Blessed One was called Sobhita, Sāgara the king was his father, Sudassanā his mother, Santa and Apasanta his chief disciples, Abhaya his servivor, Dhammā and Sudhammā his chief woman-disciples, and the Champaka his Bo-tree. His body was eighty cubits high, the glory from his body alwasys extended over a league, and his age was a hundred thousand years.

236. In the same age elect Atthadassin, best of men, Dispelled the thick darkness and attained supreme Enlightenment.

After him appeared the Teacher named Dhammadassin. He too had three assemblies of disciples; in the first were a thousand million monks, in the second seven hundred millions, in the third eight hundred millions. At that time the Bodisat, as Sakka the king of the devas, made an offering of sweet-smelling flowers from heaven, and divine music.

That Teacher also prophesied to him. The city of this Blessed One was called Saraṇa, his father was Saraṇa the king, his mother Sunandā. Paduma and Phussadeva his chief disciples, Sunetta his servitor, Khemā and Sabbanāmā his chief woman-disciples, and the red Kuravaka-tree (called also Bimbijāla) his bo-tree. His body was eighty cubits high, and his age hundred thousand years.

237. In the same age elect the far-famed Dhammadassin Dispelled the thick darkness, illuminated earth and heaven.

After him, ninety-four world-cycles ago, only one Buddha, by name Siddhattha, appeared in one Kalpa. Of his disciples too there were three assemblies; in the first were a million million monks, in the second nine hundred millions, in the third eight hundred millions.

At that time the Bodisat, as the ascetic Mangala of great glory and gifted with the powers derived from super-knowledge, brought a great jambu fruit and presented it to the Tathāgata.

The Teacher, having eaten the fruit, prophesied to the Bodisat, saying : "Ninety-four kalpas hence thou wilt become a Buddha." The city of this Blessed One was called Vebhāra, Jayasena the king was his father, Suphassā his mother, Sambla and Sumitta his chief disciples, Revata his servitor, Sīvalī and

Surāmā his chief woman-disciples, and the Kaṇikāra-tree his Bo-tree. His body was sixty cubits high, and his age hundred thousand years.

238. After Dhammadassin, the Leader named Siddhattha Rose like the sun, bringing all darkness to and end.

After him, ninety-two world-cycles ago, two Buddhas, Tissa and Phussa by name, were born in one kalpa. Tissa the Blessed One had three assemblies of disciples; in the first were a thousand million of monks, in the second nine hundred millions, in the third eight hundred millions.

At that time the Bodisat was born as the wealthy and famous warrior Sujāta. When he had taken the vows and acquired the wonderful powers of a rishi, he heard that a Buddha had been born; and taking a heaven-grown Mandārava lotus, and flowers of the Päricchattaka-tree, he offered them to thc Tathāgata as he walked in the midst of his disciples, and he spread an awning of flowers in the sky.

To him, too, the Teacher prophesied, saying : "Ninety-two kalpas hence thou wilt become a Buddha." The city of this Blessed One was called Khema, Janasandha the warrior- chief was his father, Padumā his mother, the god Brahmā and Udaya his chief disciples, Sambhava his servivor, Phussā and Sudattā his chief woman-disciples, and the Asana-tree his Bo-tree. His body was sixty cubits high, and his age a hundred thousand years.

239. After Siddhattha, Tissa, the unequalled and unrivalled, Of infinite virtue and glory, was the chief Guide of the world.

After him appeared the Teacher named Phussa. He too had three assemblies of disciples; in the first assembly were six million monks, in the second five in the third three million two hundred thousand.

At that time the Bodisat, born as the warrior Vijitavī, laid aside his kingdom and, taking the vows under the Teacher, learnt the three Piṭakas, and preached the Doctrine to the people, and fulfilled the Perfection of Moral Practice.[52]

And the Buddha prophesied to him in the samc manner. The city of this blessed One was called Kāsi (Benares), Jayasena the king was his father, Sirimā his mother, Surakkhita and Dhammasena his chief disciples, Sabhiya his servivor, Chālā and Upachālā his chief woman-disciples, and the Āmalaka-tree his Bo-tree. His body was fifty-eight cubits high, and his age ninety thousand years.

240. In the same age elect Phussa was the Teacher supreme,
Unequalled, unrivalled, the chief Guide of the world.

After him, ninety world-cycles ago, appeared the Blessed One named Vipassin.[53] He too had three assemblies of disciples; in the first assembly were six million eight hundred thousand monks, in the second one hundred thousand, in the third eighty thousand.

At that time the Bodisat, born as the mighty and powerful snake king Atula gave to the Blessed One a golden chair, inlaid with the seven kinds of gems.

To him that Teacher also prophesied, saying : "Ninety-one world-cycles hence thou wilt become a Buddha." The city of this Blessed One was called Bandhumatī, Bandhumā the king was his father, Bandhumatī his mother, Khandha and Tissa his chief disciples, Asoka his servitor, Chandā and Chandamittā his chief woman-disciples, and the Bignonia (or Pāṭali-tree) his Bo-tree. His body was eighty cubits high, the effulgence from his body always reached a hundred leagues, and his age was a hundred thousand years.

241. After Phussa, the Supreme Buddha, the best of men,
Vipassin by name, the far-seeing, appeared in the world.

After him, thirty-one world-cycles ago, there were two Buddhas, called Sikhin and Vessabhū. Sikhin too had three assemblies of disciples : in the first were a hundred thousand monks, in the second eighty thousand, in the third seventy.

At that time the Bodisat, born as king Arindama, gave a great donation of robes and other things to the Order with the Buddha at their head, and offered also a superb elephant, decked with the seven gems and provided with all things suitable. That Teacher also prophesied to him, saying : "Thirty-one world cycles hence thou wilt become a Buddha." The city of that Blessed One was called Aruṇavatī, Aruṇa warrior-chief was his father, Pabhāvatī his mother, Abhibhū and Sambhava his chief disciples, Khemankura his servivor, Makhelā and Padumā his chief woman-disciples, and the Puṇḍarīka-tree his Bo-tree. His body was thirty-seven cubits high, the effulgence from his body reached three leagues, and his age was thirty-seven thousand years.

242. After Vipassin came the Supreme Buddha, the best of men, Sikhin by name, the Conqueror, unequalled and unrivalled.

After him appeared the Teacher named Vessabhū. He also had three assemblies of disciples; in the first were eight million monks, in the second seven, in the third six.

At that time the Bodisat, born as the king Sudasana, gave a great donation of robes and other things to the Order, with the Buddha at their head. And taking the vows at his hands, he became righteous in conduct, and found great joy in meditating on the Buddha

That Teacher also prophesied to him, saying : "Thirty-one world-cycles hence thou wilt become a Buddha." The city of this Blessed One was called Anopama, Suppatīta the king was his father, Yasavatī his mother, Soṇa and Uttara his chief disciples, Upasanta his servitor, Dāmā and Sumālā his chief woman-disciples, and the Sal-tree his Bo-tree. His body was sixty cubits high, and his age sixty thousand years.

243. In the same age elect, the conqueror named Vessabhū, Unequalled and unrivalled, appeared in the world.

After him, in this world-cycle, four Buddhas have appeared–Kakusandha, Koṇāgamana, Kassapa, and our Buddha. Kakusandha the Blessed One had one assembly, at which forty thousand monks were present.

At that time the Bodisat, as Khema the king, gave a great donation, robes and bowls, to the Order, with the Buddha at their head, and having given also collyriums and medicines, he listened to the Doctrine preached by the Teacher, and took the vows.

That Teacher also prophesied to him. The city of Kakusandha the Blessed One was called Khema, Aggidatta the Brāhman was his father, Visākhā the Brahman woman his mother, Vidhura and Sanjīva his chief disciples, Buddhija his servitor, Sāmā and Campakā his chief woman-disciples, and the great Sirīsa-tree his bo-tree. His body was forty cubits high, and his age forty thousand years.

244. After Vessabhū came the perfect Buddha, the best of men,
Kakusandha by name infinite and hard to equal.

After him appeared the Teacher Koṇāgamana. Of his disciples too there was one assembly, in which were thirty thousand monks.

At that time the Bodisat, as Pabbata the king, went, surrounded by his ministers, to the Teacher, and listened to the preaching of the Doctrine. And having given an invitation to the Order, with the Buddha at their head, he kept up a great donation, giving cloths of silk, and of fine texture, and woven with gold. And he took the vows from the Teacher's hands.

That Teacher also prophesied to him. The city of this Blessed One was called Sobhavatī, Yaññadatta the Brahmin was his father, Uttarā the Brahman woman his mother, Bhiyyosa and Uttara his chief disciples, Sotthija his servivor, Samuddā and Uttarā his chief woman-disciples, and the Udumbara-tree his Bo-tree. His body was twenty cubits high, and his age was thirty thousand years.

245. After Kakusandha came the Perfect Buddha, the best of men, Koṇāgamana by name, Conqueror, chief of the world, supreme among men.

After him the Teacher named Kassapa appeared in the world. Of his disciples too there was one assembly in which were twenty thousand monks.

At that time the Bodisat, as the Brahmin youth Jotipāla, accomplished in the three Vedas, was well known in earth and sky as the friend of the potter Ghaṭīkāra. Going with him to the Teacher and hearing the Doctrine, has took the vows; and zealously learning the three Piṭakas, he glorified, by faithfulness in duty and in works of supererogation, the teaching of the Buddha.

That Teacher also prophesied to him. The birth place of the Blessed One was called Benāres, Brahmadatta the Brahmin was his father, Dhanavatī of the Brahmin caste his mother, Tissa and Bhāradvāja his chief disciples, Sabbamitta his servitor, Anuḷā, and Uruveḷa his chief woman-disciples, and the Nigrodha-tree his Bo-tree. His body was twenty cubits high, and his age was twenty thousand years.

246. After Koṇāgamana came the Perfect Buddha, best of men, Kassapa by name, that Conqueror, king of righteousness, and giver of light.

Again in the age in which Dīpankara the Buddha appeared, three other Buddhas appeared also. On their part no prophecy was made to the Bodisat, they are therefore not mentioned here; but in the commentary, in order to mention all the Buddhas from this age, it is said :

247. Tanhankara and Medhankara, and Saraṇankara, And the Perfect Buddha Dīpankara, and Koṇḍanya best of men,

248. And Mangala, and Sumana, and Revata, and Sobhita the sage, Anomadassin, Paduma, Narada, Padumuttara,

249. And Sumedha, and Sujta, Piyadassin the famous one, Atthadassin, Dhammadassin, Siddhattha guide of the world,

250. Tissa, and Phussa, the enlightened Bipassin, Sikhin, Vessabhū, Kakusandha, Koṇgamana, and Kassapa too the Guide–

251. These were the perfect Buddhas, the sinless ones, the well controlled :

Appearing like suns, dispelling the thick darkness; They, and their disciples too, blazed up like flames of fire and went out.

Thus our Bodisat has come down to us through four asankheyyas and one hundred thousand ages, making resolve in the presence of the twenty-four Buddhas, beginning with Dīpankara. But after Kassapa there is no other Buddha beside the present supreme Buddha.

So the Bodisat received a prophecy from each of the twenty-four Buddhas, beginning at Dīpankara.

And furthermore in accordance with the saying :

"The resolve (to become a Buddha) only succeeds by the combination of eight qualifications : being a man, and of the male sex, and capable of attaining arahantship, association with the Teachers, renunciation of the world, perfection in virtue, acts of self-sacrifice, and earnest determination."

he combined in himself these eight qualifications. And exerting himself according to the resolve he had made at the feet of Dīpankara, in the word :

"Come, I will search for the Buddha-making conditions, this way and that";[54]

and beholding the Perfections of Giving and the rest to be qualities necessary for the making of a Buddha, according to the words :

"Then, as I made my search, I beheld the first Perfection of Giving",[55]

he came down through many births, fulfilling these Perfections, even up to his last appearance as Vessantara.

And the rewards which fell to him on his way, as they fall to all the Bodisats who have resolved to become Buddhas, are lauded thus :

252. So the men, perfect in every part, and destined to Buddhahood, Traverse the long road through thousands of millions of ages.

253. They are not born in hell, not in the space between the worlds. They do not become consumed by hunger, thirst, and want,

And they do not become small animals, even though born to sorrow.

254. When born among men they are not blind by birth. They are not hard of hearing, they are not classed among the dumb.

255. They do not become women; among hermaphrodites and eunuchs. They are not found–these men destined to Buddhahood.

256. Free from the deadly sins, everywhere pure-living. They follow not after vain opinion, they perceive the working of karma.

257. Though they dwell in bright worlds, they are not born in the mindless. Nor are they destined to rebirth among the devas in the Pure Abodes.[56]

258. Bent upon renunciation, good men, detached from this rebirth or that. They walk as acting for the world's fulfilling all perfection.

While he was thus fulfilling the Perfections, there was no limit to the occasions on which he fulfilled the Perfection of Giving. As, for instance, in the times when he was the Brahmin Akatti, and the Brahmin Sankha, and the king Dhanañjaya, and Maha-sudassana, and Maha-govinda, and the king Nimi, and the prince Chanda, and the merchant Visayha, and the king Sivi, and Vessantara. so, certainly, in the Birth as the Wise Hare, according to the words[57] :

259. When I saw one coming for food, I offered my own self, There is no one like me in giving, such is my Perfection of Giving.

he, offering up his own life, acquired the Supreme Perfection called the Perfection of Giving.

In like manner there is no limit to the way in which he fulfilled the Perfection of Moral Practice. As, for instance, in the times when he was the snake king Sīlavat, and the snake king Campeyya, the snake king Bhūridatta, the snake king Chaddanta, and the prince Alīnasattu, son of king Jayaddisa. So, certainly, in the Sankhapāla Birth, according to the words :

260. Even when piercing me with stakes, and striking me with javelins, I was not angry with the sons of Bhoja, such is my Perfection of Moral practice.

he, offering up himself, acquired the Supreme Perfection, called the Perfection of Moral Practice.

In like manner there is no limit to the way in which, forsaking his kingdom, he fulfilled the Perfection of Renunciation. As, for instance, in the times when he was the prince Somanassa, and the prince Hatthipla, and the wise man Ayoghara–in which, forsaking his kingdom, he fulfilled the Perfection of Renunciation. So, certainly, in the Chūla-Sutasoma Birth, according to the words :

261. The kingdom, which was in my power, like spittle I rejected it, And rejecting cared not for it, such is my Perfection of Renunciation,

he, renouncing the kingdom for freedom from the ties of sin,[58] acquired the Supreme Perfection, called the Perfection of Renunciation.

In like manner, there is no limit to the ways in which he fulfilled the Perfection of Wisdom. As, for instance, in the times when he was the wise man Vidhūra, and the wise man Mahā-govinda, and the wise man Kuddāla, and the wise man Araka, and the ascetic Bodhi, and the wise man Mahosadha. So, certainly, in the time when he was the wise man Senaka in the Sattubhatta Birth, according to the words :

262. Searching the matter out by wisdom, I set the Brahmin free from pain, There is no one like me in wisdom such is my Perfection of Wisdom,

he, pointing out the snake which had got into the bellows, acquired the Supreme Perfection called the Perfection of Wisdom.

So, certainly, in the Mahā-Janaka Birth, according to the words :

263. Out of sight of the shore, in the midst of the waters, all men are as if dead, There is no other way of thinking; such is my Perfection of Resolution,

he, crossing the Great Ocean, acquired the Supreme Perfection called the Perfection of Resolution.

And so in the Khantivāda Birth, according to the words :

264. Even when he struck me with a sharp axe, as if I were a senseless thing, I was not angry with the king of Kāsi; such is my Perfection of Patience,

he, enduring great sorrow as if he were a senseless thing, acquired the Perfection of Patience.

And so in the Mahā-Sutasoma Birth, according to the words:

265. Guarding the word of Truth, and offering up my life, I delivered the hundred warriors; such is my Perfection of Truth, he, offering up his life, and observing truth, obtained the Perfection of Truth.

And in the Mūgapakkha Birth, according to the words :

266. Father and mother I hated not, reputation I hated not, But all knowledge was dear to me, therefore was I firm in duty, offering up even his life, and being resolute in duty, he acquired the Perfection of Resolution.

And so in the Ekarāja Birth, according to the words :

267. No man terrifies me, nor am I in fear of any man; Firm in the power of kindness, in purity I take delight, regarding not even his life while attaining to kindness, he acquired the perfection of Good-will.

So in the Somahaṃsa Birth, according to the words :

268. I lay me down in the cemetery, making a pillow of dead bones :

The village children mocked and praised : to all I was indifferent, he was unshaken in equanimity, even when the villagers tried to vex or please him by spitting or by offering garlands and perfumes, and thus he acquired the Perfection of Equanimity.

This is a summary only, the account will be found at length in the *Chariyā Piṭaka*,

Having thus fulfilled the Perfections, in his birth as Vessantara, according to the words :

269. This earth, unconscious though she be and ignorant of joy or grief, E'en she by my free-giving's mighty power was shaken seven times, he performed such mighty acts of virtue as made the earth to shake. And when, in the fullness of time, he had passed away, he reassumed existence in the Tusita heaven.

Thus should be understood the period, called Distant, from the Resolution at the feet of Dīpankara down to this birth in the City of Delight.

II : THE INTERMEDIATE EPOCH

Avidūre Nidāna

It was when the Bodisat was thus dwelling in the City of Delight that the so-called "Buddha proclamation" took place. For three such "Proclamations" take place on earth. These are the three. When they realize that at the end of a hundred thousand years a new dispensation will begin, devas of the next world who are called World-arrangers, with their hair flying and dishevelled, with weeping faces, wiping away their tears with their hands, clad in red garments, and with their clothes all in disorder, wander among men, and make proclamation, saying :

"Sirs, one hundred thousand years from now there will be a new dispensation; this word-system will be destroyed; even the sea will dry up; this great earth, with Sineru the monarch of mountains, will be burned up and destroyed; and the whole world up to the Brahma-realms, will pass away. And so, sirs, exercise love, pity, sympathy and equanimity, cherish the mother, cherish the father, honour the elders in your families." This is called the proclamation of an Age [Kappahalāhala].

Again, when they realize that at the end of a thousand years an omniscient Buddha will appear on earth, the deva-guardians of the world go from place to and make proclamation, saying : "Sirs, at the end of a thousand years from this time a

Buddha will appear on earth." This is called the proclamation of a Buddha [Buddha-halāhala].

Again, when devas realize that at the end of a hundred years a universal monarch will appear, they go from place to place and make proclamation, saying : "Sirs, at the end of a hundred years from this time a universal monarch will appear on earth." This is called the proclamation of a Universal monarch [Chakkavatti-halāhala].

These are the three great proclamations.

When of these three they hear the Buddha-proclamation, the devas of the entire ten thousand world systems assemble together; and having ascertained who will become the Buddha, they go to him and beseech him to do so,–so beseeching him when the first signs appear [that his present life is drawing to its close]. Accordingly on this occasion they all, with the governors in each world,[59] assembled in one world, and going to the future Buddha in the world of bliss (Tusita), they besought him, saying:

"Sir, when thou wast fulfilling the Ten Perfections thou didst not do so from a desire for the state of world-governor–Sakka, or Māra, or Brahma–or of a mighty king upon earth; thou wast fulfilling them with the hope of reaching all-knowledge for the sake of the salvation of mankind! Now has the moment come, sir, for thy Buddhahood; now, sir, has the time arrived!"

But the Great Being, as if he had not granted the prayer of the devas, reflected in succession on the following five important points, *viz.* the time; the country; the family; the mother; and her age-limit.

Of these he first reflected on the Time, thinking : "Is this the time or not?" And on this point he thought : "When the time of the span of life has grown to be upwards of a hundred thousand years, the time has not arrived. Why not? Because in such a period men perceive not that living beings are subject to birth, decay, and death; the thrice marked pearl of the preaching of the gospel of the Buddhas is not; and when the Buddhas speak of the impermanence of all things, of the universality of sorrow, and of the delusion of individuality, people will neither listen nor believe, saying : 'What is this they talk of?' At such a time there can be no understanding, and without that the teaching will not lead to salvation. That therefore is not the time. Neither is it the right time when the span of life is under one hundred years. Why not? Because then sin is rife among men; and admonition addressed to the sinners does not endure, but like a streak drawn on the water vanishes quickly away. That therefore is not the time. When, however, the span of life is under a hundred thousand and over a hundred years that is the proper time." Now at that time the span of (earth) life was one hundred years. The Great Being therefore saw that the time of his advent had arrived.

Then reflecting upon the Country, and considering the four great continents with their surrounding islands,[60] he thought : "In three of the continents the Buddhas are not born, but in Jambudvīpa they are born," and thus he decided on the country.

Then reflecting upon The District, and thinking : "Jambudvīpa indeed is large, ten thousand leagues in extent; now in which district of it do the Buddhas appear?" he fixed upon the Middle Country.[61] And calling to mind that the town named Kapilavatthu was in that country, he concluded that he ought to be born in it.

Then reflecting on The Family, he thought : "The Buddhas are not born in the Vessa caste, nor the Sudda caste; but either in the Brahmin or in the Khattiya caste, whichever is then held in the highest repute. The Khattiya caste is now predominant, I must be born in it, and Suddhodana the chief will be my father." Thus he beheld the family.

Then reflecting on The Mother, he thought : "The mother of a Buddha is not lustful, or corrupt as to drink, but has fulfilled the Perfections for a hundred thousand ages, and from her birth upwards has kept the five Precepts unbroken. Now this lady Mahā Māyā is such an one, when will be my mother." And further considering how long her life should last, he foresaw that it would still last ten months and seven days.

Having thus reflected on these five important points he favoured the devas by consenting : "The ṭime has arrived, sirs, for me to become a Buddha." He then dismissed them with the words and promise "Do you go"; and attended by the devas of the world of Bliss (Tusita), he entered the grove of Gladness (Nandånå) in the City of Bliss.

Now in each of the deva-worlds there is such a grove of Gladness; and there the devas are wont to remind any one of them who is about to depart of the opportunities he has gained by good deeds done in a former birth, saying to him : "When hence deceased go to a good destiny." And thus he also, when walking about there, surrounded by devas reminding him of his acquired merit, departed thence, and was conceived in the womb of the Lady Mahā Māyā.

In order to explain this better, the following is the account in fuller detail. At that time, it is said, the Midsummer festival was proclaimed in the City of Kapilavatthu, and the people were enjoying the feast. During the seven days before the full moon the Lady Mahā Māyā had taken part in the festivity, as free from drunkenness as it was brilliant with garlands and perfumes. On the seventh day she rose early and bathed in perfumed water : and she distributed four hundred thousand pieces in giving great largesse. Decked in her richest attire she partook of the purest food : and steadfast in the rites of the feast she entered her beautiful chamber, and lying on her royal couch she fell asleep and dreamt this dream.

The four Guardians of the world, lifting her up in her couch, carried her to the Himālaya mountains, and placing her under the Great Sāl-tree, seven leagues high, on the Crimson Plain, sixty yojanas broad, they stood respectfully aside. Their queens then came toward her, and taking her to the lake of Anotatta, bathed her to free her from human stains; and dressed her in heavenly garments; and anointed her with perfumes; and decked her with heavenly flowers. Not far from there is the Silver Hill, within which is a golden mansion; in it they spread a heavenly couch, with its head towards the East, and on it they laid her down. Then the future Buddha, who had become a superb white elephant, and was wandering on the Golden Hill, not far from there, descended thence, and ascending the Silver

Hill, approached her from the North. Holding in his silvery trunk a white lotus flower, and uttering a far-reaching cry, he entered the golden mansion, and thrice doing obeisance to his mother's couch, he gently struck her right side, and seemed to enter her womb.[62]

Thus was he conceived at the end of the Midsummer festival. And the next day, having awoke from her sleep, she related her dream to the rāja. The rāja had sixty-four eminent brahmins summoned, and had costly seats spread on a spot made ready for the state occasion with green leaves and dalbergia flowers, and he had vessels of gold and silver filled with delicate milk-rice compounded with ghee and sweet honey, and covered with gold and silver bowls. This food he gave them, and he satisfied them with gifts of new garments and of tawny cows. And when he had thus satisfied their every desire, he had the dream told to them, and then he asked them : "What will come of it?"

The brahmins said : "Be not anxious, sire! your queen has conceived : and the fruit of her womb will be a man-child; it will not be a woman-child. You will have a son. And he, if he adopts a householder's life, will become a king, a Universal Monarch; but if, leaving his home, he adopt the religious life, he will become a Buddha, who will remove from the world the veils of ignorance and sin."

Now at the moment when the future Buddha made himself incarnate in his mother's womb, the constituent elements of the ten thousand world-systems at the same instant quaked, and trembled, and were shaken violently. The Thirty-two Good Omens also were made manifest. In the ten thousand world systems an immeasurable light appeared. The blind received their sight, as if from very longing to behold this his glory. The deaf heard the noise. The dumb spake one with another. The crooked became straight. The lame walked. All prisoners were freed from their bonds and chains. In each hell the fire was extinguished. In the realm of the Petas hunger and thirst were allayed. The wild animals ceased to be afraid. The illness of all who were sick was allayed. All men began to speak kindly. Horses neighed, and elephants trumpeted gently. All musical instruments gave forth each its note, though none played upon them. Bracelets and other ornaments jingled of themselves. All the heavens became clear. A cool soft breeze wafted pleasantly for all. Rain fell out of due season. Water, welling up from the very earth, overflowed.[63] The birds forsook their flight on high. The rivers stayed their waters' flow. The sea became sweet water. Everywhere its surface was covered with lotuses of every colour. All flowers blossomed on land and in water. The trunks, and branches, and twings of trees were covered with the bloom appropriate to each. On earth tree-lotuses sprang up by sevens together, breaking even through the rocks : and handing-lotuses were born in the sky and rained down everywhere a rain of blossom. In the sky devamusic was played. The ten thousand world-systems revolved, and rushed as close together as a bunch of gathered flowers; and became as it were a woven wreath of worlds, as sweet-smelling and resplendent as a mass of garlands, or as a sacred altar decked with flowers.

From the moment of the conception, thus brought about, of the future Buddha, four devas with swords in their hands, stood guard over the Bodisat, and his mother, to shield them from all harm. Pure in thought, having reached the highest aim and the highest honour, the mother was happy and unwearied; she saw the child within her as plainly as one could see a thread passed through a transparent gem.[64] But as a womb in which a future Buddha has dwelt, like a sacred relic shrine, can never be occupied by anothei; the mother of the Bodisat, seven days after his birth, died, and was reborn in the City of Bliss.

Now other women give birth, some before, some after, the completion of the tenth month, some sitting and some lying down. Not so the mother of a Bodisat. She gives birth to the Bodisat standing, after she has cherished him in her womb for exactly ten months, this is a distinctive quality of the mother of a Buddha elect.

And queen Mahā Māyā, when she too had thus cherished the Bodīsat in her womb, like oil in a vessel, for ten months, felt herself gone with child : and wishing to go to her family home she spake to King Suddhodaṇa, and said :

"Sire, I wish to go to Devadaha, to the city of my people."

The king, saying : "It is good," consented, and had the road from Kapilavatthu to Devadaha made plain, and decked with arches of plaintain-trees, and well filled water-pots, and flags, and banners. And seating the queen in a golden palanquin carried by a thousand attendants, he sent her away with a great retinue.

Now between the two towns there is a pleasure grove of sāl-trees belonging to the people of both cities, and called the Lumbini grove. At that time, from the roots to the topmost branches, it was one mass of fruits and flowers; and amidst the blossoms and branches swarms of various-coloured bees, and flocks of birds of different kinds roamed warbling sweetly. The whole of the Lumbini grove was like a wood of variegated creepers, or the well-decorated banqueting hall of some mighty king. The queen beholding it was filled with the desire of besporting herself in the sāl-tree grove; and the attendants carrying the queen, entered the wood. When she came to the monarch sāl-tree of the glade, she wanted to take, hold of a branch of it, and the branch bending down, like a reed heated by steam, approached within reach of her hand. Stretching out her hand she took hold of the branch, and then karma-born winds shook her. The people, drawing a curtain round her, retired. Standing, and holding the branch of the sāl-tree, she was delivered.

That very moment the four pure-minded Mahā Brahmās came there bringing a golden net; and receiving the future Buddha on that net, they placed him before his mother, saying : "Be joyful, O Lady! a mighty son is born to thee!"

Now other living things, when they leave their mother's womb, leave it smeared with offensive and impure matter. Not so a Bodisat. The future Buddha left his mother's womb like a preacher descending from a pulpit or a man from a ladder, erect, stretching out his hands and feet, unsoiled by any impurities from contact with his mother's womb, pure and fair, and shining like a gem placed on fine muslin of Benares. But though this was so, two showers of water came down from heaven in honour of them and refreshed the Bodisat and his mother, and cleansed her body.

From the hands of the Brahmās who had received him in the golden net, the Four Kings received him on cloth of antelope skins, soft to the touch, such as are used on occasions of royal state. From their hands men received him on a roll of fine cloth; and on leaving their hands he stood up upon the ground and looked towards the East. Thousands of world systems became visible to him like a single open space. Men and devas offering him sweet-smelling garlands, said : "O great man, there is no other like thee, how then a greater?" Searching the ten directions[65] and finding no one like himself, he took seven strides, saying : "This is the best direction." And as he walked the Great Brahmā held over him the white umbrella, and the Suyāma followed him with the fan, and other devas with the other symbols of royalty in their hands. Then, stopping at the seventh step, he sent forth his noble voice and shouted the shout of victory, beginning with : "I am the chief of the world."[66]

Now the future Buddha in three births thus uttered his voice immediately on leaving his mother's womb; in his birth as Mahosadha, in his birth as Vessantara, and in this birth. In the Mahosadha birth the deva king Sakka came to him as he was being born, and placing some fine sandal-wood in his hand, went away. He came forth from the womb holding this in his fist. His mother asked him : "What is it you hold, dear, as you come?" He answered, "Herb medicine, mother!" So because he came holding this they gave him the name of Herb-medicine child (Osādhadāraka). Taking the medicine they kept it in a chatty (an earthenware water-pot); and it became a drug by which all the sickness of the blind and deaf and others, as many as came, was healed, so the saying sprang up : "This is a great osādha! this is a great osādha!" and hence he was called Mahosadha (The Great Herb-medicine Man).

Again, in the Vessantara birth, as he left his mother's womb, he stretched out his right hands, saying : "But is there anything in the house, mother? I would give a gift." Then his mother, saying, "You are born, dear, in a wealthy family," took his hand in hers, and placed on it a bag containing a thousand.

Lastly, in this birth he sang the song of victory.[67] Thus, the future Buddha in three births uttered his voice as he came out of his mother's womb. And as at the moment of his conception, so at the moment of his birth, the thirty-two Good Omens were seen.

Now at the very time when our Bodisat was born in the Lumbini grove, the lady mother of Rāhula,[68] Channa the attendant, Kāḷudāyi the minister, Kanthaka the royal horse, the great Bo-tree, and the four vases full of treasure, also came into being. Of these last, one was two miles, one four, one six, and one eight miles in size. These seven are called the Sahajātā, the Connatal Ones.[69]

The people of both towns took the Bodisat and went to Kapilavatthu. On that day too, companies of devas in the nest, the Tāvatiṃsa world, were astonished and joyful; and waved their robes and rejoiced, saying, "In Kapilavatthu, to Suddhodana the king a son is born, who, seated under the Bo-tree, will become a Buddha."

At that time an ascetic named Kāḷa Devala, a confidential adviser of Suddhodana the king, who had passed through the eight stages of religious attainment,[70] had eaten his midday meal, and had gone to the Tāvatiṃsa world for his midday rest. Whilst there sitting resting, he saw these devas, and asked them : "Why are you thus glad at heart and rejoicing? Tell me the reason of it."

The devas replied : "Sir, to Suddhodana the king is born as son, who, seated under the Bo-tree, will become a Buddha, and will found a Kingdom of Righteousness.[71] To us it will be given to see his infinite grace and to hear his word. Therefore it is that we are glad!"

The ascetic, hearing what they said, quickly came down from the deva-world, and entering the king's housc, set down on the seat set apart for him, and said : "A son they say is born to you, O king! let me see him."

The king ordered his son to be clad in splendour and carried in to salute the ascetic. But the future Buddha turned his feet round, and planted them on the matted hair of the ascetic.[72] For in that birth there was no one worthy to be saluted by the Bodisat, and if these ignorant ones had placed the head of the future Buddha at the feet of the ascetic, assuredly the ascetic's head would have split in two. The ascetic rose from his seat, and saying : "It is not right for me to work my own destruction," he did homage to the Bodisat. And the king also seeing this wonder did homage to his own son.

Now the ascetic had the power of calling to mind the events of forty ages (kalpas) in the past, and of forty ages in the future. Looking at the marks of future prosperity on the Bodisat's body, he considered with himself : "Will he become a Buddha or not?" And perceiving that he would most certainly become a Buddha, he smiled, saying : "This is a wonder man." Then reflecting : "Will it be given to me to behold him when he has become a Buddha?" he perceived that it would not. "Dying before that time I shall be reborn in the formless world; so that while a hundred or perhaps a thousand Buddhas appear among men, I shall not be able to go and be taught by them. And it will not be my good fortune to behold this so wonderful man when he has become a Buddha. Great, alas, is my loss!" And he wept.

The people seeing this, asked, saying : "Our master just now smiled, and has now begun to weep! Will, sir, any misfortune befall our master's child?"[73]

"There is no misfortune in him; assuredly he will become a Buddha," was the reply.

"Why then do you weep?"

"It will not be granted to me," he said, "to behold so great a man when he has become a Buddha. Great, alas, is my loss! bewailing myself, I weep."

Then reflecting : "Will it be granted or not to any one of my relatives to see him as a Buddha?" he saw it would be granted to his nephew, the boy Nālaka. So he went to his sister's house, and said to her, "Where is your son Nālaka?"

"In the house, brother."

"Call him," said he. When he came he said to him, "In the family of Suddhodana the king, dear, a son is born, a young

Buddha. In thirty-five years he will become a Buddha, and it will be granted you to see him. This very day give up the world!"

Bearing in mind that his uncle was not a man to urge him without a cause, the young man, though born in a family of incalculable wealth,[74] straightway took out of the inner store a yellow suit of clothes and an earthenware pot, and shaved his head and put on the robes. And saying : "I leave the world for the sake of him who is the greatest person on earth," he prostrated himself on the ground and raised his joined hands in adoration towards the Bodisat. Then putting the begging bowl in a bag, and carrying it on his shoulder, he went to the Himālaya mountains, and lived the life of a monk.

When the Tathāgata had attained to complete Enlightenment, Nālaka went to him and heard the way of salvation.[75] He then returned to the Himālayas and reached Arahantship. And when he had lived seven months longer as a pilgrim along the most excellent Path, he passed away when standing near a Golden Hill, by that final passing away in which no source of rebirth remains.[76]

Now on the fifth day they bathed the Bodisat's head, saying : "Let us perform the rite of choosing a name for him." So they perfumed the king's house with four kinds of odours, and decked it with Dalbergia flowers, and made ready rice well cooked in milk. Then they sent for one hundred and eight brahmins who had mastered the three Vedas, and seated them in the king's house, and gave them the pleasant food to eat, and did them great honour, and asked them to recognize the signs of what the child sould be.

Among them :

270. Rāma, and Dhaja, and Lakkhaṇa, and Mantin,
Kondanya and Bhoja, Suyāma and Sudatta
These eight brahmins then were there,
Their senses all subdued; and they declared the charm.

Now these eight brahmins were recognizers of signs; it was by them that the dream on the night of conception had been interpreted. Seven of them holding up two fingers prophesied in the alternative, saying : "If a man having such marks should remain a householder, he becomes a Universal Monarch; but if he takes the vows, he becomes a Buddha." And, so saying, they declared all the glory and power of a Chakkavatti king.

But the youngest of all of them, a young Brahmin, whose family name was Kondanya, beholding the perfection of the auspicious marks on the Bodisat raised up one finger only, and prophesied without ambiguity, and said : "There is no sign of his remaining amidst the cares of household life. Verily, he will become a Buddha, and remove the veils of sin and ignorance from the world."

This man already, under former Buddhas, had made a deep resolve of holiness, and had now reached his last birth. Therefore it was that he surpassed the other seven in wisdom; that he perceived how the Bodisat would only be subject to this one life; and that, raising only one finger, he so prophesied, saying: "The lot of one possessed of these marks will not be cast amidst the cares of household life. Verily, he will become a Buddha!"

Now those brahmins went home, and addressed their sons, saying : "We are old, dear ones; whether or not we shall live to see the son of Suddhodana the king after he has gained all-knowledge, do you, when he has gained all-knowledge, take the vows according to his religion." And after they all seven had lived out their span of life, they passed away and were reborn according to their deeds.

But the young Brahmin Kondanya was in good health; and for the sake of the wisdom of the Great Being he left all that he had and made the great renunciation. And coming in due course to Uruvela, he thought : "Behold how pleasant is this place! how suitable for the exertions of a young man desirous of wrestling with sin." So he took up his residence there.

And when he heard that the Great Being had left the world, he went to the sons of those brahmins, and said to them : "Siddhattha the prince has taken the vows. Assuredly he will become a Buddha. If your fathers were in health they would to-day leave their homes, and go forth : and now, if you should so desire, come, I will leave the world in imitation of him." But all of them were not able to agree wit one accord : three did not give up the world; the other four made Kondanya the Brahmin their leader, and left the world. It was those five who came to be called "the company of the Five Elders."

Then the king asked : "After seeing what, will my son forsake the would?"

"The four Omens" was the reply.

"Which four?"

"A man worn out by age, a sick man, a dead body, and a monk."

The king thought : "From this time let no such things come near my son. There is no good in my son's becoming a Buddha. I should like to see my son exercising rule and sovereignty over the four great continents and the two thousand islands that surround them; and walking, as it were, in the vault of heaven, surrounded by an innumerable retinue."[77] Then so saying, he placed guards two miles apart in the four directions to prevent men of those four kinds coming to the sight of his son.

That day also, of eighty thousand clansmen assembled in the festival hall, each one dedicated a son, saying : "Whether this child becomes a Buddha or a king, we give each a son; so that if he shall become a Buddha, he shall live attended and honoured by Khattiya monks, and if he shall become a king, he shall live attended and honoured by nobles."[78] And the raja appointed nurses of great beauty, and free from every fault, for the Bodisat. So the Bodisat grew up in great splendour and surrounded by an innumerable retinue.

Now one day the king held the so-called Ploughing Festival. On that day they ornament the town like a palace of the gods. All the slaves and servants, in new garments and crowned with sweet-smelling garlands, assemble in the king's house. For the king's work a thousand ploughs are yoked. On this occasion one hundred and eight minus one were, with the oxenreins and cross-bars, ornamented with silver. But the plough for the king to use was ornamented with red gold; and so also the horns and reins and goads of the oxen.

Then king leaving his house with a great retinue, took his son and went to the spot. There was a jambu-tree thick with leaves and giving a dense shade. Under it the raja had the child's couch laid out; and over the couch a canopy spread inlaid with stars of gold, and round it a curtain hung. Then leaving a guard there, the raja, clad in splendour and attended by his ministers, went away to plough.

At such a time the king takes hold of a golden plough, the attendant ministers one hundred and eight minus one silver ploughs, and the peasants the rest of the ploughs. Holding them they plough this way and that way. The raja goes from one side to the other, and comes from the other back again.

On this occasion the king had great success; and the nurses seated round the Bodisat, thinking : "Let us go to see the king's glory", came out from within the curtain, and went away. The future Buddha, looking all round, and seeing no one, got up quickly, seated himself cross-legged, and holding his breath, sank into the first Jhāna.[79]

The nurses, engaged in preparing various kinds of food, delayed a little. The shadows of the other trees turned round, but that of the jambu-tree remained steady and circular in form. The nurses, remembering their young master was alone, hurriedly raised the curtain and returned inside it. Seeing the Bodisat sitting cross-legged, and that miracle of the shadow, they went and told the raja, saying : "Sire! the prince is seated in such and such a manner; and while the shadows of the other trees have turned, that of the jambu-tree is fixed in a circle!"

And the raja went hurriedly and saw that miracle, and did homage to his son, saying : "This, dear, is the second homage paid to thee!"

But the Bodisat in due course grew to manhood. And the king had three mansions made, suitable for the three seasons, one nine stories high, one seven stories high, and one five stories high; and he provided him with forty thousand dancing girls. So the Bodisat, surrounded by well-dressed dancing girls, like a deva surrounded by troops of nymphs, and attended by musical instruments which played of themselves, lived, as the seasons changed, in each of these mansions in enjoyment of great prosperity. And the mother of Rāhula was his principal queen.

Whilst he was thus in the enjoyment of great prosperity the following talk sprang up in the public assembly of his clansmen : "Siddhattha lives devoted to pleasure; not one thing does he learn; if war should break out, what would he do?"

The king sent for the future Buddha, and said to him : "Your relations, dear one, say that you learn nothing, and are given up to pleasure : now what do you think you should do about this?"

"Sire, there is no art it is necessary for me to learn. Have the drum-beater about the city, that I may show my skill. Seven days from now I will show my kindred what I can do."

The king did so. The Bodisat assembled those so skilled in archery that they could split even a hair, and shoot as quick as lighting and then, in the midst of the people, he showed his relatives his twelve-fold skill, and how unsurpassed he was by other masters of the bow.[80] So the assembly of his clansmen doubted no longer.

Now one day the future Buddha, wanting to go to his pleasure ground, told his charioteer to harness his chariot. The latter accordingly decked the gloriously beautiful chariot with all its trappings, and harnessed to it four state horses of the Sindhi breed, and white as the leaves of the white lotus flower. And he informed the Bodisat. So the Bodisat ascended the chariot, resplendent like a mansion in the skies, and went towards the garden.

The devas thought : "The time for young Siddhattha to attain Enlightenment is near, let us show him the Omens." And they did so by making a son of the devas represent a man wasted by age, with decayed teeth and grey hair, bent and broken down in body, and with a stick in his hand. But he was only visible to the future Buddha and his charioteer.

Then the Bodisat asked his charioteer, as is told in the Mahāpadāna[89] : "What kind of man is this, whose very hair is not as that of other men?" When he heard his servant's answer, has said : "Shame then be upon life! since the old age of what is born is evident!" and with agitated heart he turned back at that very spot and re-entered his palace.

The king asked : "Why does my son turn back so hurriedly?"

"He has seen an old man," they said, "and having seen an old man, he will forsake the world."

"By this you ruin me," exclaimed the rāja; "quickly get ready plays to be performed before my son. So long as he continues in the enjoyment of pleasure, he will not turn his thoughts to forsaking the world!" Then increasing the guards, he placed them at each point of the compass, at intervals of half a league.

Again, one day, when the future Buddha, as he was going to his pleasure ground, saw a sick man represented by the devas, he made the same inquiry as before; and then, with agitated heart, turned back and re-entered his palace. The king also made the same inquiry, and gave the same orders as before; and again increasing the guard, placed them all round as far as three gavutas.

Once more, when the future Buddha, as he was going to his pleasure ground, saw a dead man represented by the gods, he made the same inquiry as before; and then, with agitated heart, turned back and re-entered his place. The king also made the same inquiry, and gave the same orders as before; and again increasing the guard, laced them all round as far as a league.

Once again, when the future Buddha, as he was going to his pleasure ground, saw one who had abandoned the world, carefully and decently clad, he asked his charioteer : "Friend, what kind of man is that?" As at that time there was no Buddha at all in the world, the charioteer understood neither what a recluse was nor what were his distinguishing characteristics; but nevertheless, inspired by the devas, he said, "That is a recluse"; and described the advantages of renouncing the world. And that day the future Buddha, cherishing the thought of renouncing the world, went on to his pleasure ground.

The repeaters of the Dīgha Nikāya,[82] however, way that he saw all the four Omens on the same say, and then went to his pleasure ground. There he enjoyed himself during the day and bathed in the beautiful like; and at sunset seated himself on the royal resting stone to be robed. Now his attendants brought robes of different colours, and various kinds of ornaments, and garlands, and perfumes, and ointments, and stood around him,

At that moment the throne on which Sakka was seated became warm.[83] And thinking to himself : "Who is it now who wants me to descend from hence?" he perceived that the time for the adornment of the future Buddha had come. And he said to Vissakamma : "Friend Vissakamma, the young noble Siddhattha, to-day, at midnight, will carry out the Great Renunciation. This is the last time he will be clad in splendour. Go to the pleasure ground and adorn him with heavenly array."

By the miraculous power which devas have, he accordingly, that very moment, drew near in the likeness of the royal barber; and taking from the barber's hand the material for the turban, he arranged it round the Bodisat's head. At the touch of his hand the Bodisat knew : "This is no man, it is a son of the devas." When the first round of the turban was put on, there arose, by the appearance of the jewel on the diadem, a thousand folds; when the turban was wrapt the second time round, a thousand folds arose again; when ten times, ten thousand folds appeared. How so many folds could seem to rise on so small a head is beyond imagination; for in size the largest of them were as the flower of the Black Piyangu creeper, and the rest even as Kutumbåka blossoms. And the head of the future Buddha became like a Kuyyåka flower in full bloom.

And when he was arrayed in all his splendour–the musicians the while exhibiting each one his peculiar skill, the Brahmins honouring him with words of joy and victory, and the men of lower station with festive cries and shouts of praise;–he ascended his superbly decorated car.

At that time Suddhodana the king, who had heard that the mother of Rāhula had brought forth a son, sent a message, saying: "Make known my joy to my son!" The future Buddha, hearing this, said : An impediment has come into being, a bond has come into being." When the king asked : "What did my son say?" and heard that saying, he gave command : "From henceforth let Rāhula (impediment) by my grandson's name." But the Bodisat, riding in his splended chariot, entered the town with great magnificence and exceeding glory.

At that time a noble maiden, Kisā Gotamī by name, had gone to flat roof of the upper story of her palace, and she beheld the beauty and majesty of the Bodisat as he was proceeding through the city. Pleased and delighted at the sight, she burst forth into this song of joy :

271. Blessed indeed is that mother–
Blessed indeed is that father–
Blessed indeed is that wife–
Of whom such an one is master!

Hearing this, the Bodisat thought to himself : "On catching sight of such an one the heart of his mother is made happy, the heart of his father is made happy, the heart of his wife is made happy! So she says. But in peace as to what can the heart be at peace?" And to him whose mind was estranged from sin the answer came : "When the fire of lust is gone out, then peace is gained; when the fires of hatred and delusion are gone out, then peace is gained; when the troubles of mind, arising from vain conceits opinion, and all other corruptions have ceased, then. peace is gained! Sweet is the lesson this singer makes me hear, for the going out which is Peace is that which I have been trying to find out. This very day I will break away from household cares! I will renounce the world! I will follow only after the Nirvāna itself![84]

Then loosing from his neck a string of pearls worth a hundred thousand, he sent it to Kisā Gotamī as a teacher's fee. Delighted at this, she thought : "Prince Siddhattha has fallen in love with me, and has sent me a present." But the Bodisat, on entering his palace in great splendour, reclined on a couch of state.

Thereupon women clad in beautiful array, skilful in the dance and song, and lovely as deva-maidens, brought their musical instruments, and ranging themselves in order, danced, and sang, and played delightfully. But the Bodisat, his heart being estranged from sin, took no pleasure in the spectacle, and fell asleep.

And the women, saying : "He for whose sake we were performing is gone to sleep? Why should we weary ourselves?" laid aside the instruments they held, and lay down to sleep. Lamps fed with sweet smelling oil were burning. The Bodisat, waking up, sat cross-legged on the couch, and saw those women with their music truck laid aside and sleeping–some drivelling at the mouth spittle-besprinked, some grinding their teeth, some snoring, some muttering in their sleep, some gaping, and some with their dress in disorder–plainly revealed as mere horrible occasions of worldly ways.

Seeing this change in their appearance, he became more and more unfain of sense-desires. To him that magnificent apartment, as splendid as Sakka's residence, began to seem like a great area laden with divers offal, like a charnel-field full of corpses. Life, whether in the worlds subject to passion, or in the other worlds of form, or in the formless worlds, seemed to him like staying in a house that had become the prey of devouring flames.[85] An utterance of intense feeling broke from him–"It all oppresses me! It is intolerable!" and his mind turned ardently to the state of those who have renounced the world. Resolving that very day to accomplish the Great Renunciation, he rose from his couch, went to the door and called out : "Who is there?"

Channa, who had been sleeping with his head on the threshold, answered : "It is I, sir, Channa."

Then said he : "I want to-day to accomplish the Great Renunciation–saddle me a horse."

So Channa saying : Very good, sire, and taking harness, went to the stable-yard, and entering the stables saw by the light of the lamps Kanthåka, prince of steeds, standing at a pleasant spot under a canopy of cloth, beautified with a pattern of jasmine flowers. "This is the very one I ought to saddle to-day," thought he; and he saddled Kanthaka.

Even whilst he was being saddled the horse knew : "He is saddling me so tightly and not as on other days for such rides as those to the pleasure grounds, because my master is about to-day to carry out the Great Renunciation." Then, glad at heart, he neighed a mighty neigh; and the sound thereof would have penetrated over all the town, had not the devas stopped the sound and let no one hear it.

Now after the Bodisat had sent Channa on this errand, he thought : "I will just look at my son." And rising from his cross-legged sitting he went to the apartments of Rāhula's mother, and opened her chamber door. At that moment a lamp, fed with sweet-smelling oil, was burning dimly in the inner chamber. The mother of Rāhula was asleep on a bed strewn with many jasmine flowers,[86] and resting her hand on the head of her son. Stopping with his foot on the threshold, the Bodisat thought, "If I lift her hand to take my son, she will awake; and that will prevent my going away. I will come back and see him when I have become a Buddha." And he left the palace.

Now what is said in the Jātaka commentary : "At that time Rāhula was seven days old," is not found in the other commentaries. Therefore the view given above should be accepted.[87]

And when the Bodisat had left the palace, he went to his horse, and said : "Dear Kanthaka, do thou bear me over this once to-night; so that I, having become a Buddha by thy help, shall bear over the world of men and devas." Then leaping up, he seated himself on Kanthaka's back.

Kanthaka was eighteen cubits in length from the nape of his neck, and of proportionate height; he was strong and fleet, and white all over like a clean chank shell. If he should neigh or paw the ground the sound would penetrate through all the town. Therefore the devas so muffled the sound of his neighing that none could hear it; and placed, at each step, the palms of their hands under his feet.

The Bodisat rode on the excellent back of the excellent steed; told Channa to catch hold of its tail, and arrived at midnight at the great gate of the city.

Now the king thinking : "In that way the Bodisat will not be able at any time to open the city gate and get away", had placed a thousand men at each of the two gates to stop him. The Bodisat was mighty and strong according to the measure of elephants as ten thousand million million men. He thought : "If the door does not open, sitting on Kanthaka's back with Channa holding his tail, I will press Kanthaka with my thighs, and jumping over the city rampart, eighteen cubits high, I will get away!" Channa though : "If the door is not opened, I will take my master on my neck, and putting my right hand round Kanthaka's girth, I will hold him close to my waist, and so leap over the rampart and get away!" Kanthaka thought : "If the door is not opened, I will spring up with my master seated as he is on my back, and channa holding by my tail, and will leap over the rampart and get away!" And if the door had not been opened, verily one or other of those three would have accomplished that whereof he had thought. But the deva residing at the gate opened it.

At that moment Māra came there with the intention of stopping the Bodisat; and standing in the air, he exclaimed : "Go not forth sir! in seven days from now the treasure-wheel will appear, and will make you sovereign over the four continents and the two thousand adjacent isles. Stop, O my lord!"

"Who are you?" said he.

"I am Vasavatti," was the reply.

"Māra! Well do I know that the treasure-wheel would appear to me; but it is not sovereignty that I desire. I shall become a Buddha, and make the ten thousand world-systems shout for joy."

Then thought the Tempter to himself : "Now, from this time forth, whenever a thought of lust or anger of malice shall arise within you, I will get to know of it." And he followed him, ever watching for some slip, as closely as a shadow which never leaves its object.

But the future Buddha, making light of the kingdom of the world, thus within his reach–casting it away as one would spittle–left the city with great honour on the full-moon day of Āsāḷhi, when the moon was in the Uttrarāsāḷha lunar mansion (*i.e.* on the 1st July). And when he had left the city a desire sprang up within him to look back upon it; and the instant he did so the broad earth revolved like a potter's wheel, and was stayed : saying as it were to him : "O great man, there is no need for you to stop in order to fulfil your wish." So the Bodisat, with his face towards the city, gazed at it; and he fixed at that place a spot for The Shrine of Kanthaka's Staying. And keeping Kanthaka in the direction in which he was going, he went on with great honour and exceeding glory.

For then, they say, devas in front of him carried sixty thousand torches, and behind him too, and on his right hand, and on his left. And while some devas undefined on the edge of the horizon, held torches aloft; other devas, and the Nāgas, and Winged Creatures, and other superhuman beings, bore him company–doing homage with heavenly perfumes, and garlands, and sandal-wood powder, and incense. And the whole sky was full of Pāricchattaka flowers as with the pouring rain when thick clouds gather. Divine songs floated around : and on every side thousands of musical instruments sounded, as when the thunder roars in the womb of the sea, or the ocean heaves against the boundaries of the world!

Advancing in this pomp and glory, the Bodisat, in that one night, passed beyond three kingdoms, and arrived, at the end of thirty leagues, at the bank of the river called Anomā. But why could not the horse go still further? It was not through want of power : for he could go from one edge of the world's disc to the other, as easily as one could step across the circumference of a wheel lying on its side;–and doing this in the forenoon, he could return and eat the food prepared for him. But on this occasion he was constantly delayed by having to drag himself along and break his way though the mass of garlands and flowers, cast down from heaven in such profusion by the devas, and the Nāgas, and the Winged Creatures, that his very flanks were hid. Hence it was that he only got over thirty leagues.

Now the Bodisat, stopping at the river side, asked Channa: "What is this river called?"

"Its name, sire, is Anomā."

"And so also our leaving our leaving the world shall be called Anomā (illustrious)," said he; and signalling to his horse, by pressing it with his heel, the horse sprang over the river, five or six hundred yards in breadth, and stood on the opposite bank.

The Bodisat, getting down from the horse's back, stood on the sandy beach, extending there like a sheet of silver, and said to Channa : "Good Channa, do thou now go back, taking my ornaments and Kanthaka. I am going to leave the world."

"But I also, sire, will leave the world."

"Thou canst not be allowed to leave the world, do thou go back," he said. Three times he refused this request of Channa's; and he delivered over to him both the ornaments and Kanthaka.

Then he thought; "These locks of mine are not suited for a recluse. Now it is not right for any one else to cut the hair of a future Buddha, so I will cut them off myself with this sword." Then, taking his sword in his right hand, and holding the plaited tresses, together with the diadem on them, with his left, he cut them off. So his hair was thus reduced to two inches in length, and curling form the right, it lay close to his head. It remained that length as long as he lived, and the beard the same. There was no need at all to shave either hair or beard any more.

The Bodisat, saying to himself : "If I am to become a Buddha, let it stand in the air; if not, let it fall to the ground", threw the hair and diadem together as he held them towards the sky. The plaited hair and the jewelled turban went a league off and stopped in the air. Sakka, the deva-king, caught sight of it with his deva-eye, and receiving it into a jewel casket, a league high, he placed it in Tāvatiṃsa, in the Dāgaba of the Diadem.

272. Cutting off his hair, with pleasant perfumes sweet,
the supreme person cast it to the sky.
The thousand-eyed one, Sakka, by his head,
Received it humbly in a golden casket.

Again the Bodisat thought : "This my raiment of Benares muslin is not suitable for a recluse." Now the great Brahmā

Ghaṭīkāra, who had formerly been his friend in the time of Kassapa Buddha,[88] was led by his friendship, which had not grown old in that long interval, to think : "To-day my friend is accomplishing the Great Renunciation, I will go and provide him with the requisites of a recluse.

273. The three robes, and the alms bowl,
Razor, needle, and girdle,
And a water strainer–these eight
Are the wealth of the monk devout.

Taking these eight requisites of a recluse, he gave them to him. The Bodisat dressed himself in the 'banner of an Arahant', and adopted the sacred garb of Renunciation; and he enjoined upon Channa to go and, in his name, assure his parents of his safety. And Channa did homage to the Bodisat reverently, and departed.

Now Kanthaka stood listening to the Bodisat as he talked with Channa. And thinking : "From this time forth I shall never see my master more!" he was unable to bear his grief. And going out of their sight, he died of a broken heart; and was reborn in Tāvatiṃsa as a deva, with the name of Kanthaka. So far the sorrow of Channa had been but single; now torn with the second sorrow of Kanthaka's death, he returned, weeping and bewailling, to the city.

But the Bodisat, having renounced the world, spent seven days in a mango grove called Anūpiya, hard by that spot, in the joy of renunciation. Then he went on foot in one day to Rājagaha, a distance of thirty leagues,[89] and entering the city, begged his food from door to door. The whole city at the sight of his beauty was thrown into commotion, as was Rājagaha by the entrance of Dhana-pālaka, or like the deva-city by the entrance of the governor of the Asuras.

The guards went to the king and said, describing him : "Sire such and such a being is coming for alms through the town. We cannot tell whether he is a deva, or a man, or a Nāga, or a Supaṇṇa,[90] or what he is."

The king, watching the great man from his palace, became full of wonder, and gave orders to his guards, and gave orders to his guards, saying, "Go, I say, and watch. If it is a superhuman being, he will disappear as soon as he leaves the city; if a deva, he will depart through the air; if a snake, he will dive into the earth; if a man, he will eat the food just as it is."

But the great man collected mixed food. And when he perceived there was enough to support him, he left the city by the gate at which he had entered. And seating himself, facing towards the East, under the shadow of the Paṇḍava rock, he began to eat his meal. His stomach, however, turned, and made as if it would come out of his mouth. Then, though distressed by that revolting food, for in that birth he had never even beheld such food with his eyes, he himself admonished himself, saying : "Siddhattha, it is true thou wast born in a family where food and drink were easily obtainable, into a state of life where thy food was perfumed third-season's rice, with various curries of the finest kinds. But ever since thou didst see one clad in a mendicant's garb, thou hast been thinking : 'When shall I become like him, and lie by begging my food? would that time were come!' And now that thou hast left all for that very purpose, what is this that thou art doing?" And overcoming his feelings, he ate the food.

The king's men saw this, and went and told him that had happened. Hearing what his messengers said, the king quickly left the city, and approaching the Bodisat, was so pleased at the mere sight of his dignity and grace, that he offered him all his kingdom.

The Bodisat said; "In me, O king! there is no desire after wealth or sinful pleasures. It is in the hope of attaining to complete enlightenment that I have left all." And when the king gained not his consent, though he asked it in many ways, he said : Assuredly thou wilt become a Buddha! Deign at least after thy Buddhahood to come to my kingdom first."

This is here concisely stated; but the full account, beginning: "I sing the Renunciation, how the Wise One renounced the world", will be found on referring to the Pabbajjā Sutta[91] and its commentary.

And the Bodisat, granting the king's request, went forward on his way. And joining himself to Āḷāra Kālāma, and to Uddaka, son of Rāma, he acquired their systems of ecstatic trance. But when he saw that was not the way to enlightenment, he left off applying himself to the realization of that system of Attainment. And with the intention of carrying out the Great Struggle against sin, and showing his might and resolution to devas and men, he went to Uruvelā. And saying : "Pleasant, indeed, is this spot!" he took up his residence there, and devoted himself to the Great Struggle.[92]

And those five recluses, Kondanya and the rest,[93] begging their way through villages, market towns, and royal cities, met with the Bodisat there. And for six years they stayed by him and served him, while he was carrying out the Great Struggle, with different kinds of service, such as sweeping out the hermitage and so on; thinking the while : "Now he will become a Buddha! now he will become Buddha!"

Now the Bodisat thought : "I will perform the uttermost penance." And he brought himself to live one seed of the oil-plant, or one grain of rice, and even to fast entirely; but devas gathered the sap of life and infused it into him through the pores of his skin. By this fasting, however, he became as thin as a skeleton; the colour of his body, once fair as gold, became dark; and the thirty-two signs of a great man disappeared. And one day, when walking up and down, plunged in intense meditation, he was overcome by severe pain; and he fainted, and fell.

Then certain of the devas began to say : "He is dead." But others said : "Such is the way of saints." And those who thought he was dead went and told Suddhodana the king, saying : "Your son is dead."

"Did he die after becoming a Buddha, or before?"

"He was unable to attain to Buddhahood, and fell down and died in the midst of the Great Struggle."

When the king heard this, he refused to credit it, saying : "I do not believe it. My son could never die without attaining to Enlightenment!"

If you ask : "Why did not the king believe it?" it was because he had seen the miracles at the foot of the jambu-tree, and on the day when Kāḷa Devla had been compelled to do homage to the Bodisat.[94]

And the Bodisat recovered consciousness again, and stood up. And those devas went and told the king, "Your son, O king, is well." And the king said : "I knew my son was not dead."

And the great being's six years' penance became noised abroad, as when the sound of a great bell is heard in the sky. But he perceived that penance was not the way to enlightenment; and begging through the villages and towns, he collected ordinary material food and lived upon it. And the thirty-two signs of a great man appeared again upon him, and his body became fair in colour, like unto gold.

Then the five attendant monks thought : "This man has not been able, eve by six years' penance, to attain all-knowledge; how can he do so now, when he goes begging through the villages, and takes meterial food? He is altogether lost in the struggle. To think of getting spiritual eminence through him is like a man, who wants to bathe his head, thinking of using a dewdrop. What could we get from him?" And leaving the great man, they took each his robes and begging bowl, and went eighteen leagues away, and entered Isipatana.[95]

Now at that time, at Uruvelā in the village Senāni, there was a girl named Sujāta, born in the house of Senāni the landowner, who, when she had grown up, made a vow at a Nigrodha-tree, saying : "If I am married into a family of equal rank, and have a son for my first-born child, then I will spend every year a hundred thousand on an offering to thee." And this her vow took effect.

And in order to make her offering, on the full-moon day of the month of May, in the sixth year of the Great Being's penance, she had driven in front of her a thousand cows into a medow of rich grass. With their milk she had fed five hundred cows, with theirs two hundred and fifty, and so on down to eight. Thus aspiring after quantity, and sweetness, and strength, she did what is called : "Working the milk in and in."

And early on the full-moon day in the month of May, thinking : "Now I will make the offering", she rose up in the morning early and milked those eight cows. Of their own accord the calves kept away from the cows' udders, and as soon as the new vessels were placed ready, streams of milk poured into them. Seeing this miracle, Sujātā, with her own hands, took the milk and poured it into new pans; and with her own hands made the fire and began to cook it. When that rice-milk was boiling, huge bubbles rising, turned to the right and ran round together; not a drop fell or was lost; not the least smoke rose from the fireplace.

At that time the four guardians of the world came and kept watch by the fireplace. A great Brahmā held over it a canopy of state. Sakka put the sticks together and lighted the fire. By their divine power the devas gathering so much of the sap of maintenance as would suffice for the support of all men and devas of the four continents, and their circumjacent two thousand isles–as easily as a man crushing the honeycomb formed round a stick would take the honey–they infused it into the milk-rice. At other times devas infused the sap into each mouthful of rice as he took it; but on the day of his Buddhahood, and on the day of his passing away, they infused it into the very vessel-full of rice itself.

Sujātā, seeing that so many wonders appeared to her on this one day, said to her slave-girl Puṇṇā : "Puṇṇā, my girl! Very gracious is our deva to-day! Never before have I seen such a wonder. Go at once and keep watch by the holy place." "Very good, madam," replied she; and ran and hastened to the foot of the tree.

Now the Bodisat had seen that night five dreams, and on considering their purport he had drawn the conclusion : "Verily this day I shall become a Buddha." And at the end of the night he washed and dressed himself, and waiting till the time should come to go round for his food, he went early, and sat at the foot of that tree, lighting it all up with his glory.

And Puṇṇā coming there saw the Bodisat sitting at the foot of the tree and lighting up all the region of the East; and she saw the whole tree in colour like gold from the rays issuing from his body. And she thought : "To-day our deva, descending from the tree, is seated to receive our offering in his own hand." And excited with joy, she returned quickly and announced this to Sujātā. Sujātā, delighted at the news, gave her all the ornaments befitting a daughter, saying : "To-day, from this time forth, be thou to me in the place of an elder daughter!"

And since, on the day of attaining Buddhahood, it is proper to receive a golden vessel worth a hundred thousand, she conceived the idea : "We will put the milk-rice into a vessel of gold." And sending for a vessel of gold worth a hundred thousand, she poured out the well-cooked food to put it therein. All the rice-milk flowed into the vessel, like water from a lotus leaf, and filled the vessel full. Taking it she covered it with a golden platter, and wrapped it in a cloth. And adorning herself in all her splendour, she put the vessel on her head, and went with great dignity to the Nigrodha-tree. Seeing the Bodisat, she was filled with exceeding joy, taking him for the tree-deva; and advanced bowing from the spot whence she saw him. Taking the vessel from her head, she uncovered it; and fetching sweet-scented water in a golden vase, she approached the Bodisat, and stood by.

The earthenware pot given him by the deva Ghaṭīkāra, which had never till then left him, disappeared at that moment. Not seeing his pot, the Bodisat stretched out his right hand, and took the water. Sujātā placed the vessel, with the milk-rice in it, in the hand of the great man. The great man looked at her. Pointing to the food, she said : "O, sir! accept what I have offered thee, and depart withersoever seemeth to thee good." And adding : "May there arise to thee as much joy as has come to me!" she went away, valuing her golden vessel, worth a hundred thousand, at no more than a dried leaf.

But the Bodisat rising from his seat, and leaving the tree on the right hand, took the vessel and went to the bank of the Neranjarā river, down into which on the day of their complete Enlightenment so many thousand Bodisats had gone. The name of that bathing place is the Supatiṭṭhita[96] ferry. Putting the vessel on the bank, he descended into the river and bathed.

And having dressed himself again in the banner of the Arahants worn by so many thousand Buddhas, he sat down with his face to the East : and dividing the rice into forty-nine balls of the size of so many single seeded palmyra fruits, he ate all that sweet-milk rice without any water.[97] Now that was the only food he had for forty-nine days, during the seven times seven days he spent, after he became a Buddha, at the foot of the Tree of Enlightenment. During all that time he had no other food; he did not bathe; nor wash his teeth; nor feel the cravings of nature. He lived on Jhāna-joy, on Path-joy, on Fruition joy.

But when he had finished eating that milk-rice, he took the golden vessel, and said : "If I shall be able to-day to become a Buddha, let this pot go up the stream : if not, let it go down the stream!" and he threw it into the water. And it went, in spite of the stream, eighty cubits up the river in the middle of the stream, all the way as quickly as a fleet horse. And diving into a whirlpool it went to the palace of Kāḷa Nāgarāja (the Black Snake King); and striking against the bowls from which the three previous Buddhas had eaten, it made them sound "killi-killi!" and stopped as the lowest of them. Kāḷa, the snake-king, hearing the noise, exclaimed : Yesterday a Buddha arose, now to-day another has arisen"; and he stood praising him in many hundred stanzas.

But the Bodisat spent the heat of the day in a grove of sāl-trees in full bloom on the bank or the river. And in the evening, when the flowers droop from their stems, he proceeded, like a lion when it is roused, towards the Tree of Enlightenment, along a path five or six hundred yards wide, decked by devas. The Snakes, and Genii, and Winged Creatures,[98] and other superhuman beings, offered him sweet-smelling flowers from heaven, and sang heavenly songs. The ten thousand world-systems became filled with perfumes and garlands and shouts of approval.

At that time there came from the opposite direction a grass-cutter named Sotthiya, carrying grass; and recognizing the great man, he gave him eight bundles of grass. The Bodisat took the grass : and ascending the rising ground round the Bo-tree, he stood at the South of it, looking towards the North. At that moment the Southern horizon seemed to descend below the level of the lowest hell, and the Northern horizon mounting up seemed to reach above the highest heaven.

The Bodisat, saying : "This cannot, methinks, be the right place for attaining Buddhahood", turned round it, keeping it on the right hand; and went to the Western side, and stood facing the East. Then the Western horizon seemed to descend beneath the lowest hell, and the Eastern horizon to ascend above the highest heaven; and to him, where he was standing, the earth seemed to bend up and down like a great cart wheel lying on its axis when its circumference is trodden on.

The Bodisat, saying : "This cannot, I think, be the right place for attaining Buddhahood", turned round it, keeping it on the right hand; and went to the Northern side, and stood facing the South. Then the Northern horizon seemed to descend beneath the lowest hell, and the Southern horizon to ascend above the highest heaven.

The Bodisat, saying : "This cannot, I think, be the right place for attaining Buddhahood", turned round it, keeping it on the right hand; and went to the Western side, and stood facing towards the East. Now in the East is the place where all the Buddhas have sat cross-legged; and that place neither trembles nor shakes.

The great being, perceiving : "This is the steadfast spot chosen by all the Buddhas, the spot for the throwing down of the cage of sin", took hold of the grass by one end, and scattered it there. And immediately there was a seat fourteen cubits long. For those blades of grass arranged themselves in such a form as would be beyond the power of even the ablest painter or carver to design.

The Bodisat turning his back upon the trunk of the Bo-tree, and with his face towards the East, made the firm resolve : "May skin, indeed, and sinews, and bones wilt away, may flesh and blood in my body dry up, but till I attain to complete enlightenment this seat I will not leave!" And he sat himself down in a cross-legged position, firm and immovable, as if welded with a hundred thunderbolts.

At that time the deva Māra, thinking : "Prince Siddhattha wants to free himself from my dominion. I will not let him get free yet!" went to the hosts of his Māras,[99] and told the news. And sounding the drum called Māra-Cry, he led forth the hosts of Māra.

That army of Māra stretches twelve leagues before him, twelve leagues to right and left of him, behind him it reaches to the rocky limits of the world, above him it is nine leagues in height; and the sound of its war-cry is heard, twelve leagues away, even as the sound of an earthquake.

Then Māra deva, mounted his elephant, two hundred and fifty leagues high, named "Girded with mountains". And he created for himself a thousand arms, and seized all kinds of weapons. And of the remainder, too, of the company of Māra, no two took the same weapon; but, assuming various colours and various forms, they went on to overwhelm the great being.

But the devas of the ten thousand world-systems continued speaking the praises of the great being. Sakka, the deva-king, stood there blowing his trumpet Vijayuttara. Now that trumpet is a hundred and twenty cubits long, and can itself cause the wind to enter, and thus itself give forth a sound which will resound for four months, when it becomes still. The Great Black One, the king of the Nāgas, stood there uttering his praises in many hundred stanzas. The Mahā Brahmā stood there, holding over him the white canopy of state. But as the army approached and surrounded the seat under the Bo-tree, not one of the hosts of Māra was able to stay, and they fled each one from the spot where the army met them. The Black One, king of the Nāgas, dived into the earth, and went to Manjerika, the palace of the Nāgas, five hundred leagues in length, and lay down, covering his face with his hands. Sakka, taking the Vijayuttara trumpet on his back, stopped on the rocky verge of the world. Mahā Brahmā, putting the white canopy of state on to the summit of the rocks at the end of the earth, went to the world of Brahma. Not a single deity was able to keep his place. The great man sat there alone.

But Māra said to his company : "Sirs! there is not other man like Siddhattha, the son of Suddhodana. We cannot give him battle face to face. Let us attack him from behind!" The great man looked round on three sides, and saw that all the devas had fled, and their place was empty. Then beholding the hosts of Māra coming thick upon him from the North, he thought: "Against me alone this mighty host is putting forth all its energy and strength. No father is here, nor mother, nor brother, nor any other relative to help me. But those ten perfections have long been to me as retainers fed from my store. So, making the perfections like a shield, I must strike this host with the sword of perfection, and thus overwhelm it!" And so he sat meditating on the Ten Perfections.[100]

Then Māra deva, saying : "Thus will I drive away Siddhattha", caused a whirlwind to blow. And immediately such winds rushed together from the four corners of the earth as could have torn down the peaks of mountains half a league, two leagues, three leagues high–could have rooted up the shrubs and trees of the forest–and could have made of the towns and villages around one heap of ruins. But through the glow of the merit of the great man, they reached him with their power gone, and even the hem of his robe they were unable to shake.

Then saying : "I will overwhelm him with water and so slay him", he caused a mighty rain to fall. And the clouds gathered, overspreading one another by hundreds and by thousands, and poured forth rain; and by the violence of the torrents the earth was saturated; and a great flood, overtopping the trees of the forest, approached the Bodhisat. But it was not able to wet on his robe even the space where a dew-drop might fall.

Then he caused a storm of rocks to fall. And mighty, mighty mountain peaks came through the air, spitting forth fire and smoke. But as they reached the Bodhisat, they changed into divine garlands. Then he raised a storm of deadly weapons. And they came–one edged, and two-edged swords, and spears, and arrows–smoking and flaming through the sky. But as they reached the Bodhisat, they became divine flowers.

Then he raised a storm of charcoal. But the embers, though they came through the sky like red kiṃsuka flowers, were scattered at the feet of the future Buddha as divine flowers.

Then he raised a storm of embers; and the embers came through the air exceeding hot, and in colour like fire; but they fell at the feet of the future Buddha as sandal-wood powder.

Then he raised a storm of sand; and the sand, exceeding fine, came smoking and flaming through the air; but it fell at the feet of the future Buddha as divine flowers.

Then he raised a storm of mud. And the mud came smoking and flaming through the air; but it fell at the feet of the future Buddha as divine unguent.

Then saying : "By this I will terrify Siddhattha, and drive him away!" he brought on a thick darkness. And the darkness became fourfold; but when it reached the future Buddha, it disappeared as darkness does before the brightness of the sun.

Thus was Māra unable by these nine–the wind, and the rain, and the rocks, and the weapons, and the charcoal, and the embers, and the sand, and the mud, and the darkness–to drive away the future Buddha. So he called on his host, and said : "Say, why stand you still? Seize, or slay, or drive away this prince!" And himself mounted the Mountain-girded, and seated on his back, he approached the future Buddha, and cried out : "Get up, Siddhattha, from that seat! It does not belong to thee! It belongs to me!"

The great being listened to his words, and said : "Māra! it is not by you that the ten Perfections have been perfected, neither the lesser Perfections, nor the higher Perfections. It is not you who have sacrificed yourself in the five great acts of renunciation, who have perfected the way of good in knowledge nor the way of good for the world nor the way of understanding. This seat does not belong to thee, it is to me that it belongs."

Then the enraged Māra, unable to endure the vehemence of his anger, cast at the great man that Sceptre-javelin of his, the barb of which was in shape as a wheel. But it became a wreath of flowers, and remained as a canopy over him, whose mind was bent upon the Ten Perfections.

Now at other times, when that Wicked One throws his Sceptre-javelin, it cleaves asunder a pillar of solid rock as if it were the tender shoot of a bambu. When, however, it thus turned into a wreath-canopy, the entire company of Māra shouted, "Now he will rise from his seat and flee!" and they hurled at him huge masses of rock. But these too fell on the ground as garlands at the feet of him whose mind was bent upon the Ten Perfections.

And the devas stood on the edge of the rocks that encircle the world; and stretching forward in amazement, they looked on, saying : "Lost! lost is the life of Siddhattha the Prince, supremely beautiful! What can he do?"

Then the great man said : "To me belongs the seat on which sit the Buddhas-to-be when they have fulfilled perfection on the day of their Enlightenment."

And he said to Māra, standing there before him : "Māra, who is witness that thou hast given alms?"

And Māra stretched forth his hand to the hosts of his followers, and said : "So many are my witnesses."

And that moment there arose a shout as the sound of an earthquake from the company of Māra, saying,

"I am his witness! I am his witness!"

Then the Tempter addressed the great man, and said : "Siddhattha! who is witness that thou hast given alms?"

And the great man answered : "Thou hast living witnesses that thou hat given alms : and I have in this place no living witness at all. But not counting the alms I have given in other births, let this great and solid earth, unconscious though it be, be witness of the seven hundredfold great alms I gave when I was born as Vessantara!"

And withdrawing his right hand from beneath his robe, he stretched it forth towards the earth, and said : "Art thou or art thou not witness of the seven hundredfold great gift I gave in my birth as Vessantara?"

And the great Earth uttered a voice, saying : "I am witness to thee of that!" overwhelming as it were the hosts of Māra as with the shout of hundreds of thousands of foes.

Then the mighty elephant "Mount-girded" as he realized what the generosity of Vessantara had been, said : "The great gift, the uttermost gift was given by thee, Siddhattha!" And he fell down on his knees before the great man. And the company of Māra fled this way and that way, so that not even two were left together : throwing off their clothes and their turbans, they fled, each one straight on before him.

But the company of devas, when they saw that the hosts of Māra had fled, cried out : Māra is overcome! Siddhattha the Prince has prevailed! Come, let us honour the victor!" And the Nāgas, and the Winged Creatures, and the Devas, and the Brahmās, each urging his comrades on, went up to the great man at the Bo-tree's foot, and as they came,

274. At the Bo-tree's foot the Nāga bands
Shouted, for joy that the Sage had won;
"The Blessed Buddha–he hath prevailed!
And the Evil Māra is overthrown!"

275. At the Bo-tree's foot the Winged Ones
Shouted, for joy that the Sage had won;
"The Blessed Buddha–he hath prevailed!
And the Evil Māra is overthrown!"

276. The Bo-tree's foot the Deva hosts
Shouted for joy that the Sage had won;
"The Blessed Buddha–he hath prevailed!
And the Evil Māra is overthrown!"

277. At the Bo-tree's foot the Brahmā Gods
Shouted, for joy that the Sage had won;
"The Blessed Buddha–he hath prevailed!
And the evil Māra is overthrown!

The other devas, too, in the ten thousand world-systems, offered garlands and perfumes and uttered his praises aloud.

It was while the sun was still above the horizon, that the great man thus pùt to flight the hosts of Māra. Then, whilst the Bo-tree paid him homage, as it were, by its shoots like springs of red coral falling over his robe, he acquired in the first watch of the night the knowledge of the past, in the middle watch the clairvoyant eye, and in the third watch the knowledge of the chain of causation.[101]

Now on his thus revolving this way and that way, and tracing backwards and forwards, and thoroughly realizing the twelvefold chain of causation, the ten thousand world-systems quaked twelve times even to their ocean boundaries. And again, when the great man, making the ten thousand world systems to shout for joy, attained at break of day to complete enlightenment, the whole ten thousand world-systems became glorious as on a festive day. The streamers of the flags and banners raised on the edge of the rocky boundary to the East of the world reached to the very West; and so those on the West and North, and South, reached to the East, and South, and North; while in like manner those of flags and banners on the surface of the earth reached to the Brahma-world, and those of flags and banners in that world swept down upon the earth. Throughout the universe flowering trees put forth their blossoms, and fruit-bearing trees were loaded with clusters of fruit; the trunks and branches of trees, and even the creepers, were covered with bloom; lotus wreaths hung from the sky; and lilies by sevens sprang, one above another, even from the very rocks. The ten thousand world-systems as they revolved seemed like a mass of loosened wreaths, or like a nosegay tastefully arranged : and the world-voids between them, the hells whose darkness the rays of seven suns had never been able to disperse, became filled with light. The sea became sweet water down to its profoundest depths; and the rivers were stayed in their course. The blind from birth received their sight; the deaf from birth heard sound; the lame from birth could use their feet; and chains and bonds were loosed and fell away.[102]

It was thus in surpassing glory and honour, and with many wanders happening around, that he attained all-knowledge, and gave vent to his emotion in the hymn of triumph uttered by all the Buddhas.

278. Long have I wandered, long,
Bound by the chain of life
Through many births,
Seeking thus long in vain,

The builder of the house. And pain
Is birth again, again.
House-maker, thou art seen!
No more a house thou It make.
Broken are all thy beams.
Thy ridge-pole shattered!
From tings that make for life my mind has past :
The end of cravings has been reached at last![103]

III : THE PROXIMATE EPOCH[104]

Santike nidāna

Now whilst he was still seated there, after he had sung the hymn of triumph, the Blessed One thought : "It is in order to attain to this seat that I have undergone successive births for so long a time,[105] that I severed my crowned head from my neck and gave it away, that I tore out my darkened eyes and my heart's flesh and gave them away, that I gave away to serve others such sons as Jāli the Prince, and such daughters as Kaṇhā Jinā the Princess, and such wives as Maddī the Queen. This seat is a seat of triumph to me, and a seat of glory; while seated on it my aims have been fulfilled : I will not leave it yet." And he sat there absorbed in many thoughts[106] for those seven days referred to in the text, beginning : "And then the Blessed One sat motionless for seven days, realizing the bliss of Nirvāna."

Now certain of the devas began to doubt, thinking : "This day also there must be something more Siddhattha has to do, for he still lingers seated there." The Master, knowing their thoughts, and to appease their doubts, rose into the air, and performed the twin-miracle.[107]

And the Master having thus by this miracle dispelled the devas' doubts, stood a little to the northeast of the seat, thinking: "It was on that seat that I attained all-knowing insight." And he thus spent seven days gazing steadfastly at the spot where he had gained the result of the deeds of virtue fulfilled through such countless years. And that spot became known as the Dāgaba of the Steadfast Gaze.

Then he created between the seat and the spot where he had stood a cloistered walk, and he spent seven days walking up and down in that treasure-cloister which stretched from east to west. And that spot became known as the Dāgaba of the Treasure-Cloister.

But for the fourth week the devas created to the north-west of the Bo-tree a Treasure-house; and he spent the week seated there cross-legged, and thinking out the Abhidhamma Piṭaka and here especially the entire Paṭṭhāna with its infinite methods. (But the Abhidhammikas[108] say that Treasure-house here means either a mansion built of the seven kinds of jewels, or the place where the seven books were thought out : and as they give these two explanations of the passage, both may be accepted as correct.)

Having thus spent four weeks close to the Bo-tree, he went, in the fifth week, to the Shepherd's Nigrodha-tree : and sat there meditating on doctrine, and experiencing the happiness of deliverance.

Now at that time the deva Māra thought to himself : "So long a time have I followed this man seeking some access to him, and find no fault in him; and now, indeed, he is beyond my power." And overcome with sorrow he sat down on the highway, and as he thought of the following sixteen things he drew sixteen lines on the ground. Thinking, "I did not attain, as he did, to the perfection of Giving; therefore I have not become like him", he draw one line. Then thinking : "I did not attain, as he did, to the Perfections of Moral Practice, and Self abnegation, and Wisdom, and Exertion, and Patience, and Truth, and Resolution, and Kindness, and Equanimity;[109] therefore I have not become like him," he drew nine more lines. Then thinking : "I did not attain the Ten Perfections, the conditions precedent to the penetration, the extraordinary knowledge of the complete way of the senses, and therefore I have not become way of the senses, and therefore I have not become like him," he drew the eleventh line. Then thinking : "I did not attain to the Ten Perfections, the conditions precedent to the penetration, the extraordinary knowledge of inclinations and latent tendencies, of the attainment of compassion, of the double miracle, of the removal of hindrances, and of all-knowing : therefore I have not become like him", he drew the five other lines. And so he sat on the highway, drawing sixteen lines for these sixteen thoughts.

At that time Craving, Discontent, and Lust,[110] the three daughters of Māra, could not find their father, and were looking for him, wondering where he could be. And when they saw him, sad at heart, writing on the ground, they went up to him, and asked : "Why, dear, are you sad and sorrowful?"

And he answered : "My women, this great recluse is escaping from my power. Long have I watched, but in vain, to find some fault in him. Therefore it is that I am sad and sorrowful."

"If that is so," replied they, "think not thus. We will subject him to our influence, and come back bringing him captive with us."

"My women," said he, "you cannot by any means bring him under your influence; this man stands firm in faith, unwavering."

"Dear one, we are women" was the reply; "even now we shall bring him bound by the sweetness of lust. Do not think so."

So they approached the Blessed One, and said : "O recluse, upon thee we humbly wait!"

But the Blessed One neither paid any attention to their words, nor raised his eyes to look at them. He sat, with a mind made free by the complete extinction of rebirth-conditions, enjoying the bliss of detachment.

Then the daughters of Māra considered with themselves : "Various are men's tastes. Some fall in love with girls, some with young women, some with mature women, some with older women. We will tempt him in various forms." So each of them assumed the appearance of a hundred women–girls, women who had never had a child, or only once, or only twice, middle-aged women, older women–and six times they went up to the Blessed One, and professed themselves his humble handmaidens; and to that also the Blessed One paid no attention, so was he made free by the complete extinction of rebirth-conditions.

Now, some teachers say that when the Blessed One saw them approaching in the form of elderly women, he commanded, saying : "Let these women remain just as they are, with broken teeth and bald heads." This should not be believed, for the Master issues not such commands.

But the Blessed One said : "Depart ye! What have ye seen that ye thus strive? Such things might be done in the presence of men who linger in the paths of sin; but by the Tathāgata lust is put away, ill-will is put away, delusion is put away." And he admonished them in those two verses from the Chapter on the Buddha in the Scripture Verses :

280. Whose conquest is not overthrown
His conquest nought on earth assails.
That Buddha, infinite in range,
Pathless, by what path will ye lead?

281. In whom there is no snare besetting.
Venomous craving any-whither leading.
That Buddha, infinite in range,
Pathless, by what path will ye lead?[111]

And they saying : "Our father spoke the truth indeed. The saint, the Well-Farer of the world is not easily led away" and so on, returned to their father.

But the Blessed One when he had spent a week at that spot, went on to the Muchalinda-tree. There he spent a week. Muchalinda, the snake-king, when a storm arose, shielding him with seven folds of his hood, so that the Blessed One enjoyed the bliss of deliverance as if he had been resting unharassed in a fragrant chamber. Thence he went away to the Kingstead-tree and there also sat down enjoying the bliss of deliverance. And so seven weeks passed away, during which he experienced no bodily wants, but fed on Jhāna-joy, Path-joy, and Fruition-joy.[112]

Now, as he sat there on the last day of the seven weeks–the forty-ninth day–he felt a desire to bathe his face. And Sakka, the deva-governor, brought a fruit of the myrobolan-tree, and gave him to eat. And Sakka, too, provided a tooth-cleanser of the thorns of the snake-creeper, and water to bathe his face. And the

Master used the tooth-cleanser, and bathed his face, and sat him down there at the foot of the Kingstead-tree.

At that time two merchants, Tapassu and Bhalluḳa by name, were travelling from Orissa to Central India,[113] with five hundred carts. And a deva, a blood relation of theirs, stopped their carts, and moved their hearts to offer food to the Master. And they took a rice cake, and a honey cake, and went up to the Master, and said : "O sir, Blessed One! out of compassion for us accept this food."

Now, on the day when he had received that sweet rice-milk, his bowl had disappeared;[114] so the Blessed One thought : "The Buddhas never receive food in their hands. How shall I accept it?" Then the four Guardians knew his thought and, coming from the four quarters of the sky, they brought bowls made of sapphire. And the Blessed One accepted them. Then they brought four other bowls, made of jade; and the Blessed one, out of kindness to the four devas, received the four, and placing them one above another commanded, saying : "Let them become one." And the four closed up into one of medium size becoming visible only as lines round the mouth of it. The Blessed One received the food into that new-created bowl, and ate it, and gave thanks.

The two brothers took refuge in the Buddha, the Doctrine, and the Order,[115] and became professed disciples. Then, when they asked him, saying : "Lord, bestow upon us something to which we may pay reverence," with his own right hand he tore from his head, and gave to them, the hair-relics. And they built a Dāgaba in their own city, and placed the relics within it.[116]

But the Perfectly Enlightened One rose up thence, and returned to the Shepherd's Nigrodha-tree, and sat down at its foot. And no sooner was he seated there, considering the depth of the Doctrine which he had gained, than there arose in his mind a doubt (felt by each of the Buddhas as he became aware of his having arrived at the Doctrine) that he had not that kind of ability necessary to explain that Doctrine to others.

Then the great Ruler of the Brahmā heavens, exclaiming : "Alas! the world is lost. Alas! the world is altogether lost!" brought with him the rulers of the worlds in the ten thousand world-systems,[117] and went up to the Master, and said : "O Blessed Lord, do thou proclaim the Doctrine! Proclaim the Doctrine, O Blessed Lord!" and in other words of like purport begged from him the preaching of the Doctrine.

Then the Master granted his request. And considering to whom he should first reveal the Doctrine, thought at first of Āḷāra, his former teacher, as one who would quickly comprehend it. But, on surveying (the country), he perceived that Āḷāra had been dead seven days. So he fixed on Uddaka. But he learnt that he too had died that very evening. Then he thought of the five mendicants : "they were very helpful!" And casting about in his mind : "where are they now dwelling?" he perceived they were at the Deer-park in Benares. And he determined, saying, "There going I will set rolling the wheel of Doctrine." But he delayed a few days, begging his daily food in the neighbourhood of the Bo-tree, with the intention : "I will go to Benares on the full moon day of Āsāḷhi."

And at dawn on the fourteenth day of the month, when the night had passed away, he took his robe and his bowl : and had gone eighteen leagues, just half way, when he met the Ājīvika friar Upākā. And he announced to him how he had become a Buddha; and on the evening of that day he arrived at the hermitage near Benares.[118]

The five elders,[119] seeing already from afar the Buddha coming, said one to another : "Brethren, here comes the recluse Gotama. He has turned back to a free use of the necessaries of life, and has recovered roundness of form, acuteness of sense, and beauty of complexion. We ought to pay him no reverence; but as he is, after all, of a good family, he deserves the honour of a seat. So we will simply prepare a seat for him."[120]

The Blessed One, casting about in his mind by the power that he had of knowing what was going on in the thoughts of all beings, as to what they were thinking, knew their thoughts. Then, concentrating that feeling of his good-will which was able to pervade generally all beings in earth and heaven, he directed it specially towards them. And the sense of his good-will diffused itself through their hearts;[121] and as he came nearer and nearer, unable any longer to adhere to their resolve, they rose from their seats, and bowed down before him, and welcomed him with every mark of reverence and respect. But, not knowing that he had become a Buddha, they addressed him, in everything they said, either by name, or as "Brother."[122] Then the Blessed One announced to them his Buddhahood, saying : "Mendicants address not a Buddha by his name, or as 'āvuso.' I, mendicants, am a perfectly awakened one, one of those who have thus come."[123]

Then, seated on the place prepared for him, and surrounded by myriads of devas, he addressed the five attendant elders, just as the moon was passing out of conjunction with the lunar mansion in Uttarasāḷha and taught them in that discourse which was *The Foundation of the Kingdom of Righteousness.*[124]

Of the five Elders, Kondanya the Believer[125] sending forth insight as the discourse went on, as it concluded, he, with myriads of devas, had arrived at the Fruit of the First Path.[126] And the Master, who remained, there for the rainy season, sat in the *vihāra* the next day, when the other four had gone a-begging, talking to Vappa : and Vappa that morning attained to the Fruit of the First Path. And, in a similar manner, Bhaddiya on the next day, and Mahā-Nāma on the next, and Assaji on the next, attained to the Fruit of the First Path. And on the fifth day, he called all five to his side, and preached to them the discourse *On the Mark of not-soul.*[127] At the end of that discourse the five elders attained to the Arahant-fruition.

Then the Master perceived that Yasa, a young man of good family, was capable of entering the Paths. And when day was breaking, he having left his home and gone away, the Master called him, saying : "Come, Yasa!" and on that very night he attained to the Fruit of the First Path, and on the next day to Arahantship. And he received also other fifty-four, his companions, into the order, with the sanction : "Come, mendicants!" and caused them to attain to Arahantship.

Now when there were thus in the world sixty-one persons who had become Arahants, the Master, after the rainy reason and the function with which it closes were over, sent out the sixty in different directions with the words : "Fare forth, mendicants." And himself going towards Uruvelā, he overcame at the Kappāsiyạ forest, half-way thither, the thirty young Bhadda-vaggiyan nobles. Of these the least advanced entered the First, and the most advanced the Third Path : and he received them all into the Order with the sanction, "Come, mendicants!" And sending them also forth into the regions round about, he himself went on to Uruvelā.

There he overcame, by performing three thousand five hundred miracles, the three Hindu ascetics, brothers–Uruvelā Kassapa and the rest–who had one thousand disciples. And he received them into the Order with the sanction : "Come, mendicants!"[128] and established them in Arahantship by his discourse, when they were seated on Gayā-head hill : "*On the Lesson to be drawn from Fire.*"[129] And attended by these thousand Arahants, he went to the grove called the Palm-grove, hard by Rājagaha, with the object of redeeming the promise he had made to Bimbisāra the king.[130]

When the king heard from the keeper of the grove the saying : "The Master is come," he went to the Master, attended by innumerable brahmins and householders, and fell down at the feet of the Buddha–those feet, which bore on their surface the pattern of the wheel, and gave forth a halo of light like a canopy of cloth of gold. Then he and his retinue respectfully took their seats on one side.

Now the question occurred to those Brahmins and householders : "How is it then? has the great recluse entered as a student in religion under Uruvelā Kassapa, or Uruvelā Kassapa under the great recluse?" And the Blessed One, becoming aware of their thus doubting within themselves, addressed the Elder in the verse–

282. What hast thou seen thou of Uruvelā,
That thou hast left the Fire, votary austere?
I ask thee, Kassapa, the meaning of this thing :
How hast renounced the sacrifice of fire?

And the Elder, perceiving what the Blessed One intended, replied in the verse :

283. Some men rely on sights, and sounds, and taste,
Desires and women, some on sacrifice;
All dross to him who knows the springs of life.
Therefore not fain am I for altar rites.

And in order to make known his discipleship he bowed his head to the Buddha's feet, saying : "The Blessed Lord is my master, and I am the disciple!" And seven times he rose into the air up to the height of one, two, three, and so on, up to the height of seven palm-trees; and descending again, he saluted the Buddha, and respectfully took a seat aside. Seeing that wonder, the multitude praised the Master, saying : "Ah! how great is the power of the Buddhas! Even so mighty a thinker as this has thought him worthy! Even Uruvelā Kassapa has broken through the net of delusion, and is tamed by the Tathāgata!"

But the Blessed One said : "Not now only have I overcome Uruvelā Kassapa; in former ages, too, he was tamed by me." And he uttered in that connexion the *Mahā-Nārada-Kassapa-Jātaka,*[131] and proclaimed the Four Truths. And the King of Magadha, with nearly all his retinue, attained to the Fruit of the First Path, and the rest became lay disciples.[132]

And the king still sitting near the Master told him of the five wishes he had; and then, confessing his faith, he invited the Blessed One for the next day, and rising from his side, departed with respectful salutation.

The next day all the men who dwelt in Rājagaha, eighteen myriads in number, both those who had already seen the Blessed One, and those who had not, came out early from Rājagaha to the Grove of Reeds to see the successor of the Buddhas. The road, six miles long, could not contain them. The whole of the Grove of Reeds became like a basket packed quite full. The multitude, beholding the exceeding beauty of him whose power is tenfold, could not contain their delight. Vaṇṇabhū was it called (that is, the Place of Praise), for at such spots all the greater and lesser characteristics of a Buddha, and the glorious beauty of his person, are to be extolled. There was not room for even a single mendicant to get out on the road, or in the grove, so crowded was it with the multitude gazing at the beautiful form of the him of the tenfold power.

So that day they say the throne of Sakka felt hot, to warn him that the Blessed One might be deprived of nourishment, which should not be. And on consideration he understood the reason; and he took the form of a young brahmin, and descended in front of the Buddha, and by deva-power made way for him, singing the praises of the Buddha, the Doctrine, and the Order :

284. The tamed together with the tamed,
men erst of the matted hair, by now set free
He who is to see like wrought gold,
The Blessed One hath entered Rājagaha.

285. The freed man together with the freed....

286. The man who has crossed over[133] together with them that have crossed over...

287. The man of way tenfold,[134] of power tenfold,
Knower of tenfold Norm, winner of ten,[135]
With retinue of ten hundred the Blessed One hath entered Rājagaha.

The multitude, seeing the beauty of the young brahmin thought : "This young brahmin is exceeding fair, and yet we have never yet beheld him." And they said : "Whence comes the young brahmin, or whose son is he?" And the young brahmin, hearing what they said, answered in the verse :

288. He who is wise, and tamed in everything,
The Buddha, the unequalled among men,
The Arahant, Wellfarer of the world,
On him I humble wait.

Then the Master entered upon the path thus made free by Sakka, and entered Rājagaha attended by a thousand mendicats. The king gave a great gift to the Order with the Buddha at their head; and had water brought, bright as jems, and scented with flowers, in a golden goblet. And he poured the water over the hand of him of the tenfold power, in token of the presentation of the Bambu Grove, saying : "I, my lord, cannot live without the Three Gems (the Buddha, the Order, and the Faith). In season and out of season I would visit the Blessed One. Now the Grove of Reeds is far away; but this Grove of mine, called the Bambu

Grove, is close by, is easy of resort, and is a fit dwelling-place for a Buddha. Let the Blessed One accept it of me!"

At the acceptance of this monastery the broad earth shook, as if it said : "Now the Religion of Buddha has taken root!" For in all India there is no dwelling-place, save the Bambu Grove, acceptance of which caused the earth to shake : and in Ceylon there is no dwelling-place, save the Great Vihāra, acceptance of which caused the earth to shake.[1]

And when the Master had accepted the Bambu Grove Monastery, and had given thanks for it, he rose from his seat and went, surrounded by the members of the Order, to the Bambu Grove.

Now at that time two ascetics, named Sāriputta and Miggallāna, were living near Rājagaha, seeking after salvation. Of these, Sāriputta, seeing the Elder Assaji[137] on his begging round, was touched and waited on him, and heard from him the verse beginning : "What things soever are produced from causes."[138] And he attained to the blessings which result from conversion; and repeated that verse to his companion Moggallāna the ascetic. And he, too, attained to the blessings which first result from conversion. And each of them left Sanjaya,[139] and with his attendants took orders under the Master. Of these two, Monggallāna attained Arahantship in seven days, and Sāriputta the elder in half a month. And the Master appointed these two to the office of his Chief Disciples; and on the day on which Sāriputta the elder attained Arahantship, he made a muster of the disciples.

Now whilst the Tathāgata was dwelling there in the Bambu Grove, Suddhodana the king heard that his son, who for six years had devoted himself to works of austerity, had attained to complete enlightenment, had founded the Kingdom of Righteousness, and was then dwelling at the Bambu Grove near Rājagaha. So he said to a certain courtier : "Come, I say, take a thousand men as a retinue, and go to Rājagaha, and say in my name : 'Your[140] father, Suddhodana the king, desires to see you'; and bring my son here."

And he respectfully accepted the king's command with the reply : So be it, sire!" and went quickly with a thousand followers the sixty leagues distance, and sat down amongst the disciples of him of the tenfold power, and at the hour of instruction entered the Vihāra. And thinking, "Let the king's message stay awhile", he stood just beyond the disciples and listened to the discourse. And as he so stood he attained to Arahantship, with his whole retinue, and asked to be admitted to the Order. And the Blessed One stretched forth his hand and said : "Come, mendicants." And all of them that moment appeared there, with robes and bowls created by miracle, like elders of a hundred years' standing.

Now from the time when they attain Arahantship the Arahants become indifferent to worldly things : so he did not deliver the king's message to him of the tenfold power. The king, seeing that neither did his messenger return, nor was any message received from him called another courtier in the same manner as before, and sent him. And he went, and in the same manner attained Arahantship with his followers, and remained silent. Then the king in the same manner sent nine courtiers each with a retinue of a thousand men. And they all, neglecting what they had to do, stayed away there in silence.

And when the king found no one who would come and bring even a message, he thought : "Not one of these brings back, for my sake, even a message : who will then carry out what I say?" And searching among all his people he thought of Kāḷudāyin. For he was in everything serviceable to the king–intimate with him, and trustworthy. He was born on the same day as the future Buddha, and had been his playfellow and companion.

So the king said to him : "Dear Kāḷudāyin, as I wanted to see my son, I sent nine times a thousand men; but there is not one of them who has either come back or sent a message. Now it is hard to know if life be in danger; and I desire to see my son before I die. Will on be able to let me see my son?"

"I can, O king!" was the reply, "if I am allowed to become a recluse."

"My dear," said the king, "whether thou become a recluse or not let me see my son!"

And he respectfully received the king's message with the words : "So be it O king!" and went to Rājagaha; and stood at the edge of the congregation at the time of the Master's instruction, and heard the gospel, and attained Arahantship with his followers, and was received with the 'come, bhikku' sanction.

The Master spent the first Lent after he had become Buddha at Isipatana; and when it was over went to Uruvelā and stayed there three months and overcame the three brothers, ascetics. And on the full-moon day of the month of Phussa, he went to Rājagaha with a retinue of a thousand mendicants, and there he dwelt two months. Thus five months had elapsed since he left Benāres, the cold season was past, and seven or eight days since the arrival of Udāyin, the Elder.

And on the full-moon day of Phaggūni Udāyin thought : "The cold season is past; the spring has come; men raise their crops and set out on their journeys; the earth is covered with fresh grass; the woods are full of flowers; the roads are fit to walk on; now is the time for the Sage to show favour to his family." And going to the Blessed One, he praised travelling in about sixty stanzas, that the Sage might revisit his native town, beginning thus :

289. Now crimson glow the trees, dear lord, and cast
In quest of fruit their sheathing coverings.
Like crests of flame they shine irradiant
And rich in tastes, great hero, is the time.

290. Not over hot, nor over cold; nor is
There dearth of food for alms. The earth is green
With verdure. This the fitting time, great sage.[141]

Then the Master said to him : "But why, Udāyin do you sing the pleasures of travelling with so sweet a voice?"

"Sir," was the reply, "your father is anxious to see you once more; will you not show favour to your relations?"

"'Tis well said, Udāyin! I will do so. Tell the Order that they will fulfil the duty (laid on all its members) of journeying from place to place."

Kāḷudāyin accordingly told the brethren. And the Blessed One attended by twenty thousand mendicants free from sin–ten thousand clansmen from Magadha and Anga, and ten thousand from Kapilavatthu–started from Rājagaha, and travelled a league a day : going slowly with the intention of reaching Kapilavatthu, sixty leagues from Rājagaha, in two months.

And the elder, thinking : "I will let the king know that the Blessed One has started", rose into the air and appeared in the king's house. The king was glad to see the elder, made him sit down on a splendid couch, filled a bowl with the delicious food made ready for himself, and gave to him. Then the elder rose up, and made as if he would go away.

"Sit down and eat," said the king.

"I will rejoin the Master, and eat then," said he.

"But where is the Master?" asked the king.

"He has set out on his journey, attended by twenty thousand mendicats, to see you, O king!" said he.

The king, glad at heart, said : "Do you eat this; and until my son has arrived at this town, provide him with food from here."

The elder agreed; and the king waited on him and then had the bowl cleansed with perfumed chunam, and filled with the best of food, and placed it in the elder's hand, saying : "Give it to the Tathāgata."

And the elder, in the sight of all, threw the bowl into the air, and himself rising up into the sky, took the food again, and placed it in the hand of the Master.

The Master ate it. Every day the elder brought him food in the same manner. So the Master himself was fed, even on the journey, from the king's table. The elder day by day, when he had finished his meal, told the king : "To-day the Blessed One has come so far, to-day so far." And by talking of the high character of the Buddha, he made all the king's family delighted with the Master, even before they saw him. On that account the Blessed One gave him pre-eminence, saying, "Pre-eminent, O mendicants, among all those of my disciples who gained over my family, was Kāḷudāyin."[142]

The Sākyas, as they sat talking of the prospect of seeing their distinguished relative, considered what place he could stay in; and deciding that the Nigrodha Grove would be a pleasant residence, they made everything ready there. And with fragrant flowers in their hands they went out to meet him; and sending in front the baby boys and girls and the boys and girls of the town and then the young men and maidens of the royal family, they themselves, decked of their own accord with sweet-smelling flowers and chunam, came close behind, conducting the Blessed One to the Nigrodha Grove. There the Blessed One sat down on the Buddha's throne prepared for him, surrounded by twenty thousand Arahants.

The Sākyas are proud by nature, and stubborn in their pride. Thinking : "Prince Siddhattha is younger than we are, standing to us in the relation of younger brother, or nephew, or son, or grandson", they said to the little children and the young people : "Do you bow down before him, we will seat ourselves behind you." The Blessed One when they had thus taken their seats, perceived what they meant; and thinking : "My relations pay me no reverence; come now, I must make them to do so," he fell into the ecstasy based on super-knowledge, and rising into the air as if shaking off the dust off his feet upon them, he performed a miracle like unto that double miracle at the foot of the Gaṇḍamba-tree.[143]

The king, seeing that miracle, said : "O Blessed One! When you were presented to Kāḷa Devala to do obeisance to him on the day on which you were born, and I saw your feet turn round and place themselves on the brahmin's head, I paid homage to you. That was my first homage. When you were seated on your couch in the shade of the jambu-tree on the day of the ploughing festival, I saw how the shadow over you did not turn, and I bowed down at your feet. That was my second homage. Now, seeing this miracle unseen before, I bow down at your feet. This is my third homage."

Then, when the king paid him homage, there was not a single Sākya who was able to refrain from bowing down before the Blessed One : and all of them did homage.

So the Blessed One, having compelled his relatives to bow down before him, descended from the sky, and sat down on the seat prepared for him. And when the Blessed One was seated, the assembly of his relatives yielded him pre-eminence; and all sat there with unity in their hearts.

Then a thunder-cloud poured forth a shower of rain, and the copper-coloured water went away rumbling beneath the earth. He who wished to get wet, did get wet; but not even a drop fell on the body of him who did not wish to get wet. And all seeing it became filled with astonishment, and said one to another : "Lo! what miracle. Lo! what wonder!"

But the Teacher said : "Not now only did a shower of rain fall upon me in the assembly of my relations, formerly also this happened." And in this connexion he told the story of his Birth as Vessantara.[144]

When they had heard his discourse they rose up, and paid reverence to him, and went away. Not one of them, either the king or any of his ministers, asked him on leaving : "To-morrow accept your meal of us."

So on the next day the Master, attended by twenty thousand mendicants, entered Kapilavatthu to beg. Then also no one came to him or invited him to his house, or took his bowl. The Blessed One, standing at the gate considered : "How then did the former Buddhas go on their begging rounds in their native town? did they go direct to the houses of the kinds, or did they beg straight on from house to house?" Then, not finding that any of the Buddhas had gone direct, he thought : "I, too, must accept this descent and tradition as my own; so shall my disciples in future, learning of me, fulfil the duty of going for alms." And beginning at the first house, he went straight on for alms.

At the rumour that the young chief Siddhattha was going for alms from door to door, the windows in the two-storied and three-storied houses were thrown open, and the multitude was transfixed at the sight. And the lady, the mother of Rāhula, thought : "My lord, who used to go to and fro in this very town with gilded palanquin and every sign of royal pomp, now with a potsherd in his hand begs his food from door to door, with shaven hair and beard, and clad in yellow robes. Is this becoming?" And she opened the window, and looked at the Blessed One; and she beheld him glorious with the unequalled majesty of a Buddha, distinguished with the Thirty-two characteristic sings and the eighty lesser marks of a Great Being, and lighting up the street of they city with a halo resplendent with many colours, proceeding to a fathom's length all round his person.

And she announced it to the king, saying : "Thy son is walking for alms from door to door; " and she magnified him with the eight stanzas on "The Lion among Men", beginning :

291. Glossy and dark and soft and curly is his hair;
spotless and fair as the sun is his forehead;
Well-proportioned and prominent and delicate is his nose;
Around him is diffused a network of rays–
The Lion among Men!

The king was deeply agitated; and he went forth instantly, gathering up his robe in his hand, and going quickly stood before the Blessed One, and said : "Why, Master, do you[145] put us to shame? Why do you walk about for alms? Do you think it impossible to provide a meal for so many monks?"

"This is our custom. O king!" was the reply.

"Not so, Master! our descent is from the royal race of the Great Elected;[146] and amongst them all not one chief has ever gone about for alms."

"This succession of kings is thy descent, O king! but mine is the succession of the Buddhas, from Dīpankara and Kondanya and the rest down to Kassapa. These, and thousands of others reckoned as Buddhas have gone about for alms, and lived on alms." And standing in the middle of the street he uttered the verse :

292. Let him rise up, and loiter not!
Let him fare the righteous faring!
Who fares in that way happy lives,
Both in this world and in the next.[147]

And when the verse was finished the king attained to the Fruit of the First, and then, on hearing the following verse, to the Fruit of the Second Path :

293. The righteous faring let him fare!
Let him not fare amiss!
The righteous farer happy lives,
Both in this world and in the next.

And when he heard the story of the Birth as the Keeper of Righteousness,[148] he attained to the Fruit of the Third Path. And just as he was dying, seated on the royal couch under the white canopy of state, he attained to Arahantship. The king never practised spiritual exertions in the forest life.

Now as soon as he had realized the Fruit of conversion, he took the Buddha's bowl and conducted the Blessed One and his retinue to the palace, and served them with savoury food, both hard and soft. And when the meal was over, all the women of the household came and did obeisance to the Blessed One, except only the mother of Rāhula.[149]

But she, though she told her attendants to go and salute their lord, stayed behind, saying : "If I have virtue in his eyes, my lord will himself come to me; and when he has come I will pay him reverence."

And the Blessed One, giving his bowl to the king to carry, went with his two chief disciples to the apartments of the daughter of the king, saying : "The king's daughter shall in no wise be spoken to, howsoever she may be pleased to welcome me." And he sat down on the seat prepared for him.

And she came quickly and held him by the ankles, and laid her head on his feet, and so did homage to him, even as she had intended. And the king told of the fullness of her love for the Blessed One, and of her goodness of heart, saying : "When my daughter heard, O Master, that you had put on the yellow robes from that time forth she dressed only in yellow. When she heard of your taking but one meal a day, she adopted the same custom. When she heard that you renounced the use of elevated couches, she slept on a mat spread on the floor. When she heard you had given up the use of garlands and unguents, she also used them no more. And when her relatives sent a message, saying, 'Let us take care of you,' she paid them no attention at all. Such are my daughter's virtues, O Blessed One!"

"'Tis no wonder, O king!" was the reply, "that she should watch over herself now that she has you for a protector, and that her wisdom is mature : formerly, even when wandering among the mountains without a protector, and when her wisdom was not mature, she watched over herself." And he told the story of his Birth as the Moonsprite;[150] and rose from his seat, and went away.

On the next day the festivals of the coronation, and of the housewarming, and of the marriage of Nanda, the king's son, were being celebrated all together. But the Buddha went to his house, and gave him his bowl to carry; and with the object of making him abandon the world, he wished him true happiness; and then, rising from his seat, departed. And (the bride) Janapada Kalyāṇī,[151] seeing the young man go away, gazed wonderingly at him, and cried out : "my lord, whither go you so quickly?" But he, not venturing to say to the Blessed One, "Take your bowl", followed him even unto the Vihāra. And the Blessed One received him, unwilling though he was, into the Order.

It was on the third day after he reached Kapilapura that the Blessed One ordained Nanda. One the seventh day the mother of Rāhula arrayed the boy in his best, and sent him to the Blessed One, saying : "Look, dear, at that monk, attended by twenty thousand monks, and beautiful in appearance as a Brahmā! That is your father. He had certain great treasures, which we have not seen since he abandoned his home. Go now, and ask for your inheritance, saying, 'Father, I am the prince. When I am crowned,

I shall become a king over all the earth. I have need of the treasure. Give me the treasure; for a son is heir to his father's property.'"

The boy went up to the Blessed one, and gained a love of his father, and stood there glad and joyful, saying : "Happy, O monk, is thy shadow!" and adding many other words befitting his position. When the Blessed One had ended his meal, and had given thanks, he rose from his seat, and went away. And the child followed the Blessed One, saying : "Monk! give me my inheritance! give me my inheritance!"

The Blessed One turned the boy not back. And the people with the Blessed One, were not able to stop him. And so he went with the Blessed One even up to the grove. Then the Blessed One thought : "This wealths, this property of his father's, which he is asking for, perishes in the using, and brings vexation with it! I will give him the sevenfold Ariyan wealth which I obtained under the Bo-tree, and make him the heir of a spiritual inheritance!" And he said to Sāriputta : "Well, then do thou, Sāriputta, receive Rāhula into the Order."

But when the child had been taken into the Order the king grieved exceedingly. And he was unable to bear his grief, and made it known to the Blessed One, and asked of him a boon, saying : "If you so please, O master, let not my lords receive a son into the Order without the leave of his father and mother." And the Blessed One granted the boon.

And the next day, as he sat in the king's house after his meal was over, the king, sitting respectfully by him, said : "Master! when you were practising austerities, a deva came to me, and said : 'Your son is dead!' And I believed him not, and rejected what he said, answering : My son will not die without attaining Buddhahood!'"

And he replied, saying : "Why should you now have believed? when formerly though they showed you my bones, and said your son was dead, you did not believe them." And in that connexion he told the story of his Birth as the Great Keeper of Righteousness.[152] And when the story was ended, the king attained to the Fruit of the Third Path. And so the Blessed One established his father in the Three Fruits; and he returned to Rājagaha attended by the company of the brethern, and resided at Cool Grove.

At that time the householder Anātha Piṇḍika, bringing merchandise in five hundred carts, went to the house of a trader in Rājagaha, his intimate friend, and there heard that a Blessed Buddha had arisen. And very early in the morning he went to the Teacher, the door being opened by the power of devas, and heard the Truth and became converted.[153] And on the next day he gave a great donation to the Order, with the Buddha at their head, and received a promise from the Teacher that he would come to Sāvatthi.

Then along the road, forty-five leagues in length, he built resting-places at every league, at an expenditure of hundred thousand for each. And he bought the Grove called Jetavana for eighteen koṭis of gold pieces, laying them side by side over the ground, and erected there a new building. In the midst thereof he made a pleasant room for him of the tenfold power, and around it separately constructed dwellings for the eighty chief elders, and other residences with single and double walls, and long halls and open roofs, ornamented with ducks and quails; and ponds also he made, and terraces to walk on by day and by night.

And so having constructed a delightful residence on a pleasant spot, at an expense of eighteen koṭis, he sent a message to him of the tenfold power that he should come.

The Master, hearing the messenger's words, left Rājagaha attended by a great multitude of monks, and in due course arrived at the city of Sāvatthi. Then the wealthy merchant decorated the monastery; and on the day on which the Tathāgata should arrive at Jetavana he arrayed his son in splendour, and sent him on with five hundred youths in festival attire. And he and his retinue, holding five hundred flags resplendent with cloth of five different colours, appeared before him of the tenfold power. And behind him Mahā-Subhaddā and Chūla-Subhaddā, the two daughters of the merchant, went forth with five hundred damsels carrying water-pots full of water. And behind them, decked with all her ornaments, the merchant's wife went forth, with five hundred matrons carrying vessels full of food. And behind them all, the great merchant himself, clad in new robes, with five hundred traders also dressed in new robes, went out to meet the Blessed One.

The Blessed One, sending this retinue of lay disciples in front, and attended by the great multitude of monks, entered the Jetavana monastery with the infinite grace and unequalled majesty of a Buddha, making the spaces of the grove bright with the halo from his person, as if they were sprinkled with gold dust.

Then Anātha Piṇḍika asked him : "How, my lord, shall I deal with this Vihāra?"

"Householder," was the reply, "give it then to the Order of Mendicants, whether now present or hereafter to arrive."

And the great merchant, saying : "So be it, my lord," brought a golden vessel, and poured water over the hand of him of the tenfold power, and dedicated the Vihāra, saying, "I give this Jetavana Vihāra to the Order of Mendicants with the Buddha at their head, and to all from every direction now present or hereafter to come."[154]

And the Master accepted the Vihāra, and giving thanks, pointed out the advantages of monasteries, saying :

294. Cold they ward off, and heat;
So also boasts of prey,
And creeping things, and gnats,
And rains in the cold season.
And when the dreaded heat and winds
Arise, they ward them off.

295. To give to monks a dwelling-place,
Wherein in safety and at ease
To think and insight gain,
The Buddha praises most of all.

296. Let therefore a wise man,
Regarding his own meal,

Have pleasant monasteries built,
And lodge there learned men.

297. Let him with cheerful mien,
Give food to them, and drink,
And clothes, and dwelling-places
To the upright in mind.

298. Then they shall preach to him the Norm–
The Norm, dispelling every grief–
Which Norm, when here he learns, he sins
No more, reaching the perfect well

(Vinaya, Chullavagga VI, 1).

Anātha Piṇḍika began the dedication festival from the second day. The festival held at the dedication of Visākhā's building ended in four months, but Anātha Piṇḍika's dedication festival lasted ninc months. At the festival, too, eighteen koṭis were spent; so on that one monastery he spent wealth amounting to fifty-four koṭis.

Long ago, too, in the time of the Blessed Buddha Vipassin, a merchant named Punabbāsu Mitta bought that very spot by laying golden bricks over it, and built a monastery there a league in length. And in the time of the Blessed Buddha Sikhin, a merchant named Sirivaḍḍha bought that very spot by spreading golden ploughshares over it, and built there a monastery three-quarters of a league in length. And in the time of the Blessed Buddha Vessabhū, a merchant named Sotthiya bought that very spot by laying golden elephant feet along it, and built a monastery there half a league in length. And in the time of the Blessed Buddha Kakusandha, and merchant named Acchūta also bought that very spot by laying golden bricks over it, and built there a monastery a quarter of a league in length. And in the time of the Blessed Buddha Koṇāgamana, a merchant named Ugga bought that very spot by laying golden tortoises over it, and built there a monastery half a league in length. And in the time of the Blessed Buddha Kassapa, a merchant named Sumangala bought that very spot by laying golden bricks over it, and built there a monastery sixty acres in extent. And in the time of our Blessed One, Anātha Piṇḍika the merchant bought that very spot by laying kahāpaṇa coins over it, and built there a monastery thirty acres in extent. For that spot is a place which not one of all the Buddhas has deserted. And so the Blessed One lived in that spot from the attainment of all-knowledge under the Bo-tree till his death.

This is the Proximate Epoch.

And now we will tell the stories of all his Births.

End of the Nidāna Kathā.

REFERENCES

1. Lit. perfected the vast constituents of Buddhahood, the Pāramitās are meant. The *Apaṇṇaka* is the title of the first Jātaka.
2. Lit. in thousands of koṭis of births (a koṭi is ten millions).
3. The above lines in the original are in verse. I have found it impossible to follow the arrangement of the stanzas, owing to the extreme involution of the style.
4. An asankheyya is a period of vast duration, lit. an incalculable.
5. Lit. "caused the drums to be beaten."
6. A poem belonging to the *Sutta-Piṭaka,* edited by Rd. Morris, Pali Text Soc., 1882.–Ed.
7. Here a gloss in the text enumerates the whole ten cries.
8. The Bodhisatta is frequently called paṇḍita, e.g. *sasapaṇḍito* (*Jāt.* No. 316), *Rāmapaṇḍito* (*Dasaratha Jāt.* No. 461).
9. *Bdhv.,* p. 7.
10. Lit. "Extinguishing".
11. Mr. Fausböll points out to me that in *tividhaggi* and *jāti* we have Vedic abbreviations.
12. *Evaṁ samāhite citte parisuddhe pariyodāte anaṅgaṇe vigatūpakkilese mudubhūte kammaniye ṭhite ānejjappatte ñāṇadassanāya cittaṁ abhinīharati* (Sāmaññaphala Sutta, see *Dīgha Nikāya,* i, 76; *Dialogues of the Buddha,* i, 86).
13. Mr. Fausböll writes to me that *guṇe* for *guṇehi* must be viewed as an old Pali form originating in the Sanskrit guṇaih.
14. Here follow four pages of later commentary or gloss, which I leave untranslated.
15. The following is what I take to be the meaning of this passage : "If I chose I could at once enter the Buddhist Order, and by the

practice of ecstatic meditation (Jhāna) free myself from human passion, and become an Arahant or saint. I should then at death at once attain Nirvāna and cease to be reborn. But this would be a selfish course to pursue, for thus I should benefit myself only. Why should I thus slip unobserved and in the humble garb of a monk into Nirvāna? Nay, let me rather qualify myself to become a Buddha, and so save others as well as myself." This is the great Act of Renunciation by which the Bodhisattva, when Nirvāna was within his grasp, preferred to endure ages of heroic trials in the exercise of the *Pāramitās,* that he might be enabled to become a Buddha, and so redeem mankind. See D'Alwis's *Introduction to Kachchāyana's Grammar,* p. vi.

16. What follows from *yasmā* to *nipajji* belongs to a later commentary. I resume the translation with p. 15, l. 11 of the text.
17. Bujjhissati.
18. Lit., "raised his right foot (to depart)."
19. Lit., "at my sitting cross-legged."
20. Mr. Fausböll writes that *yaṁ* is a mistake of the copyist for *yá* = *yáni.*
21. viz., I suppose, by dragging it forcibly away. This metaphor, which to us appears wanting in dignity, is a favourite one with the Hindus. The tail of the Yak or Tibetan ox (*Bos Grunniens*) is a beautiful object, and one of the insignia of Hindu royalty.
22. Lit., "not avoiding anything among things great, small, and middling."
23. After *kiñci* understand *kulaṁ,* as will be seen from v. 143.
24. Lit., in all postures, walking, standing, etc.
25. Lit., depart from thy course in the matter of truthful things.
26. Lit., having made its coldness exactly alike for bad people and good people, pervades them.
27. *i.e.*, alternately from the first to the tenth and from the tenth to the first.
28. *i.e.,* put the first last.
29. Vijesinha.
30. Dhamma.
31. Vijesinha writes to me : "Natural and intrinsic virtues. The Sinhalese gloss says : *paramārthavū rasasahitavū lakshaṇa oet nohot svabhāvalakshaṇa hā sarvadharmasādhāraṇalakshaṇa oeti.*

In the latter case it would mean having the quality of conformity with all laws."

32. Tena yogena. Vij. says : "In that order, viz. in the *Saraṇāgamana first,* then in the *Pañcasīla,* then in the *Dasasīla,* and so on."
33. Lit., "arithmetically innumerable."
34. The Banyan-tree.
35. The formula by which a Buddha admits a layman to the priesthood.
36. *i.e.*, the Perfections.
37. *i.e.,* his last birth before attaining Buddhahood.
38. See *Vessantara Jātaka,* vol. vi, no. 547.
39. This name means "sharp-fanged."
40. In approval of his act of faith.
41. Lit., "no grief as big as the tip of a hair."
42. Dhamma.
43. *Psalms of the Brethren,* ver. 303 (Cf. p. 416. Rukkhakathā "tree-talk" will be a scribe's mistake for rakkha-kathā "guardtalk", "ward-rune". Cf. also *Sutta-Nipāta,* ver. 181; *Jātaka,* i, 31; iv, 496.–Ed.
44. Viz. Gotama.
45. When a good man is in difficulty, Sakka is apprised of it by his marble throne becoming warm.
46. Lit., twelve or thirteen yojanas (a yojana is four leagues).
47. Used in the ecstatic meditation.
48. The Pali word for the capital of a column is ghaṭaka, "little pot."
49. *Jātaka,* no. 499.
50. According to the gloss printed in the text it is a compound of milk, rice, honey, sugar, and clarified butter.
51. Compare Jātaka no. 20.
52. See above, p. 102.
53. We now come to the 7 Buddhas recognized in the older books.–Ed.
54. See verse 125, above.
55. See verse 126, above.
56. In the four highest of the thirty-one spheres of existence the devas are mindless, and the five worlds below these are called the Pure Abodes.

57. All the following verses down to verse 269 are quotations from the Chariyāpiṭaka.
58. The Sangas, of which there are five–lust, hate, ignorance, pride, and false doctrine.
59. The names are given in the text; the four Mahārājas, Sakka, Suyāma, Santusita, Paranimitta-vasavatti, and Mahā-Brahmā. They are the governors in the different worlds (Chakkavāla) of the Buddhist cosmogony.
60. In the seas surrounding each continent (Mahādīpa) there are five hundred islands. See Hardy's *Manual of Buddhism,* p. 13.
61. *Majjhima-desa,* of which the commentator adds : "This is the country thus spoken of in the Vinaya," quoting the passage at *Mahāvagga,* v. 13, 12, which gives the boundaries as follows : "To the E. the town Kajangala, and beyond it Mahāsālā; to the S.E. the river Salalavatī; to the S. the town Setakaṇṇika; to the W. the brāhman town and district Thūṇa; and to the N. the Usīraddhaja Mountain." These are different from the boundaries of the Madhya Desa of later Brahminical literature, on which see Lassen's *Indische Alterthumskunde,* vol. i, p. 119 (2nd edition). This sacred land was regarded as the centre of Jambudvīpa; that is, of the then known world–just as the Chinese talk of China as the Middle Country, and as other people have looked on their own capital as the navel or hub of the world, and on their world as the centre of the universe.
62. It is instructive to notice that in later accounts it is soberly related as actual fact that the Bodisat entered his mother's womb as a white elephant : and the Incarnation scene is occasionally so represented in Buddhist sculptures.
63. I think this is the meaning of the passage, though Prof. Childers has a different rendering of the similar phrase at verse 104, where I would read "it" instead of "vegetation". Compare *Dāṭhāvaṃsa,* i, 45.
64. I once saw a notice of some mediaeval frescoes in which the Holy Child was similarly represented as visible within the Virgin's womb, but have unfortunately mislaid the reference.
65. N., S., E., W., four intermediate to these, the zenith and the nadir.
66. The *Madurattha Vilāsini* adds the rest : "I am supreme in the world; this is my last birth; henceforth there will be no rebirth for me."
67. Lit., roared the lion-roar; a term for a manifesto of self-confidence.– Ed.

68. Wife of Gotama Buddha.

69. There is some mistake here, as the list contains nine–or if the four treasures count as one, only six–Connatal Ones. I think before Kaḷudāyi we should insert Ānanda, the loving disciple. So Alabaster and Hardy (*Wheel of the Law,* p. 106; *Manual of Buddhism,* p. 146). Bigandet also adds Ānanda, but calls him the son of Amittodana, which is against the common tradition (*Life or Legend of Gaudama,* p. 36, comp. my *Buddhism,* p. 52). The legend is certainly, as to its main features, an early one, for it is also found, in greatly exaggerated and contradictory terms, in the books of Northern Buddhists (*Lalita Vistara,* Foucaux, p. 97, Beal, p. 53; of. Senart, p. 294).

70. *Samāpatti.*

71. *Dhammacakkaṃ pavattessati.* See my *Buddhism,* p. 45.

72. It was considered among the brahmins a sign of holiness to wear matted or platted hair. This is referred to in the striking Buddhist verse (*Dhammapada,* v, 394) : "What is the use of platted hair, O fool! What of a garment of skins! Your low yearnings are within you, and the outside you make clean!"

73. "Our master" (ayyo) is here, of course, the sage. It is a pretty piece of politeness, not unfrequent in the Jātakas, to address a stranger as a relation. See below, Jātaka no. 3.

74. Literally "worth eighty and seven times a koṭi", both eighty and seven being lucky numbers.

75. Literally "and caused him to declare, 'Nālaka-course.'" Cf. the Nāḷaka-sutta, in Sutta-Nipāka, v. 679-723. Tathagata, "gone or come, in like manner; subject to the fate of all men," is an adjective applied originally to all mortals, but afterwards used as a favourite epithet of Gotama. Childers compares the use of "Son of Man."

76. *Anupādisesāya Nibbāna-dhātuyā parinibbāyi.*

77. Literally "a retinue thirty-six leagues in circumference", where "thirty-six" is a mere sacred number.

78. Khattiya (Kshatriya) was the warrior caste.

79. A state of religious meditation. A full explanation is given in my *Buddhism,* pp. 174-6.

80. A gloss adds, "This should be understood as is related fully in the *Sarabhanga Jātaka*" (no. 522).

81. *Dialogues of the Buddha,* ii. p. 18.

82. The members of the Buddhist Order of almsmen (bhikkhus) were in the habit of selecting some book or books of the Buddhist

Scriptures, which it was their expecial duty to learn by heart, repeat to their pupils, study, expound, and preach from. Thus the *Dīgha Nikāya,* or collection of long treatises, had a special school of 'repeaters' (*bhāṇakā*) to itself.

83. At critical moments in the lives of persons of importance in the religious legends of Buddhist India, the seat of the deva-governor Sakka becomes warm. Fearful of losing his temporary bliss, he then descends himself, or sends Vissakamma, the Buddhist Vulcan, to act as *deus ex machinā,* and put things straight.

84. The force of this passage is due to the fullness of meaning which, to the Buddhist, the words *Nibbuta* and *Nibbānaṃ* convey. No words in western languages cover exactly the same ground, or connote the same ideas. To explain them fully to anyone unfamiliar with Indian modes of thought would be difficult anywhere, and impossible in a note; but their meaning is pretty clear from the above sentences. Where in them, in the song, the words *blessed, happy, peace,* and the words *gone out, ceased,* occur, *nibbuta* stands in the original in one or other of its two meanings; where in them the words *Nirvāna, going out which is Peace* occur, *Nibbānaṃ* stands in the original. *Nirvāna* is a lasting state of happiness and peace, to be reached by the extinction of the 'fires' and 'trouble' mentioned now or hereafter in this passage.

85. Lit., "The three Bhavas seemed like houses on fire." The three Bhavas are existence in the Kāma-loka, the Rūpa-loka, and the Arūpa-loka respectively; that is, existence in the worlds whose inhabitants are subject to passion, who have material forms, but not passion, and have no forms respectively.

86. Lit., "about an ammaṇa (*i.e.* five or six bushels) of the large jasmine and the Arabian jasmine."

87. The Jātaka Commentary here referred to is, no doubt, the older commentary of Elu, or old Singhalese, on which the present work is based.

88. See above, p. 51.

89. The word rendered league is *yojana,* said by Childers (*Pali Dict. s.v.*) to be twelve miles, but really only between seven and eight miles. See my *Ancient Coins and Measures,* pp. 16, 17. The thirty yojanas here mentioned, together with the thirty from Kapilavatthu to the river Anomā, make together sixty, or four hundred and fifty miles from Kapilavatthu to Rājagaha, which is far too much for the direct distance. There is here, I think, an undersigned coincidence between Northern and Southern

accounts; for the Lalita Vistara (Chap. xvi, at the commencement) makes the Bodisat go to Rājagaha *via* Vesāli, and this would make the total distance exactly sixty yojanas.

90. These are the superhuman Snakes and Winged Creatures, who were supposed, like the gods or angels, to be able to assume the appearance of men.
91. She Sutta Nipāta, vers. 405-24.
92. The Great Struggle played a great part in the Buddhist system of moral training; it was the wrestling with the flesh by which a true Buddhist overcame delusion and sin, and attained to Nirvāna. It is best explained by its four-fold division into 1. Mastery over the passions. 2. Supression of sinful thoughts. 3. Meditation of the seven kinds of Enlightenment (Bodhi-angā, see *Buddhism,* p. 173); and 4. Fixed attention, the power of preventing the mind from wandering. It is also called Sammappadhāna, Right Effort, and a formula alluded to in many Suttas. The system was, of course, not worked out at the time here referred to; but throughout the chronicle the biographer ascribes to Gotama from the beginning, a knowledge of the whole Buddhist theory as afterwards elaborated. For to our author that theory had no development, it was Eternal and Immutable Truth already revealed by innumerable previous Buddhas.
93. See above, p. 62.
94. See above, p. 157.
95. A suburb of Benāres, famous for its schools of learning.
96. 1 = well-eṣtablished.
97. The fruit of the Palmyra (Borassus flabelliformis) has always three seeds. I do not understand the allusion to a one-seeded Palmyra.
98. Nāgas, Yakkhas, and Supaṇṇas. The Yakkhas are characterized throughout the Jātaka stories by their cannibalism; the female Yakkhas as sirens luring men on to destruction. They are invisible till they assume human shape; but even then can be recognized by their red eyes. That the Ceylon aborigines are called Yakkhas in the *Mahavaṃsa* probably results from a tradition of their cannibalism. On the others, see above, p. 179.
99. Lit., to the strength of Māra(s) (Mārabala).
100. His acquisition of the Ten Perfections, or Cardinal Virtues, is described above, pp. 101 ff.
101. Pubbe-nivāsa-ñāṇa, Dibba-cakkhu, and Paṭicca-samuppāda.

102. Compare the Thirty-two Good Omens at the Buddha's Birth above, p. 160.

103. The train of thought is explained at length in my *Buddhism,* pp. 100-12. Shortly, it amounts to this. This unconscious has no pain: without consciousness, individuality, there would be no pain. What gives men consciousness,? It is due to a grasping, craving, sinful condition of heart. The absence of these cravings is Nirvāna. Having reached Nirvāna, consciousness endures but for a time (until the body dies), and it will then no longer be renewed. The beams of sin, the ridge-pole of care, give to the house of individuality its seeming strength : but in the peace of Nirvāna they have passed away. The Bodisat is now Buddha; he has reached Nirvāna : he has solved the great mystery; the jewel of salvation, sought through so many ages, has been found at last; and the long, long struggle is over.

The following is Spence Hardy's literal translation given in his *Manual of Buddhism,* p. 180, where similar version by Gogerly and Turnour will be found : but they scarcely seem to express the inner meaning of these difficult and beautiful verses :

Through many different births
I have run (to me not having found),
Seeking the architect of the (desire resembling) house,
Painful are repeated births!
O house-builder! I have seen (thee).
Again a house thou canst not build for me.
I have broken thy rafters,
Thy central support is destroyed.
To Nirvāna my mind has gone.
I have arrived at the extinction of evil desire.

(In the Theragātha (verses 183, 184) the hymn, slightly different, is ascribed to an (unknown) monk, Sivaka.–Ed.)

The figure of the house is found also in *Manu* (vi, 79-81); in the *Lalita Vistara* (p. 107 of Foucaux's *Gya Tcher Rol Pa*); and in the *Adi Granth* (Trumpp, pp. 215, 216, 471). The last passage is as follows :

A storm of divine knowledge has come!

The shutters of Delusion are all blown away–are there no longer;
The posts of Double-mindedness are broken down; the ridgepole of spiritual Blindness is shattered;

The roof of Craving has fallen on the ground; the vessel of Folly has burst!

104. See above, p. 82. A similar explanation is here repeated in a gloss.
105. Literally for four *asankheyyas* and a hundred thousand *kalpas.*
106. Anekakoṭi-sata-sahassā samāpattiyo samāpajjanto.
107. Yamaka-paṭihāriyan; Comp. pp. 88, 193, of the text, and *Mah.* p. 107. (Described in the *Patisambhidā magga,* a book of the 5th Nikāya; i, 125, as fire proceeding from the upper half of his body, water from the lower half.–Ed.) Bigandet, p. 93, has 'performed a thousand wonder.' Hardy, p. 181, omits the clause; and Beal omits the whole episode. A gloss here adds that the Buddha performed a similar miracle on three other occasions.
108. The monks whose duty it is to learn by heart, repeat, and commented upon the seven books in the *Abhidhamma Piṭaka.* See above, p. 168.
109. On these Ten Perfections, see above, pp. 101 ff.
110. Taṇhā Aratī, and Ragā. Cf. *Kindred Sayings* i, 156, giving the older version (Pali. Text Soc., 1917).–Ed.
111. Gloss : He taught the Doctrine, saying theṣe two stanzas in the Buddha-section of the *Dhammapada. Dhammapada* (verses 179, 180).
112. See above, p. 187.
113. Ukkala to Majjhima-desa. The latter included all the Buddhist Holy Land from the modern Patna to Allahabad. See above, p. 61, note.
114. See above, pp. 178, 187.
115. All three then non-existent institutions!–Ed.
116. We have here an interesting instance of the growth of legend to authenticate and add glory to local relics, of which other instances will be found in *Buddhism,* p. 195. The ancient form of this legend, as found here, must have arisen when the relics were still in Orissa. Both the Burmese and Singhalese now claim to possess them. The former say that the two merchants were Burmese, and that the Dāgaba above referred to is the celebrated sanctuary of Shooay Dagob (Bigandet, p. 101, 2nd ed.). The latter say that the Dāgaba was in Orissa, and that the hair relics were brought thence to Ceylon in 490 A.D., in the manner related in the Hair-relic chronicle *Kesa Dhātu Vaṃsa,* and referred to in the *Mahā Vaṃsa.* (See verses 43-56 of my edition of the 39th chap. of the M.V. in the J.R.A.S., 1875.) The legend in the text is found in an ancient inscription on the great bell at Rangoon (Hough's version in the

Asiatic Researches, vol. xvi; comp. Hardy, *Monastic Buddhism,* p. 183; Beal, Rom *Leg.*), p. 240.

117. In the Vinaya and Sutta accounts, the Brahmā governor comes alone.–Ed.
118. Isipatana, the hermitage in the Deer-park close to Benares, See above, p. 183.
119. Therā.
120. This snobbish allusion is not in the old (Vinaya) account.–Ed.
121. Āvuso; lit., a corruption of āyasmā, "(your) reverence."–Ed.
122. This "loving will" passage is not in the Vinaya.–Ed.
123. Tathāgato Sammāsambuddho.
124. Lit., The Rolling of the Wheel of the Norm (Dhamma).–Ed.
125. So called from his action on this occasion. See above, p. 161 f.
126. Lit., Stream-winning. Tantamount to the Christian term 'conversion'.
127. All diary and almanac allusions absent in Vinaya.–Ed.
128. Pavāraṇa.
129. They had been fire-worshippers.–Ed.
130. See above, p. 181.
131. No. 544.
132. Upāsakas; that is, those who have taken the Three Refuges and the vow to keep the Five Precepts (*Buddhism,* pp. 139, 160).
133. Tiṇṇo, crossed the ocean of transmigration.
134. That is, the Four Paths, the Four Fruits thereof, Nirvāna, and the Scriptures (or the Truth, Dhamma).
135. Dasāvāsa, probably for dasavāso (so *Vin.* i, 38) : a tenfold category taught in *Dīgha,* iii, 269; *Anguttara,* v, 29 f–Ed.
136. *Mahāvamsa,* xv, 26 f.
137. See above, p. 209.
138. The celebrated verse here referred to has been found inscribed several times in the ruins of the great Dāgaba at Isipatana, and facsimiles are given in Cunningham's *Archaeological Reports,* plate xxxiv, vol. i, p. 123. The text is given by Burnouf in the facsimiles are given in cunningham's *Archaeoloical Reports,* plate xxxiv, vol, i, p. 123. Teh text is given by Burnouf in the *Lotus de la Bonne Loi,* p. 523; and in the *Vinaya,* pp. 40, 41. (Not elsewhere in the Piṭakas.–Ed.) See also Hardy's *Manual,* p. 196.
139. Their teacher. Cf. *Dīgha,* ii, 58.

140. The Pali is also in teh 2nd person plural.–Ed.
141. His verses are in the elder's anthology. See *Psalms of the Brethren,* vers, 527-9. Only six slokas there make up his invitation; they do not contain the last two lines above.–Ed.
142. *Anguttara* i, 25.
143. See above, p. 105. The *Dhammapada Commentary,* p. 334, has a different account of the miracle performed on this occasion. It says he made a jewelled cloister (ratana-cankama) in the sky, and walking up and down in it, preached the Faith (Dhamma).
144. *Jataka,* no. 547 (the last one).
145. So also the Pali.
146. Mahā Sammata, the first king among men.
147. *Dhammapada,* ver. 168 f.
148. *Mahā-Dhammapāla Jātaka,* no. 447.
149. The following episode should be compared with the sligher sketch in Vinaya, i, 82.–Ed.
150. *Candakinnara Jātaka,* no. 485, where this episode forms the introduction to the story.
151. Lit., the lovely one of the country.
152. *Mahādhammapāla Jātaka,* no. 447. See above, p. 224.
153. See *Vin,* ii, 154 f.; *Kindred Sayings,* i, 271 f.
154. This formula has been constantly found in rock inscriptions in India and Ceylon over the ancient cave-dwellings of Buddhist hermits.

SUPPLEMENTARY TABLES

TABLES ILLUSTRATIVE OF THE HISTORY AND MIGRATIONS OF THE BUDDHIST BIRTH STORIES

Table I

INDIAN WORKS

1. The *Jātaka Atthavaṇṇanā.* A collection, probably first made in the third or fourth century B.C., of stories previously existing, and ascribed to the Buddha, and put into its present form in Ceylon, in the fifth century A.D. The Pāli text has been edited by Professor Fausböll, of Copenhagen, 1877-96. Eng. trans. Ed. cowell, Cambridge, 1895-1907.

1*a.* Singhalese translation of No. 1, called *Pan siya panas Jātaka pota.* Written in Ceylon in or about 1320 A.D.

1*b.* *Buttila Kāwyaya :* A poetical version in Elu, or old Singhalese, of one of the stories in 1*a*, by Badawaettaewa Unnānse, about 1415. Edited in Colombo, 1870, with introduction and commentary, by Baṭuwan Tuḍāwa.

1*c.* *Kusa Jātakaya :* A poetical version in Elu, or old Singhalese, of one of the stories in 1*a*, by Alagiawanna Mohoṭṭāle, 1610. Edited in Colombo, with commentary, 1868.

1*d.* *An Eastern Love Story :* Translation in verse of 1*c*, by Thomas Steele, C.C.S., London, 1871.

1*e.* *Asadisa Jātakaya :* An Elu poem, by Rājādhirāja Sinha, king of Ceylon in 1780.

2. The *Chariyā Piṭaka* : A book of the Buddhist Scriptures of the (?) fourth century B.C., containing thirty-five of the oldest stories. See Table IV.

3. The *Jātaka Mālā* : A Sanskrit work of unknown date, also containing thirty-five of the oldest stories in No.1, See Table IV.

4. The *Paṇṇāsa-Jātakaṃ,* or "50 Jātakas" : A Pāli work written in Siam, of unknown date and contents, but apparently distinct from No.1, See above, p. lxi.

5. *Pañcha Tantra* : Medieval See above, pp. lxviii-lxxii. Text edited by Kosegarten, Bonn, 1848. Kielhorn and Bühler, Bombay, 1868.

6. Translations : German, by Benfey, Leipzing, 1859.

7. French by Dubois, Paris, 1826.

8. French by Lancerau, Paris, 1871.

9. Greek by Galanos and Typaldos, Athens, 1851.

10. *Hitopadeśa* Medieval : Compiled principally from No. 5, with additions from another unknown work.

    Text edited by Carey and Colebrooke, Serampur, 1804.

    Hamilton, London, 1810.

    Bernstein, Breslau, 1823.

    Schlegel and Lassen, Bonn, 1829-31.

    Nyālankar, Calcutta, 1830 and 1844.

    Johnson, Hertford, 1847 and 1864, with English version.

    Yates, Calcutta, 1841.

    E. Arnold, Bombay, 1859.

    Max Müller, London, 1864-8.

11. Translations : English, by Wilkins, Bath, 1787; reprinted by Nyālankar in his edition of the text.

12. English by Sir. W. Jones, Calcutta, 1816.

12*a*. English by E. Arnold, London, 1861.

13. German by Max Müller, Leipzing, 1844.

13*a*. German by Dursch, Tübingen, 1853.

14. German by L. Fritze, Breslau, 1874.

15. French by Langlés, Paris, 1790.

16. French by Lancerau, Paris, 1855.

17. Greek by Galanos and Typaldos, Athens, 1851.

18. *Vetāla Pañca Viṃsati*: Twenty-five stories told by a Vetala, or demon. Sanskrit text in No. 32, vol. 11.288-93.

18*a*. Greek version of NO. 18 added to No. 17.

19. *Vethāla Kathei* : Tamil version of No. 18 Edited by Robertson in *A Compilation of Papers in the Tamil Language,* Madras, 1839.

20. No. 19, translated into English by Babington, in *Miscellaneous Translations from Oriental Languages,* London, 1831.

21. No. 18, translated into Brajbakha, by Surāt, 1740.

22. *Bytal Pachisi*: Trans. from No. 21 into Eng. by Rāja Kāli Krishna Bahadur, Calcutta, 1834. See No. 41*a*.

22*a*. *Baital pachisi* : Hindustani version of No. 21, Calcutta, 1805. Edited by Barker, hertford, 1855.

22*b*. English versions of 22*a*, by J.T. Platts, Hollings, and Barker.

22*c*. *Vikram and the Vampire,* or Tales of Hindu Devilry. Adopted from 22*b* by Richard F. Burton, London, 1870.

22*d*. German version of 22*a*, by H. Oesterley, in the *Bibliothek Orientalischer Märchen und Erzählungen,* 1873, with valuable introduction and notes.

23. *Ssidi Kür* : Mongolian version of No. 18.

24 German versions of No. 23, by Benjamin Bergmann in *Nomadische Streiferiein im Lande der Kalmücken,* i, 247 and foll., 1804; and by Juelg, 1866 and 1868.

25. German version of No. 18, by Dr. Luber, Görz, 1875.

26. *Suka Saptati* : The seventy stories of a parrot.

27. Greek version of No. 26, by Demetrios Galanos and G.K. Typaldos, *Psittakou Mythologiai Nukterinai,* included in their version of Nos. 10 and 18.

28. Persian version of No. 26, now lost; but reproduced by Nachshebi under the title Tuti Nāmeh.

28*a*. *Tota Kahani* : Hindustāni version of 26. Edited by Forbes.

28*b*. English version of 28*a*, by the Rev. G. Small.

29. *Sinhāsana Dvātriṃṣati* : The thirty-two stories of the throne of Vikramāditya; called also *Vikrama Caritra.* Edited in Madras, 1861.

29*a*. *Singhasan Battisi* : Hindī version of 29. Edited by Syed Abdoolah.

30. *Vatriṣ Singhāsan* : Bengalī version of 29, Serampur, 1818.

31. *Arji Borji Chan* : Mongolian version of 29.

32. *Vṛihat-kathā* : By Guṇādhya, probably about the sixth century; in the Paiṣacī Prākrit. See above, p. lxvii.

33. *Kathā Sarit Sāgara* : The Ocean of the Rivers of Tales. It is founded on No. 32. Includes No. 18, and a part of No. 5. The Sanskrit text edited by Brockhaus, Leipzig, vol i, with German translation, 1839; vol. ii, text only, 1862 and 1866. Original by Ṣrī Somadeva Bhaṭṭa, of Kashmīr, at the beginning of the twelfth century A.D. See above, pp. lxvi f.

34. *Vṛihat-katha* : A Sanskrit version of No. 34, by Kshemendra, of Kashmīr. Written independently of Somadeva's work, No. 32. See above, p. lxvii.

35. *Pañca Daṇḍa Chattra Prabandha* : Stories about King Vikramāditya's magic umbrella. Jain Sanskrit. Text and German version by Weber, Berlin, 1877.

36. *Vāsavadatta* By Subandhu : Possibly as old as the sixth century. Edited by Fitz-Edward Hall, in the *Bibliotheca*

Indica, Calcutta, 1859. This and the next are romances, not story-books.

37. *Kādambarī* By Bāṇa Bhaṭṭa? seventh century. Edited in Calcutta, 1850; and again, 1872, by Tarkavacaspati.

38. Bengali version of No. 37, by Tāra Shankar Tarkaratna. Tenth edition, Calcutta, 1868.

39. *Dasa-kumāra-carita* : By Daṇḍin,? sixth century. Edited by Carey, 1804; Wilson, 1846; and by Bühler, 1873.

39*a.* *Hindoo Tales,* founded on No. 39. By P.W. Jacob, London, 1873.

39*b.* *Une Tètrade* : by Hippolyte Fauche, paris, 1861-3. Contains a trans. into French of No. 39.

40. *Kathārṇava,* The Stream of Tales. In four Books; the first being No. 18, the second No. 29, the third and four miscellaneous.

41. *Purusha-parīkshā,* the Adventures of King Hammīra. Probably of the fourteenth century. By Vidyāpati.

41*a.* English translation of No. 41, by Rājā Kāli Krishna, Serampur, 1830. See No. 22.

42. *Vīra-caritan,* the Adventures of King Ṣālivāhana.

Table II

The Kalilag and Damnag Literature

1. A lost Buddhist work in a language of Northern India, ascribed to Bidpai. See above, pp. lxv-lxvii.

2. Pēlvī version, 531-79 A.D. By Barzūyē, the Court physician of Khosru Nushirvan. See above, p. xxviii,

3. *Kalilag and Damnag.* Syrian version of No. 2. Published with German trans. by Gustav Bickell, and Introduction by Professor Benfey, Leipzig, 1876. This and No. 15 preserve the best evidence of the contents of No. 2, and of its Buddhist original or originals.

4. *Kalilah wā Dimnah* (Fables of Bidpai). Arabic version of No. 3, by Abd-allah, son of Almokaffa. Date about 750 A.D. Text of one recension edited by Silvestre de Sacy, Paris, 1816. Other recensions noticed at length in Iganazio Guidi's *Studii sul testo Arabo del libro di Calila e Dimna* (Rome, 1873).

5. *Kalila and Dimna* . Eng. version of No. 4, by Knatchbull, Oxford, 1819.

6. *Das Buch des Weisen.* German version of No. 4, by Wolff, Stuttgart, 1839.

7. *Stephanitēs kai Ichvēlatēs* Greek version of No. 4, by Simeon Seth, about 1080 A.D. Edited by Seb. Gottfried Starke Berlin, 1697 (repr. in Athens, 1851), and by Aurivillius, Upsala, 1786.

8. Latin version of No. 7, by Father Possin, at the end of his edition of Pachymeres, Rome, 1866.

9. Persian translation of No. 4, by Abdul Maali Nasr Allah, 1118-53. Exists, in MS. only, in Paris, Berlin, and Vienna.

10. *Anvār i Suhaili.* Persian translation, through the last, of No. 4, by Husain ben Ali el Vāiz U'l-Kāshifī; end of the fifteenth century.

11. *Anvār i Suhaili, or the Lights of Canopus.* Eng. version of No. 10, by Edward Eastwick, Hertford, 1854.

11*a*. Another Eng. version of No. 10, by Arthur N. Wollaston (London, Allen).

12. *Livre des Lumières.* French version of No, 10, by David Sahid, d'Ispahan, Paris, 1644, Svo.

13. *Del Governo de Regni.* Italian version of No. 7, Ferrara, 1853; by Giulio Nūti. Edited by Teza, Bologna, 1872.

14. Hebrew version of No, 4, by Joel (?), before 1250. Exists only in a single MS. in Paris, of which the first part is missing.

15. *Directorium Humanoe Vitoe.* Latin version of No. 14, by John of Capua. Written 1263-78. Printed about 1480,

without date or name of place. Next to No. 3 it is the best evidence of the contents of the lost books Nos. 1 and 2.

16. German version of No. 15, also about 1480, but without date or name of place.

17. Version in Ulm dialect of No. 16. Ulm, 1483.

18. Baldo's *Alter Aesopus.* A translation direct from Arabic into Latin (? thirteenth century). Edited in du Meril's *Poesies inédites du moyen age,* Paris, 1854.

19. *Calila é Dymna.* Spanish version of No. 4 (? through an unknown Latin version). About 1251. published in *Biblioteca de Autores Españoles,* Madrid, 1860, vol. 51.

20. *Calila et Dimna.* Latin version of the last, by Raimond de Beziers, 1313.

21. *Conde Lucanor.* By Don Juan Manuel (died 1347), grandson of St. Ferdinand of Spain. Spanish source not certain.

22. *Sinbad the Sailor,* or *Book of the Seven Wise Masters.* See Comparetti, *Ricerche intorno al Libro di Sindibad,* Milano, 1869.

23. *Contes et Nouvelles.* By Bonaventure des Periers, Lyons, 1587.

24. *Exemplario contra los Engaños.* 1493. Spanish version of the Directorum.

25. *Discorse degli Animali.* Italian of last, by Ange Firenzuola, 1548.

26. *La Filoso Fia Morale.* By Doni, 1552. Italian of last but one.

27. North's English version of last, 1570.

28. *Fables,* by La Fontaine.

    First edition in vi books, the subjects of which are mostly taken from classical authors, and from Planudes' Aesop, Paris, 1668.

Second edition in xi books, the five later taken from Nos. 12 and 23, Paris, 1678.

Third edition in xii books, Paris, 1694.

Table III

1. *St. John of Damascus's Greek Text.* Seventh century, A.D. First edited by Boissonade in his *Anecdota Graeca,* Paris, 1832, vol. iv. Reprinted in Migne's *Patrologia Cursus Completus, Series Graeca,* tom. xcvi, pp. 836-1250, with the Latin translation by Billy[1] in parallel columns. Boissonade's text is reviewed, and its imperfections pointed out, by Sehubart (who makes use of six Vienna MSS.) in the *Wiener Jahrbücher,* vol. lxiii.
2. Syriac version of No. 1 exists only in MS.
3. Arabic version of No. 2 exists only in MS., one MS. being at least as old as the eleventh century.
4. Latin version of No. 1 of unknown data and author of which MSS. of the twelfth century are still extant. There is a black-letter edition (? Spiers, 1470) in the British Museum. It was adopted, with abbreviations in several places, by Vincentius Bellovicensis, in his *Speculum Historiale* (lib. xv, cap. 1-63); by Jacobus a Voragine, in his *Legenda Aurea* (ed. Grässe, 1846); and was reprinted in full in the editions of the works of St. John of Damascus, published at Basel in the sixteenth century.[2] From this Latin version all the later medieval works on this subject are either directly or indirectly derived.

4*a*. An abbreviated version in Latin of the fourteenth century in the British Museum. Arundel MS. 330, fol. 51-7. See Koch, No. 9, p. xiv.

German :

5. *Barlaam and Josaphat.* A poem of the thirteenth century, published from a MS. in the Solms-Laubach Library by L. Diefenbach, under the title *Mittheilungen über eine noch ungedruckete m.h.d. Bearbeitung des B. and J.* Giessen, 1836.

6. Another poem, partly published from an imperfect MS. at Zürich, by Franz Pfeiffer, in Haupt's *Zeitsch. f. d. Alterthum,* i, 127-35.

7. *Barlaam and Josaphat.* By Rudolf von Ems. Written about 1230. Latest and best edition by Franz pfeiffer, in *Dichtungen des deutschen Mittelalters,* vol. iii, Leipzig, 1843. This popular treatment of the subject exists in numerous MSS.

7*a.* *Die Hÿstori Josaphat und Barlaam.* Date and author not named. Black-letter. Woodcuts. Title on last page. Fiftysix short chapters. Quaint and forcible old German. A small folio in the British Museum.

8. *Historia von dem Leben der Zweien H. Beichtiger Barlaam Eremiten, und Josaphat des König's in Indien Sohn* etc. Translated from the Latin by the Counts of Helffenstein and Hohenzollern, München, 1684. In 40 long chapters, pp. 602, 12 mo.

Dutch :

9. *Het Leven en Bedryf van Barlaam den Heremit, en Josaphat Koning van Indien.* Noo in Nederduits vertaalt door F. v. H., Antwerp, 1593, 12mo.

   A new edition of this version appeared in 1672. This is a long and tedious prose version of the holy legend.

French :

10. Poem by Gui de Cambray (1200-50). Edited by Hermann Zotenberg and Paul Meyer in the *Bibliothek des Literarischen Vereins,* in Stuttgart, vol. lxxv, 1864. They mention also (pp. 318-25) :

11. *La Vie de Seint Josaphaz.* Poem by Chardry. Edited by John Koch, Heilbronn, 1879, who confirms the editors of No. 8 as to the following old French versions, 10-15; and and further adduces No. 11*a.*

12. A third poem by an unknown author.

13. A prose work by an unknown author–all three being of the 13th cent.

13*a*. Another in MS. Egerton, 745, British Museum.

14. A poem in French of the fifteenth century, based on the abstract in Latin of No. 4, by Jacob de Voragine.

15. A Provencal tale in prose, containing only the story of Josafat and the tales told by Barlaam, without the moralizations.

16. A miracle play of about 1400.

17. Another miracle play of about 1460.

Italian :

18. *Vita di san Giosafat convertito da Barlaam.* By Geo. Antonio Remondini. Published about 1600, at Venezia and Bassano, 16mo. There is a second edition of this, also without data; and a third, published in Modena in 1768, with illustrations.

19. *Storia de' SS. Barlaam e Giosafatte.* By Bottari, Rome, 1734, 8vo, of which a second edition appeared in 1816.

20. *La santissima vita di Santo Josafat, figlulo del Re Avenero, Re dell' India, da che ei nachque per infino ch'ei mori.* A prose romance, edited by Telesforo Bini from a MS. belonging to the Commendatore Frencesco de Rossi, in pp. 124-52 of a collection, *Rime e Prose,* Lucca, 1852, 8vo.

21. A prose *Vita da Santo Josafat.* In MS. Add. 10902 of the British Museum, which Paul Mayer (see No. 8) says begins exactly as No. 18, but ends differently. (See Koch, No. 9 above.)

22. A *Rappresentatione di Barlaam e Josafat* is mentioned by Federigo Palermo in his *I manuscritti Palatini de Fireneze,* 1860. vol. ii, p. 401.

Skandinavian :

A full account of all the Skandinavian versions is given in *Barlaam's ok Josaphat's Saga,* by C.R. Unger, Christiania, 1851, 8vo.

Spanish :

Honesta, etc, historia de la rara vida de los famosos y singulares sanctos Barlaam, etc. By Baltasat de Santa Cruz. Published in the Spanish dialect used in the Phillipine Islands at Manila, 1692. A literal translation of Billius (No. 1).

English :

In Horstmann's *Altenglische Legenen,* Paderborn, 1875, an Old English version of the legend is published from the Bodleian MS. No. 779. There is another recension of the same poem in the Harleian MS. No. 4196. Both are of the fourteenth century; and of the second there is another copy in the Vernon MS. See further, Warton's *History of English Poetry,* i, 271-9, and ii, 30, 58, 308.

Horstmann has also published a Middle English version in the *Program of the Sagan Gymnasium,* 1877.

The History of the Five Wise Philosophers; or, the Wonderful Relation of the Life of Jehoshaphat the Hermit, Son of Avenerian, King of Barma in India, etc. By N.H. (that is, Nicholas Herick), Gent., London, 1711, pp. 128, 12mo. This is a prose romance, and an abridged translation of the Italian version of 1600 (No. 16), and contains only one fable (at p. 46) or the Nightingale and the Fowler.

The work referred to on p. xliii, under the title *Gesta Romanorum,* a collection of tales with lengthy moralizations (probably sermons), was made in England about 1300. It soon passed to the Continent, and was repeatedly re-written in numerous MSS., with additions and alteration. Three printed editions appeared between 1472; and one of these, containing 181 stories, is the source of the work now known under this title. Tale No. 168 quotes Barlaam. The best edition of the Latin version is by H. Oesterley, Berlin, 1872. The last English traslation is Hooper's, Bohn's Antiquarian Library, London, 1877. The Early English versions have been edited by Sir F.

Madden; and again, in vol. xxxiii of the Extra Series of the Early English Text Society, by S.J.H. Herrtage.

The Seven Sages (edited by Thomas Wright for the Percy Society, 1845) also contains some Buddhist tales.

REFERENCES

1. Billy (1535-77) was Abbot of St. Michael's, in Brittany. Another edition of his Latin version, by Rosweyd, is also reprinted in Migne, *Series Latina,* tom. lxxiii; and several separate editions have appeared besides (Antwerp, 1602; Cologne, 1624, etc.).
2. The British Museum copy of the first, undated, edition, has the date 1539 written in ink on the title-page. Rosweyd, in Note 4 to his edition of Billius (Migne, vol. lxxiii, p. 606), mentions an edition bearing the date 1548. In the British Museum there is a third, dated 1575 (on the last page).

Table IV

Comparison of the Cariyā Pitaka and the Jātaka Mālā

1. Akitte-cariyan	Vyāghī-jātakan
2. Sankha-c°	Sivi-j° (8)
3. Danañjaya-c°	Kulmāṣapiṇḍi-j°
4. Mahā-sudassana-c°	Ṣreshthi-j° (21)
5. Mahā-govinda-c°	Avisajyaṣreshthi-j°
6. Nimi-rāja-c°	Ṣaṣa-j° (10)
7. Canda-kumāra-c°	Agastya-j°
8. Sivi-rāja-c° (2)	Maitribala-j°
9. Vessantara-c°	Viṣvantara-j° (9)
10. Sasa-paṇḍita-c° (6)	Yajña-j°
11. Sīlava-nāga-c° (J. 72)	Sakra-j°
12. Bhuridatta-c°	Brāhmaṇa-j°
13. Campeyya-nāga-c°	Ummādayanti-j°
14. Cūḷa-bodhi-c°	Suparāga-j°
15. Mahiṃsa-rāja-c° (27)	Matsya-j° (30)
16. Ruru-rāja-c°	Vartaka-potaka-j° (29)
17. Mātanga-c°	Kacchapa-j°
18. Dhammādhamma-devaputta-c°	Kumbha-j°
19. Jayadisa-c°	Putra-j°
20. Sankhapāla-c°	Visa-j°
21. Yudañjaya-c°	Ṣreshthi-j° (4)
22. Somanassa-c°	Suddhabodhi-j°
23. Ayoghara-c° (33)	Haṃsa-j°
24. Bhisa-c°	Mahābodhi-j°
25. Soma-paṇḍita-c° (32)	Mahākapi-j° (27, 28)
26. Temiya-c°	Ṣarabha-j°
27. Kapi-rāja-c° (25, 28)	Ruru-j° (16)
28. Saccasavhaya-paṇḍita-c°	Mahākapi-j° (25, 27)
29. Vattaka-potaka-c° (15)	Kshānti-j°

30.	Maccha-rāja-c° (15)	Brahma-j°
31.	Kaṇha-dipāyana-c°	Hasti-j°
32.	Sutasoma-c° (25, 32)	Sutasoma-j° (25, 32)
33.	Suvaṇṇa-sāma-c°	Ayogṛiha-j° (23)
34.	Ekarāja-c°	Mahisha-j°
35.	Mahā-lomahaṃsa-c° (J. 94)	Ṣatatra-j°

For the above lists see Feer, *Etude sur les jātakas,* p. 58; Gogerly, *Journal of the Ceylon Branch of the Royal Asiatic Society,* 1853; Fausböll, *Five Jātakas,* p. 59; 'A Chinese Pilgrim on the Jātaka-mālā,' *Ind. Antiquary,* xi, 44; and also above, pp. xlviii-1. It will be seen that there are seven tales with identical, and one or two more with similar titles, in the two collections. The former was edited by Rd. Morris, P.T.S., 1882, the latter by E. Kern, H.O.S. 1891, trs, by J.S. Speyer, S.B. Buddhists, 1895. The Cambridge Unicersity Library possesses a MS. of the former, with the various readings of several other MSS. noted, for me, by Dewa Aranolis.

Table V

Alphabetical List of Jātaka Stories in the Mahāvastu

Aranged from Cowell and Eggelling's *Catalogue of Buddhist Sanskrit MSS. in the Possession of the Royal Asiatic Society (Hodgson Collection).*

Amarāye karmārakādhītāye jatākṃa	Rakshito-nāma-ṛishi-j°
	Ṛishabasya-j°
Arindama-j°	Ṣakuntaka-j°
	(Two with this title.)
Asthisenasya-j°	
Bhadravargikānan-j°	Ṣarakshepanan-j°
Campaka-nāgarāja-j°	Ṣaratān-j°
Godhā-j°	Sārthavāhasya-j°
Hastinī-j°	Ṣirī-j°
Kāka-j°	Ṣirī-prabhasya mṛiga-rājasya-j°
Uruvilva-kāṣyapādi-kāṣyapānan-j°	Ṣyāma-j°[1] (Car. Piṭ. 33)
	Ṣyāmaka-j°
Ājnāta-Kauṇḍinya-j°	Triṇakunīyan nāma-j°
Kinnari-j°[1]	Upali gaṅga palānan-j°
Kṛicchapa-j°	Vānarādhipa-j°
Kuṣa-j°	Vara-j°
Mañjerī-j°	Vijitāvasya Vaideha-rājño-j°
Markaṭa-j°	Yaṣoda-j°
Mṛigarājño surūpasya-j°	Yosodharāye hārapradāna-j°
Nalnīye rājakumārīye-j°	Yosodharāye vyaghribhūtāya-j°
Puṇyavanta-j°	
Pūrṇasya Maitrāyaṇīputrasya-j°	

Footnote

1. These two Jātakas also from the contents of a separate MS. int eh Royal Asiatic society's Library (*Catalogue*, p. 14).

Table VI

Places at which the Jātaka Tales were Told

M. Léon Feer as taken the trouble to count the number of times each of the follwoing places is mentioned at the commencement of the Comentary.

Jetavana monastery	410	
Sāvatthi	6	416
Veḷuvana	49	
Rājagaha	5	55
Laṭṭhivanuyyāna	1	
Vesāli		4
Kosambi		5
Āḷavī		3
Kuṇḍāladaha		3
Kusa		2
Magadha		2
Dakkhiṇāgiri		1
Migadāya		1
Mithila		1
By the Ganges		1
		494
To wich we may add from pp. 124-8 below :		
Kapilavatthu		4
		498

Table VII

The Bodisats

At his request the Rev. Spence Hardy's 'paṇḍit' made an analysis of the number of times in which the Bodisat appears in the Buddhist Birth Stories in each of the following characters :

An ascetic	83	An iguana	3
A king	85	A fish	2
A tree god	43	An elephant driver	2
A teacher	26	A rat	2
A courtier	24	A jackal	2
A brāhman	24	A crow	2
A king's son	24	A woodpecker	2
A nobleman	23	A thief	2
A learned man	22	A pig	2
Sakka	20	A dog	1
A monkey	18	A curer of snake bites	1
A merchant	13	A gambler	1
A man of property	12	A mason	1
A deer	11	A smith	1
A lion	10	A devil dancer	1
A wild duck	8	A student	1
A snipe	6	A silvermith	1
An elephant	5	A carpenter	1
A cock	5	A water-fowl	1
A slave	5	A frog	1
An eagle	5	A hare	1
A horse	4	A kite	1
A bull	4	A jungle cock	1
Brahma	4	A fairy	1
A peacock	4		
A serpent	4	–	
A potter	3		530
An outcast	3		

Table VIII

Jatakas Illustrated in Bas-Relief on the Ancient Monuments

Arranged from General Cunnigham's *Stūpa of Bharhut*

No.	*Plate.*	*Title inscribed on the stone.*	*Title in the Jātaka Book.*
1.	xviii.	Vitura-panakaya Jātaka[1]	Vidhura Jātaka
2.	xxv.	Miga Jātaka	Nigrodha-miga Jātaka[2]
3.	xxv.	Nāga[3] Jātaka	Kakkataka Jātaka
4.	xxv.	Yava-majhakiya Jātaka	?[4]
5.	xxv.	Muga-pakhaya Jātaka	Muga-pakkha Jātaka
6.	xxvi.	Laṭuva Jātaka	Laṭukika Jātaka
7.	xxvi.	Cha-dantiya Jātaka	Chad-danta Jātaka
8.	xxvi.	Isi-singiya Jātaka	Isi-singa Jātaka
9.	xxvi (?)	Yaṃbamaṇo-ayavesi Jātaka	Andha-bhuta Jātaka
10.	xxvii.	?[5]	Kurunga-miga Jātaka
11.	xxvii.	Haṃsa Jātaka	Nacca Jātaka
12.	xxvii.	Kinara Jātaka	Canda-kinnara Jātaka[6]
13.	xxvii.	?[5] Jātaka	Aśadisa Jātaka[6]
14.	xxvii.	?[5] Jātaka	Dasaratha Jātaka
15.	xxviii.	Janako Rāja Jātaka Sivala-Devī Jātaka	Janaka Jātaka
16.	xxxiii.	Maha Kapi Jātaka	Camma-Sataka Jātaka
17.	xliii.	Isi-migo Jātaka	Miga potaka Jātaka
18.	xliv.	Janako rājā Sivali devī Jātaka	Mahājanaka Jātaka
19.	xlv.	Aramadūsaka Jātaka	Kapota Jātaka
20.	xlvi.	Uda Jātaka	Dabbha puppha Jātaka
21.	xlvi.	Secha Jātaka	Dūbhiya-makkata Jātaka
22.	xlvii.	Sujato gahuto Jātaka	Sujāta Jātaka
23.	xlvii	Biḍala Jātaka Kukuta Jātaka	 Kukkuṭa Jātaka
24.	xlviii.	Magha-deviya Jātaka	Makhā-deva Jātaka
25.	xlviii.	Bhisa-haraṇiya Jātaka	Bhisa Jātaka

There are numerous other scenes without titles, and not yet identified in the Jātaka Book, but which are almost certainly illustrative of Jātaka Stories; and several scenes with titles illustrative of passages in the Nidāna Kathā of the Jātaka Book. So, for instance, Pl. xvi, fig. 1, is the worship in heaven of the Buddha's Head-dress, the reception of which into heaven is described above, p. 178; and the heavenly mansion, the Palace of Glory, is inscribed *Vejayanto Pāsādo,* the origin of which name is explained below, p. 287. Plate xxviii has a scene entitled *Bhagavato Okkanti* (The Descent of the Blessed One),[7] in illustration of Māyā Devī's Dream (above, pp. 148 f.); and Plate lvii is a representation of the Presentation of the Jetavana Monsatery (above, p. 178). The identifications of Nos. 12 and 13 in the above list are very doubtful.

Besides the above, Mr. Fergusson, in his *Tree and Serpent Worship,* has identified bas-reliefs on the Sanchi Tope in illustration of the Sama and Asadisa Jātakas (Pl. xxxvi, p. 181) and of the Vessantara Jātaka (Pl. xxiv, p. 125); and there are other Jātaka scenes on the Sanchi Tope not yet identified.

Mr. Simpson also has been kind enough to show me drawings of bas-reliefs he discovered in Afghanistān, two of which I have been able to identify as illustrations of the Sumedha Jātaka and another as illustrative of the scene described above, pp. 222f.

REFERENCES

1. There are four distinct bas-reliefs illustrative of this Jataka.
2. This is one of those which General Cunningham was unable to identify.
3. General Cunningham says (p. 52) : "The former [Nāga, jataka, i.e. Elephant Jātaka] is the correct name, as in the legend here represented Buddha is the King of the Elephants, and there for the Jātaka, or Birth, must of necessity have been named after him." The title of each Jataka, or Birth Story, is chosen not by any means from the character which the Bodisat fills in it, but indifferently from a variety of other reasons. General Cunningham himself gives the story called Isī-singiya Jātaka (No. 7 in the above list), in which the ascetic after whom the Jātaka is named is not the Bodisat.

4. Not as yet found in the Jātaka Book; but Dr. Bühler has shown in the *Indian Antiquary,* vol. i, p. 305, that it is the first tale in the *Vrihat Kathā* of Kshemendra (Table I, No. 34), and in the *Kathā Sarit Sāgara* of Somadeva (Table I, No. 33), and was therefore probably included in the *Vrihat Kathā* of Guṇadhya (Table I, No. 32).
5. The part of the stone supposed to have contained the inscription is lost.
6. It is mentioned above, p. 225, and is included in the Mahāvastu (Table V), and forms the subject of the carving on one of the rails at Buddha Cayā (Rajendra Lāl Mitra, pl. xxxiv, fig. 2).
7. General Cunningham's reading of this inscription as *Bhagavato rukdanta* seems to me to be incorrect, and his translation of it ('Buddha as the sounding elephant') to be grammatically impossible.

Table IX

Former Buddhas

1-3. Taṇhankara Medhankara Saraṇankara
4. Dīpankara
5. Kondañña
6. Mangala
7. Sumana
8. Revata
9. Sobhita
10. Anomadassin
11. Paduma
12. Nārada
13. Padumuttara
14. Sumedha
15. Sujāta
16. Piyadassin
17. Atthadassin
18. Dhammadassin
19. Siddhattha
20. Tissa
21. Phussa
22. Vipassin
23. Sikhin
24. Vessabhu
25. Kakusandha
26. Koṇāgamana
27. Kassapa